EIGHTH DAY PRAYERS

DAILY JOY *FOR* ORDINARY TIME

Sally Breedlove, Willa Kane,
Madison Perry, and Alysia Yates

Forefront
BOOKS

Dedication

For Lekita Essa, widowed young, who turned grief into
a way to love others. She heard the Holy Spirit's call
to prayer and shared it with an anxious world.

And for Beatrice Rose Dasher, whose brief eighty-eight
days helped those who knew her steadfast peace
learn to hope in the resurrection of the body
and the life of the world to come.

Contents

Introduction

MADISON PERRY

*W*HAT DAY IS IT? No matter the week or season, there is another name for the day we are living: the eighth day. Jesus Christ was resurrected the day after the last day of the week. If the first day was a day of creation, the eighth day was one of new creation and life in Christ on the far side of the grave. By the power of the Holy Spirit, we can join Christ and live in this new day, even in the midst of the old order.

This book is an invitation to live like eighth-day people. We are invited to a banquet, to feast in the halls of Zion and dwell forever in the kingdom of God. At this table lies nothing less than everything, no matter what we have lost or suffered, or even what we have inflicted on the world around us.

This invitation is present on every page of the Bible. However, left to our own devices, we do not have eyes to see God's glory or ears to hear God's call. Adrift in the imagination of our hearts, we wander through the ruins of another age.

How do we enter this realm of God's resurrection glory? By the work of the Holy Spirit through God's Word. His Word is living and active, capable of piercing even to the dividing of soul and spirit, and his mercies are new every morning.

You likely recognize that you are in the same decaying world that we all experience, where our sense of history comes from the news cycle and to-do lists. This is the stale kingdom of the age that is passing away. What will quicken our hearts, rebuild our imaginations, and pull us back toward our God on a daily basis? Surely God's Word is up to the challenge.

Within *Eighth Day Prayers* you will find passages of Scripture that pull you into the world of God's Word, new landscapes of fresh truth where the Holy Spirit will equip you for friendship with God. We hope that this book moves you to engage with Scripture and that our words will recede, leaving you open to God's Word and its power. We cannot set the terms of your engagement with God, but we hope to guide you into what may feel like new terrain and prepare you for real life—life with Christ.

We have ordered *Eighth Day Prayers* to follow the church's calendar, and the newly revised format comprises three volumes: the Incarnation Cycle contains Advent, Christmas, and Epiphany; the Paschal Cycle contains Lent, Holy Week, Easter, and Pentecost; and the final volume contains Ordinary Time. Each season begins with a brief introduction, and we have added a calendar at the beginning of each page for your convenience. Following the church's calendar will give you the opportunity to connect your daily exposure to God's Word with the expansive story of God's redeeming work. Here we find an older, truer way of living, one that draws its momentum from the arc of salvation and discovers deep wells of rest and strength in Christ.

As you immerse yourself in the Word of God, open yourself to his Spirit, and orient yourself within the life of Jesus, we pray that you will move into a new and richer reality. The kingdom of God is near. Repent, believe, and find your life in the gospel!

Entering In
STEPHEN A. MACCHIA

*T*HE BEST PART OF CONVERSATION with friends is the give-and-take—we don't already know what they are going to say. We notice things about them that we enjoy even as we converse. We are curious, we ask questions, we share real things. We listen intently because the person matters to us. They are not a book we have already read; they are not present merely to tell us what to do or what is wrong with us. They want to know us, and we want to know them.

The ancient practice of *lectio* is like that—it's listening to God's Word, listening to what arises in our hearts as we hear God's Word, and responding in prayer to the Author of these words with real words of our own. *Lectio* is conversation between the triune God and us, the children he so deeply loves, in the context of his beautiful Word.

Consider these ancient words used to describe this way of being with God during *lectio*:

- We pause for silence and still our hearts to receive God's Word (*silencio*).
- We receive a sacred reading of the text (*lectio*).
- We notice a particular word or image that has leapt off the page into our hearts, and we meditate on that word or image (*meditatio*).
- We prayerfully respond to what we notice stirring in our own heart (*oratio*).
- We linger in silence, noticing more deeply how this particular scripture is speaking to us (*contemplatio*).
- We say yes to the transforming work God is seeking to do in us as we hold this word from him. How is our soul being nourished and transformed? How are we called to be and what are we called to do in this world (*incarnatio*)?

In many ways this book is designed to guide you into a time of *lectio* so you can focus on a small portion of God's Word and enter into a prayerful encounter with the living God. When Bible reading becomes prayer, you know you've touched a nerve the Spirit is inviting you to consider. There is a fresh wind of God's Spirit when we genuinely receive the living Word, and it is profoundly good for our souls.

You are blessed to be holding this resource in your hands. May the words of your mouth and the meditations of your heart be inspired by the Word and then multiplied in your soul and in service to others. Receive what God has in store for you like you've never heard the Word before. Such joy!

Introduction to the Christian Year
STEVEN E. BREEDLOVE

*F*ROM THE MOMENT GOD CREATED THE WORLD, he rooted it in time. The six days of creation are endowed with beauty, meaning, and purpose, leading us to the seventh day of divine rest. But what of the eighth day? For Christians the eighth day is the day of Jesus's resurrection from the dead—Easter—on the first day after the Jewish Sabbath. The eighth day marks a new way of keeping time shaped by the inbreaking of a new creation.

Time tells a story. And the way we keep time inscribes that story in us. As Christians we are eighth-day people, thus the inspiration for eight-sided churches, pulpits, stained glass windows, and the emblem that adorns the cover and pages of this book. We have titled this book *Eighth Day Prayers* as an invitation to a new way of keeping time, one rooted in the rhythm of creation that nonetheless draws us on toward new creation.

In so many ways we have lost our ability to keep time. Perhaps this loss results from the movement away from an agricultural world, where land was left fallow for a season before it was sown and where sowing necessarily preceded growing, which resulted in harvest. It was impossible in the agricultural world to divorce one season from another; each season contributed its own gift and preparation to the next. But this loss of connection between the seasons is also the result of trading the church calendar for the economic calendar, where every season is harvest and none is planting.

The church calendar is not a series of discrete seasons, yet the tyranny of the economic calendar makes it initially difficult to see this. Throughout the centuries, the church has recognized that the Christian year consists of two cycles. In other words, we don't have Advent, Christmas, and Epiphany in isolation. Instead, we have the Incarnation Cycle, which consists of Advent, Christmas, and Epiphany. And we don't have Lent, Easter, and Pentecost. Instead, we have the Paschal Cycle, which consists of the three together. In each of these cycles, the seasons are intricately connected to and dependent on one another, and in each, the pattern is the same—preparation, celebration, and growth. Growth is also the focus in Ordinary Time, which concludes the church year. During Ordinary Time, the people of God are invited to live for the sake of the world as they wait for the return of their King.

In a previous age, we might have simply said that mortification and repentance must precede rejoicing because they sow the seeds for it, and that rejoicing is the foundation for growth, discipleship, and mission because we reap a harvest from the object of our rejoicing. We cannot divorce Lent from Easter, and we cannot divorce Easter from Pentecost.

Each season prepares for the next, and trying to live the spiritual life in only one season is like trying to have only harvest without sowing. We need to be planted anew each year. The Christian year offers us the framework for this.

As you let *Eighth Day Prayers* help shape your daily prayers, notice how your response to Scripture and your prayers change as you hold in mind what season it is. Is it a time for preparation? For rejoicing? For a rekindled awareness of God's presence and his call to us?

God has given us the gift of agricultural seasons and the rhythm of the Christian year. Let that rhythm draw you more deeply into a prayer-filled life with God.

Introduction to Ordinary Time
STEVEN E. BREEDLOVE

*T*HE SEASON AFTER PENTECOST, commonly called "Ordinary Time," is the longest and final season of the Christian year. It completes the three-season cycle that began in Advent, and it offers us the chance to live as Christians in the here and now. In spite of the term *Ordinary Time* (which simply refers to the way the Sundays were ordered), the here and now is anything but ordinary because the life, death, and resurrection of Jesus Christ changes everything.

In the season after Pentecost, the church is called to be Christ's presence in this world by the power of the Holy Spirit. This is what the disciples did in the days following Pentecost. They were living Jesus's life, as his body, in the strength and presence of the Holy Spirit. This is also what we are called to do, week after week. We are called to be faithful disciples in this season, through the Spirit given at Pentecost.

Ordinary time is lived out week by week, but it ends with an extraordinary Sunday, one we often overlook. The last Sunday of Ordinary Time is Christ the King Sunday. The setting apart of this day began only in the early 20th century, but we can see the wisdom of the church. For as our modern world has grown increasingly secular, we need to be reminded that at the end of the ages, Christ will truly reign as King forever, world without end.

The prayers and readings of this season are thus focused on growing in the faith and being witnesses to the world. We read the Scriptures and pray in response to the readings so that we will grow in understanding, devote ourselves to prayer, come to the Lord's table, and take care of each other in love. The life of the church, in all its aspects, is our focus during this season. As we read, our prayer ought to be, "Lord, strengthen and sanctify your body, filling it with your Spirit, so that we might be your witnesses in the world!"

Ordinary Time Day 1

KARI WEST

Read: *Psalm 90:1–6, 12–17*

Lord, you have been our dwelling place
    in all generations.
Before the mountains were brought forth,
        or ever you had formed the earth and the world,
        from everlasting to everlasting you are God.
You return man to dust
        and say, "Return, O children of man!"
For a thousand years in your sight
        are but as yesterday when it is past,
        or as a watch in the night.
You sweep them away as with a flood; they are like a dream,
        like grass that is renewed in the morning:
in the morning it flourishes and is renewed;
        in the evening it fades and withers....
So teach us to number our days
        that we may get a heart of wisdom.
Return, O Lord! How long?
        Have pity on your servants!
Satisfy us in the morning with your steadfast love,
        that we may rejoice and be glad all our days.
Make us glad for as many days as you have afflicted us,
        and for as many years as we have seen evil.
Let your work be shown to your servants,
        and your glorious power to their children.
Let the favor of the Lord our God be upon us,
        and establish the work of our hands upon us;
        yes, establish the work of our hands!

Reflect:

Do you see how the psalmist looked to the Lord for everything? God gives wisdom. God satisfies with his love. God makes us glad. God shows his work and glorious power. God establishes the work of our hands.

As you step into a new season in the liturgical year, pause and consider: Do you come to the Father with the same kind of neediness, the same kind of expectancy? Do you plead for his return, for a deeper experience of his presence?

There is no life apart from the Lord. There is no lasting gladness apart from his steadfast love. We are like flowers that will wither and die without the sun. Nothing we do or build will last without his blessing; he is the one who establishes the work of our hands. He is our dwelling place from everlasting to everlasting.

As you pray, step into the dependance the psalmist modeled. Abandon all pretense of self-sufficiency. Pray this psalm to the Lord, asking him to mold you more and more in humility and give you a true understanding of the impossibility of life without his abiding presence.

Pray:

O Lord the God of our salvation, you are the hope of all the ends of the earth. Upon you the eyes of all do wait; for you give unto all life and breath and all things. You still watch over us for good; you daily renew us to our lives and your mercies. And you have given us the assurance of your Word, that if we commit our affairs to you, if we acknowledge you in all our ways, you will direct our paths. We desire, O Lord, to be still under your gracious conduct and fatherly protection. We beg the guidance and help of your good Spirit, to choose our inheritance for us, and to dispose of us, and all that concerns us, to the glory of your name. Amen.

(John Wesley)

Ordinary Time Day 2

KARI WEST

Read: *Psalm 119:33–40*

> Teach me, O LORD, the way of your statutes;
>> and I will keep it to the end.
> Give me understanding, that I may keep your law
>> and observe it with my whole heart.
> Lead me in the path of your commandments,
>> for I delight in it.
> Incline my heart to your testimonies,
>> and not to selfish gain!
> Turn my eyes from looking at worthless things;
>> and give me life in your ways.
> Confirm to your servant your promise,
>> that you may be feared.
> Turn away the reproach that I dread,
>> for your rules are good.
> Behold, I long for your precepts;
>> in your righteousness give me life!

Reflect:

What are the prayers that come up from the depths of your heart? Are they in tune with the requests found here in Psalm 119?

In these words, the psalmist displayed a soul-deep conviction of the goodness, beauty, and worth of God's law. He delighted in God's commands; he sought understanding to better follow the Lord with all his heart; he trusted that true life is found in the words of God.

Pause and reflect. Do you possess the psalmist's love for the law of God?

One of the beautiful aspects of prayer is that when we offer verses like these up to the Lord, he will work within us to make them our true desires. If we ask for understanding so that we may grow in obedience, God delights not only to answer that prayer but also to slowly transform us into the kind of people who want that more than anything else.

When we ask for our eyes to be turned away from worthless things and to instead hold to the supremacy of God's Word, we slowly become people who know, deep in our bones, that "everything else is worthless when compared with the infinite value of knowing Christ Jesus" (Philippians 3:8 NLT), the Word made flesh.

Offer up each of these requests to your Father and ask him to transform your heart to want the best things. Trust by the power of his Spirit that he is indeed forming you as his beloved disciple and child. Be at peace.

Pray:

Some of us are trying, striving after some excellent virtue. Lord, help strugglers; enable those that contend against great difficulties only to greater grace, more faith, and so to bring them nearer to God. Lord, we will be holy; by your grace we will never rest until we are. You have begun a good work in us, and you will carry it on. You will work in us to will and to do of your own good pleasure. Amen.

(Charles Spurgeon)

Ordinary Time Day 3

MARY RACHEL BOYD

Read: *Psalm 119:73–88*

Your hands have made and fashioned me;
    give me understanding that I may learn your commandments.
Those who fear you shall see me and rejoice,
    because I have hoped in your word.
I know, O LORD, that your rules are righteous,
    and that in faithfulness you have afflicted me.
Let your steadfast love comfort me
    according to your promise to your servant.
Let your mercy come to me, that I may live;
    for your law is my delight.
Let the insolent be put to shame,
    because they have wronged me with falsehood;
    as for me, I will meditate on your precepts.
Let those who fear you turn to me,
    that they may know your testimonies.
May my heart be blameless in your statutes,
    that I may not be put to shame!
My soul longs for your salvation;
    I hope in your word.
My eyes long for your promise;
    I ask, "When will you comfort me?"
For I have become like a wineskin in the smoke,
    yet I have not forgotten your statutes.
How long must your servant endure?
    When will you judge those who persecute me?
The insolent have dug pitfalls for me;
    they do not live according to your law.
All your commandments are sure;
    they persecute me with falsehood; help me!
They have almost made an end of me on earth,
    but I have not forsaken your precepts.
In your steadfast love give me life,
    that I may keep the testimonies of your mouth.

Reflect:

We live in an age obsessed with image. We are expected to construct a perfect facade and to curate beautiful lives. But our inner worlds tend to go unseen, which complicates knowing and being known. And where there is a lack of knowing, loneliness is close at hand. Loneliness stirs fear, grief, anxiety, and a host of other challenging feelings.

But the psalmist unabashedly proclaimed a different possibility: the achingly deep beauty of knowing God and of being known by him. This knowing God and letting God know us strengthens us and equips us to embrace the truth. And truth, as Jesus said, will set us free—not just despite our circumstances but in the mess of them.

In the cross, we are reminded that we do not rest in our own ability or capacity to fashion peace or comfort. We can rejoice with the psalmist that there is a Creator who powerfully, delicately, and intentionally crafted each one of us into existence in our mothers' wombs.

Our Creator's heart has an unlimited capacity for compassion. He possesses an unshakable sense of justice that gives dignity to the weak and lowly, and he hears the cry of the lonely and needy.

As humans, we run dry and grow weary when confronted with challenges. The psalmist declared that it is God's unfailing love that preserves us.

As you pray, confess your weariness to your Creator. Think of others you know who are struggling as well. Then thank your Father for his unfailing love, made known in Jesus Christ.

Pray:

Heavenly Father, you see us and know us. You created us and you reign gloriously over all creation with grace and compassion. Remind us of your decrees and of how deeply you love us, this earth, and all who dwell on it. Enable us to hope in faith, rejoice in life, and thrive in obedience. Preserve and protect our lives; all for your love's sake. Amen.

Ordinary Time Day 4

KARI WEST

Read: *Psalm 119:129–136*

Your testimonies are wonderful;
    therefore my soul keeps them.
The unfolding of your words gives light;
    it imparts understanding to the simple.
I open my mouth and pant,
    because I long for your commandments.
Turn to me and be gracious to me,
    as is your way with those who love your name.
Keep steady my steps according to your promise,
    and let no iniquity get dominion over me.
Redeem me from man's oppression,
    that I may keep your precepts.
Make your face shine upon your servant,
    and teach me your statutes.
My eyes shed streams of tears,
    because people do not keep your law.

Reflect:

O how we need hearts that stand in awe of God's words! Too often we find other things to admire and seek after—power, reputation, family, rest, friendships, knowledge, sex, or pleasure. We orchestrate our lives around our awe of lesser gods. We worship the idols we make for ourselves.

But Psalm 119 teaches us another way. The psalmist delighted in Scripture like one who had come upon unexpected treasure. He proclaimed that God's "testimonies are wonderful; therefore my soul keeps them" (v. 129); he described the light and understanding that God's words endow (v. 130). He longed for God's Word as the thirsty long for water (v. 131).

God speaks to his people. However, we are often so familiar with this idea that it loses its incandescence and unfathomability. God speaks to us, his people. God wants to talk with us. We have his words as a light to our

20

paths, as honey on our tongues, as diamonds in our hands, as the embrace of a father, as thunder.

Sit with this psalm and ask God to give you rightly attuned awe.

Ask him to mend again the broken compass of your soul. Pray for ordered loves and a heart that seeks him foremost. Ponder the glory of this reality—God speaks to you. Thank him for the precious gift of Scripture and the precious incarnation of Christ the Word.

Pray:

Blessed Lord, who caused all Holy Scriptures to be written for our learning: Grant us so to hear them, read, mark, learn, and inwardly digest them, that by patience and the comfort of your Holy Word we may embrace and ever hold fast the blessed hope of everlasting life, which you have given us in our Savior Jesus Christ; who lives and reigns with you and the Holy Spirit, one God, for ever and ever. Amen.

(Anglican Church in North America Book of Common Prayer)

Ordinary Time Day 5

MARY RACHEL BOYD

Read: *Psalm 119:161–168*

> Princes persecute me without cause,
>   but my heart stands in awe of your words.
> I rejoice at your word
>   like one who finds great spoil.
> I hate and abhor falsehood,
>   but I love your law.
> Seven times a day I praise you
>   for your righteous rules.
> Great peace have those who love your law;
>   nothing can make them stumble.
> I hope for your salvation, O LORD,
>   and I do your commandments.
> My soul keeps your testimonies;
>   I love them exceedingly.
> I keep your precepts and testimonies,
>   for all my ways are before you.

Reflect:

Like all Jewish children, Jesus memorized, sang, and prayed the words of Scripture. Read back through this stanza from Psalm 119 in light of what you know about the life, death, and resurrection of Jesus Christ. What was it like for him to speak and pray these words? How might these words have given him hope, joy, and confidence?

Too often we read Scripture as a means of self-reflection or as a way to make sense of our own lives, but this psalmist had a far greater landscape in mind. He proclaimed honor and awe for God's righteousness and its effect in his life; he knew God was his only hope for salvation; he determined to pursue a life of obedience. The psalmist loved Scripture "exceedingly" (v. 167) and placed his full confidence in God's law. Those who love God's law have great peace, he declared, and "nothing can make them stumble" (v. 165).

Pause and reflect. Doesn't this psalm sound like the heart of Jesus? His soul was shaped by the Scriptures. In his final days before the crucifixion, Jesus prayed as this psalmist prayed. He spoke of his love for God and his determination to obey.

As you pray, read again these words from Psalm 119. Let the triune God bring comfort and strength to your anxious heart. Remember that all of your ways are before God (v. 168) and that he will keep you from stumbling.

Pray:

Write your blessed name, O Lord, upon my heart, there to remain so indelibly engraven, that no prosperity, no adversity shall ever move me from your love. Be to me a strong tower of defense, a comforter in tribulation, a deliverer in distress, a very present help in trouble, and a guide to heaven through the many temptations and dangers of this life. Amen.

(Thomas à Kempis)

Ordinary Time Day 6

KARI WEST

Read: *Psalm 119:169–176*

Let my cry come before you, O Lord;
    give me understanding according to your word!
Let my plea come before you;
    deliver me according to your word.
My lips will pour forth praise,
    for you teach me your statutes.
My tongue will sing of your word,
    for all your commandments are right.
Let your hand be ready to help me,
    for I have chosen your precepts.
I long for your salvation, O Lord,
    and your law is my delight.
Let my soul live and praise you,
    and let your rules help me.
I have gone astray like a lost sheep; seek your servant,
    for I do not forget your commandments.

Reflect:

Listen to some of the psalmist's requests of God:

- "Let my cry come before you" (v. 169).
- "Give me understanding" (v. 169).
- "Deliver me" (v. 170).
- "Help me" (v. 173).
- "Seek your servant" (v. 176).

One thing we never learn from this holy prayer book is independence. The Psalms continually put us in the place of the supplicant, asking God for what we need. They repeatedly teach us that we are not enough on our own.

There is freedom in the knowledge that we are dependent creatures. We need the gracious care of our Father, which he promises to give us. There is freedom in not having to posture and pretend that we are fully capable in every way.

Choose a verse from this stanza of Psalm 119 that captures your most pressing spiritual need. Do you need fresh assurance that God hears you? Do you need to confess your straying and ask him to seek you again? Do you need understanding? Do you need lips that overflow in praise?

Come to your good heavenly Father and pray the verse you have chosen. Trust that he will give you all you require for life and godliness. Then praise him for his gracious and perfect provision for you and for all his people.

Pray:

O Lord bless us and keep us;

O Lord make your face to shine upon us and be gracious to us;

Lord, turn your countenance upon us and give us peace.

For Jesus's sake. Amen.

(Adapted from Numbers 6:24–26)

Trinity Sunday: 1st Sunday of Ordinary Time

SALLY BREEDLOVE

Read: *Psalm 100:1–5*

> Make a joyful noise to the LORD, all the earth!
> > Serve the LORD with gladness!
> > Come into his presence with singing!
> Know that the LORD, he is God!
> > It is he who made us, and we are his;
> > we are his people, and the sheep of his pasture.
> Enter his gates with thanksgiving,
> > and his courts with praise!
> > Give thanks to him; bless his name!
> For the LORD is good;
> > his steadfast love endures forever,
> > and his faithfulness to all generations.

Reflect:

Gladness is in short supply these days. But this psalm instructs us to choose gladness and exuberant joy. Can you hear how the psalmist's delight overflowed? He exhorted us: Shout out how good things are! Sing joyful songs to God! Come near to him with praise and thanksgiving!

This psalm and Psalm 23 endure as two of the most beloved of all psalms. Could it be that at the core of our beings we need to know we are cared for by the Good Shepherd? Could it be that we need deep gladness?

The seriousness and distress of our world lead people to scoff at the idea that joy is meant to have a central place in our lives. But we were made for joy. The work of being changed into the likeness of Jesus is growth toward joy. Paul put it this way in 2 Corinthians 1:24: "We work with you for your joy."

Could it be that the mark of true Christlikeness is not just love and peace but also joy? Dare we hope that the trajectory of a life of faith is a movement toward greater and greater joy?

We belong to God. He takes care of us. We are safe. He chooses us. We are beloved.

Belongingness, safety, belovedness. If our life with God is our truest reality, then all will indeed be well.

Will you let joy find you?

As you pray, let this psalm lead you into joy, thanksgiving, and praise.

Pray:

O heavenly Father, you have filled the world with beauty: Open our eyes to behold your gracious hand in all your works; that, rejoicing in your whole creation, we may learn to serve you with gladness; for the sake of him through whom all things were made, your Son Jesus Christ our Lord. Amen.

(Anglican Church in North America Book of Common Prayer)

Ordinary Time Day 8

KARI WEST

Read: *Galatians 1:1–9*

Paul, an apostle—not from men nor through man, but through
Jesus Christ and God the Father, who raised him from the dead—
and all the brothers who are with me,
To the churches of Galatia:

Grace to you and peace from God our Father and the Lord Jesus
Christ, who gave himself for our sins to deliver us from the present
evil age, according to the will of our God and Father, to whom be
the glory forever and ever. Amen.

I am astonished that you are so quickly deserting him who
called you in the grace of Christ and are turning to a different
gospel—not that there is another one, but there are some who
trouble you and want to distort the gospel of Christ. But even if we
or an angel from heaven should preach to you a gospel contrary to
the one we preached to you, let him be accursed. As we have said
before, so now I say again: If anyone is preaching to you a gospel
contrary to the one you received, let him be accursed.

Reflect:

In this opening passage of Galatians, notice that Paul didn't see the gospel as
a disembodied idea. It is not an interesting theological concept to bat around
in our minds or debate in our seminary classes.

The Lord Jesus Christ gave himself for our sins to rescue us from the
present evil age. Christ presents himself in the gospel. It is the story of his
life, death, and resurrection. Through it, we encounter a person who is very
alive and very real.

This is why Paul was so incensed in these beginning verses. If the
Galatians deserted the gospel, if they turned from the atoning sacrifice of
Jesus and began to believe there were other avenues to friendship with God,
they would lose everything. In turning from the gospel, Paul said, they were
deserting the one who called them to live in the grace of Christ.

They weren't simply swapping out one philosophy of life for another. They were turning from the one living, reigning Lord who bridged the chasm between their souls and their souls' Maker. They were turning toward spiritual death.

We run the risk of making the same mistake today. Jesus offers himself to us through the gospel. Do not turn from him to any other savior. Embrace him as your Lord and live in the grace he gives. As you pray, confess any wanderings from Christ. Ask for fresh faith to see the gospel as the one beautiful, true way to eternal life with God.

Pray:

Gracious Father, we pray for your holy Catholic Church. Fill it with all truth, in all truth with all peace. Where it is corrupt, purify it; where it is in error, direct it; where in anything it is amiss, reform it. Where it is right, strengthen it; where it is in want, provide for it; where it is divided, reunite it; for the sake of Jesus Christ your Son our Savior. Amen.

(William Laud)

Ordinary Time Day 9

SALLY BREEDLOVE

Read: *Galatians 1:10–24*

For am I now seeking the approval of man, or of God? Or am I trying to please man? If I were still trying to please man, I would not be a servant of Christ.

For I would have you know, brothers, that the gospel that was preached by me is not man's gospel. For I did not receive it from any man, nor was I taught it, but I received it through a revelation of Jesus Christ. For you have heard of my former life in Judaism, how I persecuted the church of God violently and tried to destroy it. And I was advancing in Judaism beyond many of my own age among my people, so extremely zealous was I for the traditions of my fathers. But when he who had set me apart before I was born, and who called me by his grace, was pleased to reveal his Son to me, in order that I might preach him among the Gentiles, I did not immediately consult with anyone; nor did I go up to Jerusalem to those who were apostles before me, but I went away into Arabia, and returned again to Damascus.

Then after three years I went up to Jerusalem to visit Cephas and remained with him fifteen days. But I saw none of the other apostles except James the Lord's brother. (In what I am writing to you, before God, I do not lie!) Then I went into the regions of Syria and Cilicia. And I was still unknown in person to the churches of Judea that are in Christ. They only were hearing it said, "He who used to persecute us is now preaching the faith he once tried to destroy." And they glorified God because of me.

Reflect:

We have just finished remembering and celebrating Christ's death and resurrection, and now we turn to consider a man wholly changed by the power of that death and resurrection.

Paul experienced an about-face in his life—he turned from hating Jesus Christ to worshipping Jesus and loving the message that was made real in his death and resurrection. Paul abandoned the life of intense religious observance that had morphed into a murderous hatred of the new Christian believers, and he became instead a man determined to proclaim Jesus as the only one who could give "himself for our sins to deliver us from the present evil age" (Galatians 1:4).

Do you ever wish that you yourself could be so radically changed? Are you ever sick and hopeless because you keep on being the same person and doing the same thing?

Look at what changed Paul—a powerful encounter with Jesus on the road to Damascus, where he saw the depth of his own sin and the deeper reality of Christ and his mercy. Are you willing to turn from your sin and say yes to God's mercy?

Something else reshaped Paul's life. He made time after his Damascus road encounter to listen long to Jesus. Paul wrote that he went to the Arabian Desert for three years to be with Jesus in solitude and to be taught by him.

As you start this new season, are there any about-face decisions you need to make concerning how you treat your family, your own body, or the community around you? Will you encounter Jesus and let him be Lord? Are you willing to make time regularly to be with Jesus in quiet and let the Spirit teach you?

As you pray, ask God to help you repent where you need to repent. Thank him for his great mercy. Ask him for the will to make time to simply be with him each day.

Pray:

Thanks be to thee, My Lord Jesus Christ, for all the pains and insults thou hast borne for me, and for all the benefits thou hast given me. O most merciful Redeemer, Friend, and Brother: Grant that I may see thee more clearly, love thee more dearly, and follow thee more nearly, day by day. Amen.

(Richard of Chichester)

Ordinary Time Day 10
SALLY BREEDLOVE

Read: *Galatians 2:17–21*

> But if, in our endeavor to be justified in Christ, we too were found to be sinners, is Christ then a servant of sin? Certainly not! For if I rebuild what I tore down, I prove myself to be a transgressor. For through the law I died to the law, so that I might live to God. I have been crucified with Christ. It is no longer I who live, but Christ who lives in me. And the life I now live in the flesh I live by faith in the Son of God, who loved me and gave himself for me. I do not nullify the grace of God, for if righteousness were through the law, then Christ died for no purpose.

Reflect:

We have a new phrase in our culture: *virtue signaling*. It's a rampant game, easy to play. Pick an issue that's important to you—whether it is morality, politics, how to raise your children, or how you treat your dog—and then find those who see things differently and deride them for their opposing view. Perhaps you've been a victim of this game, or perhaps you've been the instigator.

What can we do about our fractured society, the judging that is done against us as believers in Jesus and the judging we do of others?

Our friend the apostle Paul invited us to join him in a new freedom, the freedom of not having to be the person who's always at the top of the virtue pecking order. What do we need to do to join him in this spacious new life?

We need the humility to know we are broken people who hurt others. We need to confess our ego and our desire to be seen as the right one, the best one, or the one who is trying the hardest.

But if we let go of our pride of place and our desire to be praised and vindicated, how can we know we matter? How can we be safe? Once again Paul's letters are instructive for us. He said that Christ lived in him. Christ loved him and gave his life for Paul—and he did the same for you. If you belong to Christ, the truest thing about you is not how virtuous you are but how much you are loved.

As you go to prayer, will you join the tax collector in Luke 18:13 and pray his prayer: "God, have mercy on me, a sinner" (NIV)? Will you thank your Father that his mercy toward you overflows? When he sees you, he sees his beautiful Son alive in you; he does not see your battle-weary, battle-stained soul. He does not see your protests that you are trying as hard as you can. He simply sees his beloved Son's love for you.

Lay down your ego and come to him. Pray.

Pray:

Lord Jesus, Master Carpenter of Nazareth, on the Cross through wood and nails you wrought our full salvation: Wield well your tools in this, your workshop, that we who come to you rough-hewn may be fashioned into truer beauty by your hand; who with the Father and the Holy Spirit live and reign, one God, world without end. Amen.

(Anglican Church in North America Book of Common Prayer)

Ordinary Time Day 11

SALLY BREEDLOVE

Read: *Galatians 3:1–6*

O foolish Galatians! Who has bewitched you? It was before your
eyes that Jesus Christ was publicly portrayed as crucified. Let me ask
you only this: Did you receive the Spirit by works of the law or by
hearing with faith? Are you so foolish? Having begun by the Spirit,
are you now being perfected by the flesh? Did you suffer so many
things in vain—if indeed it was in vain? Does he who supplies the
Spirit to you and works miracles among you do so by works of the
law, or by hearing with faith—just as Abraham "believed God, and
it was counted to him as righteousness"?

Reflect:

Have you ever daydreamed about what it would be like to receive an enormously
large, unexpected inheritance? Perhaps a far-flung childless great-aunt leaves you
her fortune. Stay with that imagining. What if you barely made enough for rent
each month and knew you would never have the money for a down payment
on a home of your own? What if you depended on the government for food
programs and health care? What if you worked every job you could find, but they
were always temporary minimum wage jobs, offering no hope of advancement?

What if you went by your post office box one day and found a notice
for a certified letter? When you retrieved the letter from the postal clerk, you
learned an estate lawyer wanted you to call him because you had an inheritance in store.

What would you do? Would you leave the post office, pray your car
would start, and drive to your next odd job? Or would you find a way to call
the lawyer? Would you start dreaming about a whole new life—an education,
a dependable car, a home of your own, and new clothes that didn't come
from the thrift store?

Paul took pains in Galatians 3 to explain how this gift of new life in
Christ is utterly comprehensive and transformative. It began with the death

of Christ on the cross, and it is sustained daily by the Spirit. It is an abundant inheritance we did not earn; it is treasure beyond all imagining.

It's as if Paul was saying, "Live like a person who's just received that certified letter. Start making plans to become the well-resourced person you actually are. And look around you—everyone who has received this same inheritance is your sibling, your equal. Be encouraged and encourage each other!"

As you pray, ask God to help you lay down all your striving to save yourself or remake your life. Thank him that you have so much more than an earthly inheritance. Thank him for the lavish gift of the Father, Son, and Holy Spirit in your life.

Pray:

What shall I render to the LORD for all his benefits to me? I will lift up the cup of salvation and call on the name of the LORD, I will pay my vows to the LORD in the presence of all his people. Amen.

(Psalm 116:12–14)

Ordinary Time Day 12

MATT HOEHN

Read: *Galatians 3:25–27*

But now that faith has come, we are no longer under a guardian, for in Christ Jesus you are all sons of God, through faith. For as many of you as were baptized into Christ have put on Christ.

Reflect:

While what we wear may seem like an inconsequential topic, the apostle Paul maintained that clothing is crucially significant for the Christian.

In today's passage, Paul wasn't so concerned with *what* one wears: togas, tunics, or trousers (which were actually highly unfashionable in his day). He was much more concerned with *who* one wears—namely, Jesus Christ himself.

Paul said that being baptized into Christ necessarily entails clothing yourself with Christ. Baptism means undergoing a symbolic death to the old age of the law, sin, and death in order to rise to life as a member of God's family and a participant in new creation. When we rise from the waters of baptism, we no longer wear the old self of our former sinful flesh; rather, we have been clothed with Christ.

What does it mean to be clothed with Christ?

It means *protection*. The Lord is our shield (Psalm 33:20), and he hides us in the shadow of his wings (Psalm 17:8), even though the world at our doorstep seems threatening.

It means *witness*. The good news of the gospel is on display as we exhibit the fruit of the Spirit to the watching world: "love, joy, peace, patience, kindness, goodness, faithfulness, gentleness, self-control" (Galatians 5:22–23).

It means *loving embrace*. Regardless of the future, nothing in all creation "will be able to separate us from the love of God in Christ Jesus our Lord" (Romans 8:39).

Even though our world has overwhelming issues, our spiritual clothing with Christ is a reminder of our status as God's beloved children who have been adopted into his family. It is an assurance of our eternal inheritance with him. This clothing never changes, never wears out, and never goes out of fashion.

As you pray, ask that God would remind you of the incredible assurances that accompany being clothed with Christ. Ask that those who are fearful will be comforted by the protection and loving embrace of our Father.

Pray:

Father, help me to trust in you and to root my life in you today. When the things of this world threaten to overwhelm me, give me your peace. Remind me that you never change. Clothe me with Christ so that I may experience your loving embrace today. Amen.

Ordinary Time Day 13

SALLY BREEDLOVE

Read: *Galatians 4:1–7, 28–29*

I mean that the heir, as long as he is a child, is no different from a slave, though he is the owner of everything, but he is under guardians and managers until the date set by his father. In the same way we also, when we were children, were enslaved to the elementary principles of the world. But when the fullness of time had come, God sent forth his Son, born of woman, born under the law, to redeem those who were under the law, so that we might receive adoption as sons. And because you are sons, God has sent the Spirit of his Son into our hearts, crying, "Abba! Father!" So you are no longer a slave, but a son, and if a son, then an heir through God....

Now you, brothers, like Isaac, are children of promise. But just as at that time he who was born according to the flesh persecuted him who was born according to the Spirit, so also it is now.

Reflect:

Adoption has always been part of this world.

In Galatians 4, as Paul explained how fully our adoption into God's family has changed us, he turned to the Genesis account of Abraham's two sons, Ishmael and Isaac. Their story was full of all the relational brokenness we encounter so often in our world. At the heart of this story was the reality that although Abraham had two sons, he had only one real son, Isaac. All of Abraham's blessings and wealth would be inherited by Isaac, the son of the promise.

If you have an adopted child, or if you yourself are adopted, then you know the deep longing an adopted child has to know that he or she is indeed a real son or real daughter. No matter how much the adoptive parents love their child, their love and the legal paperwork are not enough. Something in the heart of an adopted child has to shift. The child has to submit to how deeply he or she has been longed for, chosen, and loved.

Paul's longing for the Galatians to accept the truth that they are real sons and daughters of their heavenly Father was so intense that it was painful—as painful as childbirth, he said. Likely he had watched or heard of the intensity of a woman in labor and had experienced some of the agony that precedes the gift of a new life.

Paul's longing was just a shadow of God's longing for you and for me. God's heart is in agony as he waits for us to submit to being loved, wanted, and made into a family with him.

The Spirit wants to help you receive and trust the reality that God loves you as his beloved child. As you pray, ask the Spirit to help you cry out to God, "Abba, Father." As you pray, lift before God someone who needs to know the Father love of God. Put the person's name in the appropriate places in this prayer:

Pray:

Watch over your child_____, O Lord, as [his/her] days increase; bless and guide and keep [him/her] unspotted from the world. Strengthen _____ when [he/she] stands; comfort [him/her] when discouraged or sorrowful; and raise [him/her] up if [he/she] falls. And in [his/her] heart, may your peace that passes understanding abide all the days of [his/her] life, through Jesus Christ our Lord. Amen.

(Anglican Church in North America Book of Common Prayer)

2nd Sunday of Ordinary Time

WILLA KANE

Read: *Psalm 4*

> Answer me when I call, O God of my righteousness!
>> You have given me relief when I was in distress.
>> Be gracious to me and hear my prayer!
> O men, how long shall my honor be turned into shame?
>> How long will you love vain words and seek after lies?   *Selah*
> But know that the LORD has set apart the godly for himself;
>> the LORD hears when I call to him.
> Be angry, and do not sin;
>> ponder in your own hearts on your beds, and be silent.   *Selah*
> Offer right sacrifices,
>> and put your trust in the LORD.
> There are many who say, "Who will show us some good?
>> Lift up the light of your face upon us, O LORD!"
> You have put more joy in my heart
>> than they have when their grain and wine abound.
> In peace I will both lie down and sleep;
>> for you alone, O LORD, make me dwell in safety.

Reflect:

In this prayer for help, David called with passion to God, his defender. God was his protector. The Lord helped him in times of trouble.

Trouble is promised as part of our earthly existence. Most of us know trouble all too well. Today may have been such a day, filled with trouble for you and those you love. Illness, broken relationships, job loss, food insecurity, and political instability wrap cords of grief around us.

Predictably but sadly, trouble is our companion.

In the day of trouble, whom do you trust and where do you turn? Do you first look for the sort of help and answers the world offers? Do you count on your own ingenuity? Or do you turn to God?

The psalmist's enemies loved what was worthless and went after what was false. Examine your heart. What do you love? What do you seek? The world is filled with worthless and false things we use as substitute saviors. But they cannot save, and they never satisfy.

David knew there was a better way. God is our righteousness. In Jesus Christ, he has chosen us and made us his own. He hears when we call. When the Lord himself claims us as his own, substitute saviors lose their allure.

Meditate on this good news and offer a sacrifice of praise to God. Then offer your life itself as a sacrifice. Take your everyday, ordinary, "sleeping, eating, going to work, and walking around" life and place it before God as an offering.

As you pray, be like David; cry to God your defender, your helper. Thank him for the ways he has helped you in the past and for the joy of being kept by him. Trust him to do the same tomorrow. Because he never slumbers, you can lie down and sleep in peace.

Pray:

I adore you, O Lord, my helper, my defender, and lover of my soul.
I rest in the safety of your embrace and praise you as my King. Amen.

Ordinary Time Day 15

SALLY BREEDLOVE

Read: *Galatians 5:13–15, 19–24*

For you were called to freedom, brothers. Only do not use your freedom as an opportunity for the flesh, but through love serve one another. For the whole law is fulfilled in one word: "You shall love your neighbor as yourself." But if you bite and devour one another, watch out that you are not consumed by one another.

Now the works of the flesh are evident: sexual immorality, impurity, sensuality, idolatry, sorcery, enmity, strife, jealousy, fits of anger, rivalries, dissensions, divisions, envy, drunkenness, orgies, and things like these. I warn you, as I warned you before, that those who do such things will not inherit the kingdom of God. But the fruit of the Spirit is love, joy, peace, patience, kindness, goodness, faithfulness, gentleness, self-control; against such things there is no law. And those who belong to Christ Jesus have crucified the flesh with its passions and desires.

Reflect:

Christ offers us freedom from having to prove our own goodness and promises a new kind of freedom beyond our imagining. It is a freedom to learn to love well. It is the only freedom that can't be taken from us, and it is ours as we let God love us. We can't churn out love on our own. But if the Spirit is alive in us, this love will begin to reveal itself in our lives, just as truly as new life erupts in a summer garden.

Here is what God longs to grow in our hearts, things he tends in us by his Spirit:

- *Love*: Affection for others

  Do you really like the people in your life?

- *Joy*: Exuberance about life

  Is your life characterized by hope and gratitude?

- *Peace*: Serenity

  Does peace keep you even when things are unsettled?

- *Patience*: A willingness to persevere
  Are you easily frustrated? Do you give up easily?
- *Kindness*: A sense of compassion in the heart
  Are you tenderhearted?
- *Goodness*: A conviction that a basic holiness permeates things and people
  Do you respect people, or are you plagued by contempt for them?
- *Faithfulness*: Loyalty to commitments
  Do you easily give up on people? Family? Your church?
- *Gentleness*: The ability not to force your way in life
  What do you do when things don't go your way?
- *Self-control*: The ability to marshal your energies wisely
  Do you live wisely and sanely? Do you take Sabbath times?

It's the beginning of Ordinary Time. All around us, we see meadows, farmlands, and gardens teeming with new growth. Let the life around you teach you. You, too, are to be a garden of life and love that God is tending.

Walk with him around your heart right now. Ask God to show you what is growing in your life that you haven't created on your own. Ask God to help you see the tenacious weeds and briars that need rooting out. Confess the barren places in your heart. Ask your Father to change you. Thank God for the ways he is teaching you to love, confess the ways your love needs to grow, and ask him to increase your love.

Pray:

O Lord, you have taught us that without love, all our deeds are worth nothing: Send your Holy Spirit and pour into our hearts that most excellent gift of charity, the true bond of peace and of all virtues, without which whoever lives is counted dead before you; grant this for the sake of your Son Jesus Christ, who lives and reigns with you and the Holy Spirit, one God, for ever and ever. Amen.

(Anglican Church in North America Book of Common Prayer)

Ordinary Time Day 16
SALLY BREEDLOVE

Read: *Galatians 6:1–8*

Brothers, if anyone is caught in any transgression, you who are spiritual should restore him in a spirit of gentleness. Keep watch on yourself, lest you too be tempted. Bear one another's burdens, and so fulfill the law of Christ. For if anyone thinks he is something, when he is nothing, he deceives himself. But let each one test his own work, and then his reason to boast will be in himself alone and not in his neighbor. For each will have to bear his own load.

Let the one who is taught the word share all good things with the one who teaches. Do not be deceived: God is not mocked, for whatever one sows, that will he also reap. For the one who sows to his own flesh will from the flesh reap corruption, but the one who sows to the Spirit will from the Spirit reap eternal life.

Reflect:

Paul used every means at his disposal to teach us about grace: his own story, arguments from law courts and inheritance rights, the story of Abraham and his sons, and metaphors from the agricultural world. Everywhere Paul looked, he saw the freedom grace brings, the freedom a beloved son has to learn to love like his father loves.

Ordinary Time calls us into a life of daily discipleship so that we become more like Jesus—and Jesus lived a life of love.

Paul's aim in this final chapter of Galatians was to teach us how to get about the business of everyday loving. If you make your days about yourself, Paul said, you'll watch everything collapse into corruption in the end.

Or you can face the things that keep you from love and learn how to love in the complexity and brokenness of your own world. A life of love is a mosaic shaped by repeated daily decisions. It is a life of humility, a life of taking risks to help people who are living in destructive ways. It is a life of bearing the burdens of others and carrying your own daily burden.

It is a life where you quit ranking yourself and instead ask God to show you the truth about yourself. It is a life where you don't give up and where you keep doing good.

Jesus is the glorious interjection of love into our futility. He has loved us and loved this world in far greater ways than we will ever be called on to love, so don't be afraid to be the first one to love in your own broken and pain-filled relationships. Be like Jesus, and peace and mercy will flood into your life.

As you pray, ask God to give you new and specific ways to love the people in your world.

Pray:
Lord, make me an instrument of your peace,
Where there is hatred, let me sow love;
Where there is injury, pardon;
Where there is doubt, faith;
Where there is despair, hope;
Where there is darkness, light;
Where there is sadness, joy;
O Divine Master,
Grant that I may not so much seek
To be consoled as to console;
To be understood as to understand;
To be loved as to love.
For it is in giving that we receive;
It is in pardoning that we are pardoned;
And it is in dying that we are born to eternal life.
Amen.

(Saint Francis of Assisi)

Ordinary Time Day 17
WILLA KANE

Read: *Galatians 6:1–2, 9–10*

Brothers, if anyone is caught in any transgression, you who are spiritual should restore him in a spirit of gentleness. Keep watch on yourself, lest you too be tempted. Bear one another's burdens, and so fulfill the law of Christ....

And let us not grow weary of doing good, for in due season we will reap, if we do not give up. So then, as we have opportunity, let us do good to everyone, and especially to those who are of the household of faith.

Reflect:

The call to bear each other's burdens applies to us as it did to believers in Galatia almost two thousand years ago. Theirs was a time when religious zealots tried to add requirements to the freedom promised by grace alone in Christ alone. Ours is often a season of division and unrest when the needs within and around us seem to far exceed our resources.

Many of us are weary. How are we to bear our own burdens, much less help shoulder the burdens of those around us?

In the sacrificial simplicity of his love, Jesus said, "Come to me, all who labor and are heavy laden, and I will give you rest. Take my yoke upon you, and learn from me, for I am gentle and lowly in heart, and you will find rest for your souls. For my yoke is easy, and my burden is light" (Matthew 11:28–30).

Rest for the weary is more than a physical need. It's a deep desire of our souls that is satisfied only in Christ. As we come to him with empty hands and on bended knee, his love pours rest into our weary souls. Jesus's love is selfless, sacrificial, sympathetic, and sure.

- Jesus's love is selfless. When we come, Jesus gives.
- Jesus's love is sacrificial. He bore in his body the crushing burden of sin for all humanity.

- Jesus's love is sympathetic. He was tempted in every way as we are, so he knows our pain and struggle.
- Jesus's love is sure. Our hope in him is an anchor for the soul.

This Jesus, our burden-bearer, admonishes us to bear each other's burdens and in so doing fulfill the law of Christ. Galatians 5:14 reads, "For the whole law is fulfilled in one word: 'You shall love your neighbor as yourself.'"

To obey the law of Christ is to love one's neighbors with his love: selfless, sacrificial, sympathetic, and sure. This is possible only as Jesus pours his love through us. Though expressed in myriad practical ways, this love always draws us and points others to a relationship with Christ—to know Jesus and grow in him.

Where is God calling you to extend this kind of love? What opportunities to fulfill the law of Christ are right in front of you? Pray and listen. The Spirit will lead you.

Pray:

Heavenly Father, we are weary. These times are hard, and we are broken. Would you give us humility to lay our burdens down at the foot of the cross, to receive help and rest in Jesus, and to receive strength and compassion to stoop low to bear the burdens of those around us, especially our brothers and sisters in Christ? Amen.

Ordinary Time Day 18

SALLY BREEDLOVE

Read: *Galatians 6:1–5 & Proverbs 14:8*

Brothers, if anyone is caught in any transgression, you who are spiritual should restore him in a spirit of gentleness. Keep watch on yourself, lest you too be tempted. Bear one another's burdens, and so fulfill the law of Christ. For if anyone thinks he is something, when he is nothing, he deceives himself. But let each one test his own work, and then his reason to boast will be in himself alone and not in his neighbor. For each will have to bear his own load.

The wisdom of the prudent is to discern his way,
but the folly of fools is deceiving.

Reflect:

Pause and ask yourself, "How have I been changed recently?"

As you begin your time of prayer, would you be willing to ask yourself a few questions about your current season of life?

Don't try to dress up your answers, don't resist what comes to you, and don't move into self-condemnation as you respond. Simply ponder your responses to the following questions:

- If Jesus Christ were to ask you what has been the hardest thing about this season, what would you tell him?
- What are you afraid Jesus might ask of you in this season?
- What do you wish Jesus would ask you or tell you about this time?
- Is there something this season has given you that you are deeply grateful for? If so, what is it?
- Is there some new way of living or small habit you have learned that you want to take into future seasons?

As you move into prayer, read these verses from Psalm 103 aloud and thank the Lord for his presence and provision.

Pray:

Bless the Lord, O my soul,
>and all that is within me,
>>bless his holy name!

Bless the Lord, O my soul,
>and forget not all his benefits,

who forgives all your iniquity,
>who heals all your diseases,

who redeems your life from the pit,
>who crowns you with steadfast love and mercy,

who satisfies you with good
>so that your youth is renewed like the eagle's. . .

The Lord is merciful and gracious,
>slow to anger and abounding in steadfast love.

He will not always chide,
>nor will he keep his anger forever.

He does not deal with us according to our sins,
>nor repay us according to our iniquities.

For as high as the heavens are above the earth,
>so great is his steadfast love toward those who fear him;

as far as the east is from the west,
>so far does he remove our transgressions from us.

As a father shows compassion to his children,
>so the Lord shows compassion to those who fear him.

For he knows our frame;
>he remembers that we are dust. . .

Bless the Lord, O you his angels,
>you mighty ones who do his word. . .

Bless the Lord, all his works,
>in all places of his dominion.

Bless the Lord, O my soul! Amen.

Ordinary Time Day 19
BRANDON WALSH

Read: *Ecclesiastes 6*

There is an evil that I have seen under the sun, and it lies heavy on mankind: a man to whom God gives wealth, possessions, and honor, so that he lacks nothing of all that he desires, yet God does not give him power to enjoy them, but a stranger enjoys them. This is vanity; it is a grievous evil. If a man fathers a hundred children and lives many years, so that the days of his years are many, but his soul is not satisfied with life's good things, and he also has no burial, I say that a stillborn child is better off than he. For it comes in vanity and goes in darkness, and in darkness its name is covered. Moreover, it has not seen the sun or known anything, yet it finds rest rather than he. Even though he should live a thousand years twice over, yet enjoy no good—do not all go to the one place?

All the toil of man is for his mouth, yet his appetite is not satisfied. For what advantage has the wise man over the fool? And what does the poor man have who knows how to conduct himself before the living? Better is the sight of the eyes than the wandering of the appetite: this also is vanity and a striving after wind.

Whatever has come to be has already been named, and it is known what man is, and that he is not able to dispute with one stronger than he. The more words, the more vanity, and what is the advantage to man? For who knows what is good for man while he lives the few days of his vain life, which he passes like a shadow? For who can tell man what will be after him under the sun?

Reflect:

Sometimes it's hard to trust what we know. We know a second dessert is rarely a good idea, but we go back anyway. We know we need more sleep to feel better in the morning, but we stay up longer than we should.

In the same way, most of us know that wealth, honor, and security are not satisfying ends in and of themselves, but we long for them anyway. Yet it is all vanity and vapor—here today, gone tomorrow.

Ecclesiastes 6 warns of the dangers of placing our hope in wealth. Jesus, too, had harrowing things to say about wealth and its dangers. He admonishes us that pride, self-righteousness, and the desire for wealth are destructive to our souls.

What is it about a longing for material wealth that it so dangerous? God created the world good. Food for feasting, clothes for wearing, and gold for artistry are part of his creation. Jesus himself turned water into wine for a wedding and was accused of gluttony (see Luke 7). But he also fasted for forty days in the wilderness and had no place to lay his head.

Wealth is not dangerous because physical things are bad. Wealth proves dangerous because it falsely promises us that it can satisfy our deep longing for security, affection, glory, and power. But only God can fill our hearts. Material things must be seen for what they are: blessings, yes, but never blessings that can satisfy our longings.

As you pray, ask God to show you where you are too eager for material blessings. Ask him where you can be a generous person instead. The best cure for your fixation on your needs or wants is often generosity. It's hard to be possessed by something and to obsess about it if you give it away. Nothing puts wealth in its proper place more than sharing it with others. Pray for the grace of generosity. Then ask God to meet your deep longings and heal your fears and insecurities.

Pray:

Eternal Word, only begotten Son of God,
Teach me true generosity.
Teach me to serve you as you deserve.
To give without counting the cost,
To fight heedless of wounds,
To labor without seeking rest,
To sacrifice myself without thought of any reward
Save the knowledge that I have done your will. Amen.

(Saint Ignatius of Loyola)

Ordinary Time Day 20

KARI WEST

Read: *Jeremiah 29:4–14*

"Thus says the LORD of hosts, the God of Israel, to all the exiles whom I have sent into exile from Jerusalem to Babylon: Build houses and live in them; plant gardens and eat their produce. Take wives and have sons and daughters; take wives for your sons, and give your daughters in marriage, that they may bear sons and daughters; multiply there, and do not decrease. But seek the welfare of the city where I have sent you into exile, and pray to the LORD on its behalf, for in its welfare you will find your welfare. For thus says the LORD of hosts, the God of Israel: Do not let your prophets and your diviners who are among you deceive you, and do not listen to the dreams that they dream, for it is a lie that they are prophesying to you in my name; I did not send them, declares the LORD.

"For thus says the LORD: When seventy years are completed for Babylon, I will visit you, and I will fulfill to you my promise and bring you back to this place. For I know the plans I have for you, declares the LORD, plans for welfare and not for evil, to give you a future and a hope. Then you will call upon me and come and pray to me, and I will hear you. You will seek me and find me, when you seek me with all your heart. I will be found by you, declares the LORD, and I will restore your fortunes and gather you from all the nations and all the places where I have driven you, declares the LORD, and I will bring you back to the place from which I sent you into exile."

Reflect:

The Lord Almighty carried his people into exile and promised to return them to their homeland. In the meantime, while they waited in a land not their own, he commanded them to seek the welfare of their captors. He told them to pray for the peace and prosperity of those who had inflicted massive suffering on them.

On the heels of this seemingly impossible charge, God gave them a promise that we often hear quoted today: He knows the plans he has for his people. He plans to care for them, to give them hope, and to give them a future. He promises to bow low and hear each prayer offered to him. He promises to be found by those who seek him with their whole hearts.

His deep and powerful words of promise were not given to populate a floral-decorated Instagram post or to make us feel good about ourselves. They were meant to propel the Israelites to love their enemies and seek the peace and prosperity of the group who had wreaked havoc on them.

By the great work of Christ, we have been grafted in as part of God's people, so we can take these words of promise to the Israelites and embrace them as a promise for ourselves. But we must also let these beautiful words lead us where they were always designed to lead God's people—to seek the peace and goodness of those who despise, mistreat, malign, or disregard us.

Meditate on God's great and powerful words and ask him to propel you toward love for your enemies. Hope in this great promise—God will be found by his people.

Pray:

Proceeding Spirit, our defense…
Refine and purge our earthly parts;
But, oh, inflame and fire our hearts!
…And, lest our feet should step astray,
Protect and guide us in the way.
Make us eternal truths receive,
And practice all that we believe:
Give us thyself, that we may see
The Father and the Son, by thee.
Amen.

("Come, Creator Spirit," John Dryden)

3rd Sunday of Ordinary Time
SALLY BREEDLOVE

Read: *Psalm 4:3–5*

> But know that the LORD has set apart the godly for himself;
>> the LORD hears when I call to him.
> Be angry, and do not sin;
>> ponder in your own hearts on your beds, and be
>> silent. *Selah*
> Offer right sacrifices,
>> and put your trust in the LORD.

Reflect:

We may miss the opportunity the turbulence of our time offers us. In an age of endless ways to connect, endless things to blog about, endless material to read online, endless movies, and endless phone calls with people we love, we may miss or resist the invitation right in front of us.

Could it be we are ignoring (or bolting shut) the door that would lead us into silence and stillness?

We could sit and be still at some point in the twenty-four hours that each day offers. We could be undistracted and quiet and ponder the mystery that God is always present. We could give our own souls room to speak the prayers we would pray if we were entirely honest. We could make enough space to find out what we really want to say to each other. And we could find that silence is not emptiness nor a terrifying loneliness. We could discover, if we linger in silence, that it is brimming with the presence of the good and beautiful God.

What do you really want?

Will you choose to stop for ten minutes or even an hour and observe silence each day? Will you make space to be with your own soul and to seek the triune God, who is always present even when our hurried and distracted lives tell us otherwise?

Be still; be silent. Let there be spaces that aren't filled with connecting, with internet information, or with words.

Pray for yourself. Are there places where God is calling you to simply stop and be with him? Pray for those who are lonely and terrified of being alone. Pray they will know the goodness of God, who is always present.

Pray:

King of kings and Lord of lords, our striving, searching, and toil brings us back to where we started today: in your hands and sheltered by you. We praise you, the one who is everywhere present, filling all things. Protect the physicians and caretakers who tend to the sick. Open the mouths of your people so that we can sing your praises; give us strong and gentle hands to lift up the hurting. Grant us peaceful sleep tonight, the hope and faith to do your will tomorrow, and life without end in your kingdom. Amen.

Ordinary Time Day 22
BILL BOYD

Read: *Luke 1:26–38*

> In the sixth month the angel Gabriel was sent from God to a city of Galilee named Nazareth, to a virgin betrothed to a man whose name was Joseph, of the house of David. And the virgin's name was Mary. And he came to her and said, "Greetings, O favored one, the Lord is with you!" But she was greatly troubled at the saying, and tried to discern what sort of greeting this might be. And the angel said to her, "Do not be afraid, Mary, for you have found favor with God. And behold, you will conceive in your womb and bear a son, and you shall call his name Jesus. He will be great and will be called the Son of the Most High. And the Lord God will give to him the throne of his father David, and he will reign over the house of Jacob forever, and of his kingdom there will be no end."
>
> And Mary said to the angel, "How will this be, since I am a virgin?"
>
> And the angel answered her, "The Holy Spirit will come upon you, and the power of the Most High will overshadow you; therefore the child to be born will be called holy—the Son of God. And behold, your relative Elizabeth in her old age has also conceived a son, and this is the sixth month with her who was called barren. For nothing will be impossible with God." And Mary said, "Behold, I am the servant of the Lord; let it be to me according to your word." And the angel departed from her.

Reflect:

When angels appeared in the Bible, they reassured those who encountered them that they need not be afraid. Mary was open to the Lord, willing to receive his message and hold it in her heart. Her response revealed her quiet confidence in the inherent goodness of the Almighty.

How does one cultivate a heart that is open to the Word of the Lord? Luke wrote that Mary was disturbed by the angel's words, but she tried to discern what he meant. She was willing to listen, to consider.

"Willing to listen" would be a fine epitaph for any of us, a succinct summary of a life well lived. The Scriptures present God himself as quite willing to listen. The Spirit listens to the groans and utterances of our souls. God listens to the distress of his people. And to Mary the richest reward was bestowed, the heart-wrenching honor of hearing Christ and then bearing Christ within her, the same honor given this and every day to any and all willing to listen to the Lord.

As you pray, consider Mary's response to the angel Gabriel's annunciation. Ponder these words as one of the finest affirmations of faith. Pray these words as a way to actively practice listening to the Lord.

Pray:

My soul glorifies the Lord
and my spirit rejoices in God my Savior,
for he has been mindful
of the humble state of his servant.
From now on all generations will call me blessed,
for the Mighty One has done great things for me—
holy is his name.
His mercy extends to those who fear him,
from generation to generation.
He has performed mighty deeds with his arm;
he has scattered those who are proud in their inmost thoughts.
He has brought down rulers from their thrones
but has lifted up the humble.
He has filled the hungry with good things
but has sent the rich away empty.
He has helped his servant Israel,
remembering to be merciful
to Abraham and his descendants forever,
just as he promised our ancestors. Amen.

(Luke 1:46–55 NIV)

Ordinary Time Day 23
KARI WEST

Read: *Luke 5:27–32*

> After this he went out and saw a tax collector named Levi, sitting at the tax booth. And he said to him, "Follow me." And leaving everything, he rose and followed him.
>
> And Levi made him a great feast in his house, and there was a large company of tax collectors and others reclining at table with them. And the Pharisees and their scribes grumbled at his disciples, saying, "Why do you eat and drink with tax collectors and sinners?" And Jesus answered them, "Those who are well have no need of a physician, but those who are sick. I have not come to call the righteous but sinners to repentance."

Reflect:

"Follow me" (v. 27). How succinct and how powerful were Christ's words to Levi.

Our Lord held out this invitation to Levi despite the man's despised job description, his dishonest dealings, his greed, and his disreputability. Tax collectors, corrupt instruments of foreign Roman rule, were universally hated by their fellow Jews for their disloyalty and greed. They wielded the borrowed power of the oppressor to cheat their own people and line their own pockets.

In fact, Christ spoke these words because of these things and their underlying cause. The Great Physician knows the outward symptoms of a decrepit heart. He unapologetically and graciously holds out the remedy—*Follow me.*

The cure is simple: repentance. Jesus called Levi out of his old sinful ruts and onto a path of discipleship. Levi immediately heeded the call.

But, as a warning to all of us, the Pharisees refused to acknowledge that such a profound diagnosis of sin could apply to them. "We are well," they maintained. "We have no need of a doctor's care." Rejecting Jesus's gracious cure, they were left in their own self-deception, decay, and whitewashed tombs.

By contrast, a life of repentance and renewal fueled by the healing power of the Spirit—like Levi's—spills over into generosity, thankfulness, and celebration.

As you pray, inhabit the place of Levi. Reject the lie of the Pharisees. You are not well. Embrace the reality that sin's infection has spread in you and that there is no thought, word, or deed that is free of decay.

And then embrace the cure of the Great Physician. Believe the gospel. Follow hard after Jesus. Leave behind every weight and all entangling sin and throw a party to celebrate the elaborate grace Jesus offers.

Pray:

Christ, our healer, let us remember how much we need you. Keep us from believing the lie of our own self-righteousness. Thank you for your shed blood that covers us and empowers us to heed your call of repentance; in your precious and powerful name. Amen.

Ordinary Time Day 24

KARI WEST

Read: *Luke 6:1–11*

On a Sabbath, while he was going through the grainfields, his disciples plucked and ate some heads of grain, rubbing them in their hands. But some of the Pharisees said, "Why are you doing what is not lawful to do on the Sabbath?" And Jesus answered them, "Have you not read what David did when he was hungry, he and those who were with him: how he entered the house of God and took and ate the bread of the Presence, which is not lawful for any but the priests to eat, and also gave it to those with him?" And he said to them, "The Son of Man is lord of the Sabbath."

On another Sabbath, he entered the synagogue and was teaching, and a man was there whose right hand was withered. And the scribes and the Pharisees watched him, to see whether he would heal on the Sabbath, so that they might find a reason to accuse him. But he knew their thoughts, and he said to the man with the withered hand, "Come and stand here." And he rose and stood there. And Jesus said to them, "I ask you, is it lawful on the Sabbath to do good or to do harm, to save life or to destroy it?" And after looking around at them all he said to him, "Stretch out your hand." And he did so, and his hand was restored. But they were filled with fury and discussed with one another what they might do to Jesus.

Reflect:

In this passage, much of the action stemmed from need. Christ's disciples were hungry, so they stretched out their hands for grain. In the Old Testament, David needed sustenance, so he stretched out his hand for holy bread. The helpless man in the synagogue stretched out his withered hand for healing.

Stretching out our hands is a humble action, one that acknowledges our dependence. One of the Sabbath's key lessons is that we need to learn to rely on God. Don't work constantly. Give a day to rest and worship. Recall your creatureliness, your need for respite, your utter lack of self-sufficiency. Recall that God is Lord and that your place is at his feet with outstretched hands, asking for provision and restoration. The Lord of the Sabbath will give you what you need.

Pause a moment and consider the implications of what Christ said about himself. To be the Lord of the Sabbath means that true rest describes the nature of his reign. Christ bid all who are weary to come, lay down their burdens, and find a lighter yoke. We all carry a yoke; no one is free of all burden. However, the yoke of submission to right lordship—the lordship of Christ—is easy and light.

Come and bow before the Lord of the Sabbath. Confess the ways you have again taken up the heavy yoke of self-sufficiency and pride. Confess that your failure to show humility, love, and a desire for true life is the reason you have not been guided into Sabbath living. Confess that you've followed in the paths of the Pharisees and set yourself against the preeminence of Christ.

And then, rejoice! Christ has purchased your future shalom at great cost to himself. Rejoice that he comes with healing in his wings. Rejoice that though we come with hunger and disease, our Lord of Sabbath gives us bread and restoration. Rejoice that his coming kingdom will be full of feasting and rest.

Pray:

O Christ, as the eyes of servants look to the hand of their master, as the eyes of a maidservant to the hand of her mistress, so our eyes will look to you, O Lord our God, till you have mercy upon us. Bless us and keep us, Lord of the Sabbath. Amen.

Ordinary Time Day 25

KARI WEST

Read: *Luke 7:1–10*

After he had finished all his sayings in the hearing of the people, he entered Capernaum. Now a centurion had a servant who was sick and at the point of death, who was highly valued by him. When the centurion heard about Jesus, he sent to him elders of the Jews, asking him to come and heal his servant. And when they came to Jesus, they pleaded with him earnestly, saying, "He is worthy to have you do this for him, for he loves our nation, and he is the one who built us our synagogue." And Jesus went with them. When he was not far from the house, the centurion sent friends, saying to him, "Lord, do not trouble yourself, for I am not worthy to have you come under my roof. Therefore I did not presume to come to you. But say the word, and let my servant be healed. For I too am a man set under authority, with soldiers under me: and I say to one, 'Go,' and he goes; and to another, 'Come,' and he comes; and to my servant, 'Do this,' and he does it." When Jesus heard these things, he marveled at him, and turning to the crowd that followed him, said, "I tell you, not even in Israel have I found such faith." And when those who had been sent returned to the house, they found the servant well.

Reflect:

What could cause the Maker of the stars to marvel? Christ, who created all things and who holds all things together, the Son of the Most High God—is there something that can make him wonder?

And if so, would it not be worth all the riches in the world to possess it? In these verses, we behold a mystery—Jesus marveled at a man's humble faith.

This centurion was a man of some human importance and power. He had soldiers at his command, enough wealth to build the Jewish synagogue, and enough social clout for the Jewish leaders to beg a favor of Christ on his behalf.

62

Yet this pagan Roman warrior comprehended something that the religious leaders missed. He had the correct assessment of his own worth, and it was the opposite of what the Jewish leaders said of him. He was not worthy for Christ to enter his home. His words echoed those of John the Baptist when he said he wasn't worthy to untie the sandals of Jesus.

But with this recognition of Christ's supremacy came the assurance that Jesus could do great and marvelous works. The centurion understood that while he had the authority to tell his servants what to do, Christ's words—even spoken from afar—could banish death.

It is a supremely precious gift to have this kind of faith—a faith that recognizes one's unworthiness to call on the name of Jesus and yet trusts that he is powerful and gracious to answer one's humble asking.

As you pray, ask for this priceless faith. Ask Christ to help you better comprehend his greatness and your smallness. Ask him, out of his might and love, to listen to your prayer and give you what is best.

Pray:
Christ, you are so great, and I am so small. I lay my desires before you.
I long for the heart to receive whatever you give. Amen.

Ordinary Time Day 26
KARI WEST

Read: *Luke 7:18–23*

> The disciples of John reported all these things to him. And John, calling two of his disciples to him, sent them to the Lord, saying, "Are you the one who is to come, or shall we look for another?" And when the men had come to him, they said, "John the Baptist has sent us to you, saying, 'Are you the one who is to come, or shall we look for another?'" In that hour he healed many people of diseases and plagues and evil spirits, and on many who were blind he bestowed sight. And he answered them, "Go and tell John what you have seen and heard: the blind receive their sight, the lame walk, lepers are cleansed, and the deaf hear, the dead are raised up, the poor have good news preached to them. And blessed is the one who is not offended by me."

Reflect:

Our faith is not steady.

In the beginning of John's Gospel, John the Baptist bellowed, "Behold, the Lamb of God, who takes away the sin of the world!" (John 1:29). A bit later on, in Luke 7:28, Christ said, "Among those born of women none is greater than John."

And yet here in these verses, we see John waver. He sent his disciples to Christ for confirmation. He asked of Jesus, "Are you the one who is to come, or should we expect someone else?" (v. 19 NIV).

Are you familiar with the lingering doubt that John expressed? Do you wrestle with similar misgivings, even if you will not say them aloud?

Jesus, are you truly who you say you are? Are you our Messiah, our rescuer, our Savior? Will you repair the ruined road that leads to friendship with God? Will you keep me until the end? Will you never leave, never forsake? Will you remake the world?

Let this passage teach you. John laid his question at Christ's feet. And Christ answered, *Look around. The blind see, the lame walk, the deaf hear, the lepers dance, and the dead breathe again. And if you aren't offended by me, if you accept my words and my lordship, you will know the very blessing of God.*

Jesus didn't crush John in his wavering. Instead, Jesus told John to listen to the shouts of surprise and joy, to see the tears of gladness, to taste these firstfruits of his coming reign. Yet in the mystery of his goodness and sovereignty, he did not promise John's release from prison. Instead, he called him to learn a deeper trust.

The Gospels promise a coming kingdom where all disease is undone and where death will be trampled. In this present world, some of that good work is already taking place. But much remains deeply broken. Christ calls to us, "Don't be offended. Trust me."

As you pray, voice your doubts to the Lord and then listen for his invitation to learn a deeper trust. Sit long with the Gospels and let Christ's works of grace permeate your imagination and your soul. Hold fast to Jesus.

Pray:

O Christ, we believe. Help our unbelief. We are bruised reeds and smoldering wicks. Be gracious to us. Give us the courage for honest prayers and the patience to meditate, long and slow, on Scripture. Let us consider you, Jesus, and be renewed. Give us the deep faith that holds to you always. Amen.

Ordinary Time Day 27

KARI WEST

Read: *Luke 7:36–50*

One of the Pharisees asked him to eat with him, and he went into the Pharisee's house and reclined at table. And behold, a woman of the city, who was a sinner, when she learned that he was reclining at table in the Pharisee's house, brought an alabaster flask of ointment, and standing behind him at his feet, weeping, she began to wet his feet with her tears and wiped them with the hair of her head and kissed his feet and anointed them with the ointment. Now when the Pharisee who had invited him saw this, he said to himself, "If this man were a prophet, he would have known who and what sort of woman this is who is touching him, for she is a sinner." And Jesus answering said to him, "Simon, I have something to say to you." And he answered, "Say it, Teacher."

"A certain moneylender had two debtors. One owed five hundred denarii, and the other fifty. When they could not pay, he cancelled the debt of both. Now which of them will love him more?" Simon answered, "The one, I suppose, for whom he cancelled the larger debt." And he said to him, "You have judged rightly." Then turning toward the woman he said to Simon, "Do you see this woman? I entered your house; you gave me no water for my feet, but she has wet my feet with her tears and wiped them with her hair. You gave me no kiss, but from the time I came in she has not ceased to kiss my feet. You did not anoint my head with oil, but she has anointed my feet with ointment. Therefore I tell you, her sins, which are many, are forgiven—for she loved much. But he who is forgiven little, loves little." And he said to her, "Your sins are forgiven." Then those who were at table with him began to say among themselves, "Who is this, who even forgives sins?" And he said to the woman, "Your faith has saved you; go in peace."

Reflect:

Our love for Christ will depend in part on how much we acknowledge our sinfulness and then forget about ourselves and the esteem of others.

This prostitute, knowing that she would face utter contempt from those watching, wept freely at the feet of Christ, used her own hair to wipe his feet clean, kissed his feet, and then poured out costly ointment on his skin.

She wept because she knew her own moral bankruptcy. She kissed and anointed because she knew Christ was worthy of all her adoration. Her actions aroused the scorn of the other guests. But Jesus's supremacy freed her from being controlled by the opinions of others and enabled her to worship.

Simon, by contrast, was the exalted center of his own world. He sat in judgment over both the woman and Jesus. He knew she was a sinful woman, and he assumed that Jesus wasn't a prophet because he did not push her away.

Simon was encased in pride, so the faults of others, perceived or real, only reinforced his high view of himself. The woman, however, revealed Simon's self-importance, judgment, and lack of hospitality. Simon withheld honor; he appraised and evaluated but he did not love. The woman humbly gave Christ the adoration he was due. It was only the woman who left that evening with her sins forgiven and her faith alive.

As you pray, ask God to kill your pride and give you a right understanding of yourself. Ask for the kind of blessed self-forgetfulness that allowed the woman to deny all social convention for the greater good of true worship. Thank Jesus for canceling your massive debt of sin at the cross. Then join this prostitute in the new life of forgiveness and faith.

Pray:

Father, lift our eyes to you. In the light of your presence, let our pride wilt and our humility flourish. Give us tears of repentance. Let us know you as worthy of any price and any sacrifice. Thank you for free and full forgiveness bought by Jesus, in his most precious name. Amen.

4th Sunday of Ordinary Time
BRANDON WALSH

Read: *Psalm 7:1-11*

O Lᴏʀᴅ my God, in you do I take refuge;
    save me from all my pursuers and deliver me,
lest like a lion they tear my soul apart,
    rending it in pieces, with none to deliver.
O Lᴏʀᴅ my God, if I have done this,
    if there is wrong in my hands,
if I have repaid my friend with evil
    or plundered my enemy without cause,
let the enemy pursue my soul and overtake it,
    and let him trample my life to the ground
    and lay my glory in the dust.   *Selah*
Arise, O Lᴏʀᴅ, in your anger;
    lift yourself up against the fury of my enemies;
    awake for me; you have appointed a judgment.
Let the assembly of the peoples be gathered about you;
    over it return on high.
The Lᴏʀᴅ judges the peoples;
    judge me, O Lᴏʀᴅ, according to my righteousness
    and according to the integrity that is in me.
Oh, let the evil of the wicked come to an end,
    and may you establish the righteous—
you who test the minds and hearts,
    O righteous God!
My shield is with God,
    who saves the upright in heart.
God is a righteous judge,
    and a God who feels indignation every day.

Reflect:

Christians often speak about "intimacy" with God. Most of the time they mean a sense of the Lord's consoling nearness, a place where the Lord speaks, or a place where we know the Spirit's peace. But this is not the only kind of intimacy with the Lord that the Scriptures offer us.

Psalm 7 describes an intimacy with the Lord that has room for brutal honesty and frustration.

First, the psalmist named the atrocities the wicked committed. They oppressed the poor and allowed their pride to swell. When would God act? The writer didn't bridle the anger, frustration, and confusion stirring inside his heart.

Often when we speak to a superior or casual acquaintance, our words may be calculated or restrained. But words flow more freely with the people we trust. The same can be said of this psalmist and the Lord; theirs was a relationship close enough for brutal honesty.

In truth, it sometimes feels as if the Lord is far off and oblivious to injustice. When we doubt, when our frustration and anger rise up, we have a choice: We can turn away from the Lord and be silent or lean in and speak honestly with him. This second option is a path to deep faithfulness and intimacy.

The church calendar calls this time of year "Ordinary Time." Sadly, it seems our ordinary is often a long walk through frightening and unsettling days. We are anxious about finances, health, the stability of our world, and the future. As you pray, move toward the Lord with your true heart, no matter how brutal and messy. Choose intimacy with your God.

Pray:

Give me, O Lord, a steadfast heart, which no unworthy thought can drag down; an unconquered heart, which no tribulation can wear out; an upright heart, which no unworthy purpose can tempt aside. Bestow upon me understanding to know you, diligence to seek you, wisdom to find you, and faithfulness that finally may embrace you. Amen.

(Thomas Aquinas)

Ordinary Time Day 29

KARI WEST

Read: *Luke 8:4–15*

And when a great crowd was gathering and people from town after town came to him, he said in a parable, "A sower went out to sow his seed. And as he sowed, some fell along the path and was trampled underfoot, and the birds of the air devoured it. And some fell on the rock, and as it grew up, it withered away, because it had no moisture. And some fell among thorns, and the thorns grew up with it and choked it. And some fell into good soil and grew and yielded a hundredfold." As he said these things, he called out, "He who has ears to hear, let him hear."

And when his disciples asked him what this parable meant, he said, "To you it has been given to know the secrets of the kingdom of God, but for others they are in parables, so that 'seeing they may not see, and hearing they may not understand.' Now the parable is this: The seed is the word of God. The ones along the path are those who have heard; then the devil comes and takes away the word from their hearts, so that they may not believe and be saved. And the ones on the rock are those who, when they hear the word, receive it with joy. But these have no root; they believe for a while, and in time of testing fall away. And as for what fell among the thorns, they are those who hear, but as they go on their way they are choked by the cares and riches and pleasures of life, and their fruit does not mature. As for that in the good soil, they are those who, hearing the word, hold it fast in an honest and good heart, and bear fruit with patience."

Reflect:

How generative is the Word of God received in a soul ready to listen and obey; but how barren, complicated, and shallow is a life without Christ.

Do you hear both the danger and the promise brimming in these words of Jesus? The parable of the sower is so familiar to us that we are in danger of growing deaf to both its warning and its glory.

Pause and let these divinely chosen images take root in your mind: Seed is trampled on the ground and devoured by birds; seedlings sprout up between rock crevices, only to wilt and then die without water; fresh green shoots are choked and shredded by encroaching thorns.

These pictures are meant to alarm us. Satan, the evil one, hates life itself. Hardships have the power to undo us if we let them. The world, if we are not diligent, will choke and smother our very souls. May we heed these warnings!

But now listen to the last part of this parable: A seed falls into dense, nurturing soil, and over time it grows straight and strong, vibrant and green, until it yields abundant, rich fruit.

Indeed, this is a life open to the Word of God, one ready to hear, ready to do, and eager to know the Lord. This is a heart where the seeds of Scripture are planted deep, where they can flourish into abundance and new life.

As you pray, ask for a heart of tender, attentive receptivity to the Word of God. Ask the Good Sower to plant seeds deeply and to keep the soil rich and ample. Thank him for his good promises.

Pray:

I ask you, most gracious God, preserve me from the cares of this life, lest I should be too much entangled in them; and from the many necessities of the body, lest I should be ensnared by pleasure; and from whatsoever is an obstacle to the soul, lest, broken with troubles, I should be overthrown. Amen.

(Thomas à Kempis)

Ordinary Time Day 30
KARI WEST

Read: *Luke 8:26–39*

Then they sailed to the country of the Gerasenes, which is opposite Galilee. When Jesus had stepped out on land, there met him a man from the city who had demons. For a long time he had worn no clothes, and he had not lived in a house but among the tombs. When he saw Jesus, he cried out and fell down before him and said with a loud voice, "What have you to do with me, Jesus, Son of the Most High God? I beg you, do not torment me." For he had commanded the unclean spirit to come out of the man. (For many a time it had seized him. He was kept under guard and bound with chains and shackles, but he would break the bonds and be driven by the demon into the desert.) Jesus then asked him, "What is your name?" And he said, "Legion," for many demons had entered him. And they begged him not to command them to depart into the abyss. Now a large herd of pigs was feeding there on the hillside, and they begged him to let them enter these. So he gave them permission. Then the demons came out of the man and entered the pigs, and the herd rushed down the steep bank into the lake and drowned.

When the herdsmen saw what had happened, they fled and told it in the city and in the country. Then people went out to see what had happened, and they came to Jesus and found the man from whom the demons had gone, sitting at the feet of Jesus, clothed and in his right mind, and they were afraid. And those who had seen it told them how the demon-possessed man had been healed. Then all the people of the surrounding country of the Gerasenes asked him to depart from them, for they were seized with great fear. So he got into the boat and returned. The man from whom the demons had gone begged that he might be with him, but Jesus sent him away, saying, "Return to your home, and declare how much God has done for you." And he went away, proclaiming throughout the whole city how much Jesus had done for him.

Reflect:

When we neglect the Scriptures, we find it easy to remake Christ in our image, as a smaller, less commanding, and more easily explained Savior. Stories like this one shake us awake again. We need to remember again and again the true nature of the God-man to whom we pray; we need to see Christ anew in his power, lordship, and great mercy.

Though many people in Luke's Gospel questioned Christ's authority and word, the demons did not doubt his identity. They knew the far-reaching domain of Christ's rule, and they were powerless to disobey his word. These demons could not escape the kingship of Christ or his command. This Jesus is the warrior king in whose name we pray.

Christ is not only powerful but he uses that authority to restore right order, to bring about goodness and life. Demons had wreaked havoc on this man. He enjoyed no community and wore no clothing. He was out of his mind. Tellingly, he took up residence among tombs.

Christ wielded his power for the purposes of love. He gave this man back his mind and his life and seated him at his feet. He overturned the destructive work of Satan and reinstated a taste of shalom. This is the merciful Savior we call on.

As you pray, embrace the power and the mercy of Christ. Sit with these words from Luke's Gospel until they work fresh wonder in your soul at your great and loving Savior.

Pray:

Blessed Jesus! We can add nothing to you, nothing to your glory, but it is a joy of heart to us that you are what you are, that you are so gloriously exalted at the right hand of God. We long more fully and clearly to behold that glory, according to your prayer and promise. Amen.

(John Owen)

Ordinary Time Day 31
SALLY BREEDLOVE

Read: *Luke 8:42–48*

> As Jesus went, the people pressed around him. And there was a woman who had had a discharge of blood for twelve years, and though she had spent all her living on physicians, she could not be healed by anyone. She came up behind him and touched the fringe of his garment, and immediately her discharge of blood ceased. And Jesus said, "Who was it that touched me?" When all denied it, Peter said, "Master, the crowds surround you and are pressing in on you!" But Jesus said, "Someone touched me, for I perceive that power has gone out from me." And when the woman saw that she was not hidden, she came trembling, and falling down before him declared in the presence of all the people why she had touched him, and how she had been immediately healed. And he said to her, "Daughter, your faith has made you well; go in peace."

Reflect:

The crowd was pushing Jesus along. Jairus was afraid; his daughter was dying. He was desperate for Jesus to get to his house as quickly as he could. Nothing else mattered. Peter also was insistent for them to hurry. Perhaps he was impressed that the leader of a synagogue was asking for help. It could have been quite an opportunity for Jesus.

But in that crowd was a woman with a secret plan. She had bled for twelve years, and the doctors hadn't been able to help her. She was almost bankrupt. Her bleeding made her unclean and isolated her from every part of society. She knew no one wanted to be near her, but still she pressed through the crowd. Perhaps it parted as she came near. Finally, she managed to touch the tassels on Jesus's garment. Her bleeding stopped. She realized at last she could be free from the bondage of illness and the shame of being unclean, flawed, and outcast.

But then Christ did the most unexpected thing. He knew healing had gone out from his body, and he stopped to find out who had touched him. Peter wanted him to keep moving, but Christ insisted: *Who touched me?*

The woman had a choice. Would she step forward and confess why she needed healing? Would she admit what she had done? Would she step into the shame of exposure?

This woman took the first risk by touching Jesus's robe. Then she took a second risk: She stepped forward and owned the shame of her own story. And Jesus? He called her "daughter." He declared she belonged in the family. He blessed her with peace.

Could the door to our own freedom possibly be to admit our shame and come face-to-face with Jesus and his mercy?

As you pray, sit with your own story. Do you hide from yourself, from those around you, from God? Do you believe you are fundamentally flawed by things you have done or by what has been done to you? Reach out to Jesus. He will not hurry past you. He forgives you; he heals you; he calls you his own.

Pray:

Lord, you know everything about me. You know my shame, my hiding, and my pretense. Forgive the stubborn and resistant ways I keep you at a distance. Heal the broken places in me. Help me to know your mercy. Thank you that you have made me part of your family for Jesus's sake. Amen.

Ordinary Time Day 32
SALLY BREEDLOVE

Read: *Luke 8:40–42, 49–56*

Now when Jesus returned, the crowd welcomed him, for they were all waiting for him. And there came a man named Jairus, who was a ruler of the synagogue. And falling at Jesus' feet, he implored him to come to his house, for he had an only daughter, about twelve years of age, and she was dying....

While he was still speaking, someone from the ruler's house came and said, "Your daughter is dead; do not trouble the Teacher any more." But Jesus on hearing this answered him, "Do not fear; only believe, and she will be well." And when he came to the house, he allowed no one to enter with him, except Peter and John and James, and the father and mother of the child. And all were weeping and mourning for her, but he said, "Do not weep, for she is not dead but sleeping." And they laughed at him, knowing that she was dead. But taking her by the hand he called, saying, "Child, arise." And her spirit returned, and she got up at once. And he directed that something should be given her to eat. And her parents were amazed, but he charged them to tell no one what had happened.

Reflect:

Did Jesus take too long? It certainly seemed so. The only daughter of an important family was dying. In a world where big families symbolized God's blessing, she was all they had. Her parents had probably hoped that she would marry and give them a houseful of grandchildren.

Her father, Jairus, was the ruler of the synagogue, and he had likely opposed Jesus. He heard the conversation among his peers in neighboring towns and suspected that this would-be Messiah needed to be silenced, perhaps (as was being discussed behind closed doors) even eliminated.

But now Jairus was desperate. He found Jesus, fell at his feet, and begged him to come to his house and save his daughter.

For some of us, asking for help, even for small things, is hard. But asking for help from someone we look down on, someone we oppose? That's almost impossible. Unless desperation drives us to throw away our pride and beg.

So Jairus did that, but then Jesus got caught up in an event in the crowd around him. He was delayed. How did that feel to Jairus? Was desperation morphing into anger or doom? As they finally arrived at his home, Jairus heard the mourners and saw the grief etched on his wife's face. It was too late.

But Jesus said, "Do not fear; only believe, and [your daughter] will be well" (v. 50). Then he led them inside to the child's corpse.

Death is not the end. Jesus pulled her back from death and restored her to her family.

The questions also fall to us: Will we humble ourselves before our gracious God and cry out, "Help me!"? Will we be willing to wait, even when Jesus seems to take too long? Our own circumstances may appear beyond help. The world around us seems to be spinning into chaos and anger and despair. How can we hang on to hope?

As you pray, ask Jesus for the faith to accept his invitation: "*Do not fear; only believe*" (v. 50).

We do not know how or when Christ will fulfill his promises. But are we willing to turn to Jesus, to wait with him while he seems to delay, and then to enter in with him to the broken and ruined places of our lives and world?

Pray:

Restore my soul, O God. There are green pastures around me for which my eye has no lens; there are quiet waters beside me for which my ear has no chord; restore my soul. The path on which I go is already the path of your righteousness; open my eyes, that I may behold its windows. The place I call dreadful is even now the house of the Lord; the heavens shall cease to hide you when you have restored my soul. May I be content to know that goodness and mercy shall follow me without waiting to see them in advance of me. Amen.

(George Matheson)

Ordinary Time Day 33

SALLY BREEDLOVE

Read: *Luke 9:10–17*

On their return the apostles told him all that they had done. And he took them and withdrew apart to a town called Bethsaida. When the crowds learned it, they followed him, and he welcomed them and spoke to them of the kingdom of God and cured those who had need of healing. Now the day began to wear away, and the twelve came and said to him, "Send the crowd away to go into the surrounding villages and countryside to find lodging and get provisions, for we are here in a desolate place." But he said to them, "You give them something to eat." They said, "We have no more than five loaves and two fish—unless we are to go and buy food for all these people." For there were about five thousand men. And he said to his disciples, "Have them sit down in groups of about fifty each." And they did so, and had them all sit down. And taking the five loaves and the two fish, he looked up to heaven and said a blessing over them. Then he broke the loaves and gave them to the disciples to set before the crowd. And they all ate and were satisfied. And what was left over was picked up, twelve baskets of broken pieces.

Reflect:

Could it be that the disciples were tired of other people's needs? As evening drew near, they urged Jesus to send the crowds away to find food.

But Jesus pushed back. "You give them something to eat" (v. 13).

Was there sarcasm, or irritated exhaustion, in the disciples' response? It was as if they were asking, "*So, you want us to walk to the next village, then buy and bring back enough food for five thousand men and their kids and their wives? What village would have food for five thousand extra people at a moment's notice? You must be kidding, Jesus.*"

Christ's only response was to instruct them, "Have them sit down in groups of about fifty each" (v. 14).

That was a job the disciples could do—direct people where to go and where to sit—but to what end?

While the disciples were busy arranging the crowd, Jesus gathered the small bit of food they had scavenged. He looked upward to heaven and blessed the food before him. Then he began to break it and give it away, and then break it and give it away, and then break it and give it away, until everyone had eaten and what was left over was gathered up into twelve baskets.

It never looked like a gigantic buffet or feast. As the disciples came back to Jesus again and again for another basket of food to distribute, did they ever wonder if the next time there wouldn't be any left?

It was an impossible situation. But somehow the need was met, and leftovers abounded.

We live in a world of impossible needs. Who has the answers? Who has the means? Who can solve the hatred, the contempt, the division, the disease, and the distrust that threaten to consume us? Does Jesus expect any one of us to come up with a large enough answer to set this world right? If we can't do that, what can we do?

Perhaps we need to do what the disciples did: Keep returning to Jesus, time after time, day after day. Receive from him a basket's worth of wisdom, love, patience, compassion, and trust. Go give today's provision away and come back again tomorrow.

As you pray, name one or two of the impossible needs that burden your heart and mind. Then hold your hands up to Jesus and ask him to carry what you cannot carry. Ask him to do his perfect will in an "impossible place" in your life.

Pray:

Blessed be the Lord, who daily bears us up; God is our salvation. Our God is a God of salvation, and to GOD, the Lord, belong deliverances from death. Amen.

(Psalm 68:19–20)

Ordinary Time Day 34

SALLY BREEDLOVE

Read: *Luke 9:18–22*

Now it happened that as he was praying alone, the disciples were with him. And he asked them, "Who do the crowds say that I am?" And they answered, "John the Baptist. But others say, Elijah, and others, that one of the prophets of old has risen." Then he said to them, "But who do you say that I am?" And Peter answered, "The Christ of God."

And he strictly charged and commanded them to tell this to no one, saying, "The Son of Man must suffer many things and be rejected by the elders and chief priests and scribes, and be killed, and on the third day be raised."

Reflect:

Prayer is meant to change us. As we sit with God, we see more clearly how we need to care for those around us. Jesus prayed, and then he turned his attention to his disciples and asked them if they understood who he was.

Jesus did what we often do in an important conversation: He asked a less significant question to set the stage for the real question. The first question seemed almost casual: "Who do the crowds say that I am?" (v. 18).

The disciples gave all sort of answers. Theorizing and reporting is easy. Data and intellectual queries can be simple. Nothing gets personal. Nothing is aimed at the heart.

But then Jesus went deeper and confronted his disciples with a question: "Who do you say that I am?" (v. 20).

A world of difference lies between these two questions: "Who do *they* say?" and "Who do *you* say?" For centuries people have asked, "Who is Jesus?" But only Jesus can look deep into our hearts and ask us, "*Who do you say I am?*"

Peter answered with insight that the Father gave him: "God's Messiah" (v. 20 NIV). What was it like for someone to finally see Jesus for who he really was? Did Christ shout in triumph and praise?

No. Look at what followed. Jesus gave his disciples more information than they could comprehend, telling them he was not the Messiah they had expected: "The Son of Man must suffer many things and be rejected by the elders and chief priests and scribes, and be killed, and on the third day be raised" (v. 22).

What a devastating and confusing reply.

The truth is, Christ never leads us on. He never pretends to be who he isn't. He never glibly promises an easy road. As long as we live in this world, suffering and then glory will be the arc of our story.

The world is so very broken. We are at odds with each other, within ourselves, with creation, and with God. The suffering in our world comes as no surprise to the God we abandoned. But the God we walked away from has walked into our world. He is indeed the God-man Jesus Christ.

He is the Messiah. After the resurrection, Peter understood: All the suffering we are experiencing will be healed by the suffering Messiah.

As you pray, let Jesus ask you, "Who do you say I am?" What answer rises up in you? Take your heart to Jesus.

Pray:

Almighty God, whom truly to know is everlasting life: Grant us so to perfectly know your Son Jesus Christ to be the way, the truth and the life, that we may steadfastly follow his steps in the way that leads to eternal glory; through Jesus Christ your Son our Lord, who lives and reigns with you, in the unity of the Holy Spirit, one God, for ever and ever. Amen.

(Anglican Church in North America Book of Common Prayer)

5th Sunday of Ordinary Time

KARI WEST

Read: *Psalm 7:10–17*

> My shield is with God,
> > who saves the upright in heart.
>
> God is a righteous judge,
> > and a God who feels indignation every day.
>
> If a man does not repent, God will whet his sword;
> > he has bent and readied his bow;
>
> he has prepared for him his deadly weapons,
> > making his arrows fiery shafts.
>
> Behold, the wicked man conceives evil
> > and is pregnant with mischief
> > and gives birth to lies.
>
> He makes a pit, digging it out,
> > and falls into the hole that he has made.
>
> His mischief returns upon his own head,
> > and on his own skull his violence descends.
>
> I will give to the LORD the thanks due to his righteousness,
> > and I will sing praise to the name of the LORD, the
> > Most High.

Reflect:

We prefer to meditate on a God of love more than on a God of justice. We like to consider forgiveness and mercy, and we might feel uncomfortable reading passages like this one. Here we see a God who sharpens his sword and strings his bow, readying deadly weapons to wield against those who love evil and perpetrate injustice.

But the psalmist took refuge in the justice of God. He called God a shield because God saves the upright in heart and will ultimately destroy those who persist in opposing his goodness with open rebellion.

When we witness widespread injustice, when we encounter evil men and women thriving, when we see the innocent trodden down and the wicked plotting more destruction, we need a deep, weighty belief in God's commitment to justice and goodness so we don't despair. We need to contemplate these images of God and take them up as our shields against hopelessness in a dark world.

And in God's righteousness, we need to have the right kind of fear before him. Not one that cowers, but one that takes our own sin and his holiness seriously. God is opposed to the wicked, including the wickedness that lurks in our own hearts. Though we are made upright through Christ and are being made upright by the Spirit, we are far from perfect. God's holiness should draw us to awe of him, confession to him, gratitude for Jesus, and humility toward others.

As you pray, reflect on the justice of God. Do you need to see God's justice as a banner of hope, as his commitment to righting a wrong world in his good time? Do you need to grasp his righteousness as a warning to your own wayward heart? Ask the Lord to use his Word and his Spirit to convict, change, and strengthen you.

Pray:
O Father, thank you that you will bring about justice in the world. Let us remember your holiness. Thank you, Christ, that by your blood we are made righteous. Give us hearts that trust you and hope in you above all things. Amen.

Ordinary Time Day 36
SALLY BREEDLOVE

Read: *Luke 9:23–27*

> And he said to all, "If anyone would come after me, let him deny himself and take up his cross daily and follow me. For whoever would save his life will lose it, but whoever loses his life for my sake will save it. For what does it profit a man if he gains the whole world and loses or forfeits himself? For whoever is ashamed of me and of my words, of him will the Son of Man be ashamed when he comes in his glory and the glory of the Father and of the holy angels. But I tell you truly, there are some standing here who will not taste death until they see the kingdom of God."

Reflect:

Peter had just confessed that Jesus was the Messiah. But Jesus's response was not to explain in detail the great story of his crucifixion, resurrection, ascension, and coming kingdom. Instead, he took pains to teach his friends that the road of following him could be a hard road.

The disciples were confused. They wanted to be with Jesus; his authority, his miracles, and his compelling presence could not be denied. But he kept driving home his point: If they wanted to be with him, they must follow him on the path he chose.

What does it look like to follow Jesus?

It's a life of imitating Christ. His cross was a suffering chosen for the healing of others. How might you need to suffer so that others can be healed?

It's a life where you let go of your own preferences, your privileges, your pride. What would it be like not to insist on having things your way?

It's a life of steadfast loyalty to Jesus, no matter what the world thinks of him. We live in a world where people are fine with personal spiritual beliefs. But Christianity is centered on the real historical Jesus Christ—fully God and fully man—who came into this world to die and rise again so that all people could find salvation in him. In a world where no one is supposed to make a truth claim, holding to the reality of Jesus Christ often provokes anger, scorn, and ostracism. Are you willing to stand with him?

If you were Jesus, would you have laid out the cost of following before the disciples experienced Easter morning? Wouldn't it have been smarter to wait until after the resurrection?

Perhaps Christ was asking these first disciples, *Will you follow me by faith, despite your limited understanding? Will you follow me to the cross when it looks like all is lost? Will you follow me even though I will not guarantee you a happy ending to your life on this planet?*

Doesn't he ask us those same questions?

We have to make up our minds about Jesus. Do we expect this world to save us? Jesus unabashedly calls us to follow him. Will we follow him, regardless of the cost?

Pray for Christians everywhere. Pray we will be loyal to the Son of God no matter the cost.

Pray:

O God, the author of peace and lover of concord, to know you is eternal life and to serve you is perfect freedom: Defend us, your humble servants, in all assaults of our enemies; that we, surely trusting in your defense, may not fear the power of any adversaries, through the might of Jesus Christ our Lord. Amen.

(Anglican Church in North America Book of Common Prayer)

Ordinary Time Day 37

SALLY BREEDLOVE

Read: *Luke 9:28–36*

Now about eight days after these sayings he took with him Peter and John and James and went up on the mountain to pray. And as he was praying, the appearance of his face was altered, and his clothing became dazzling white. And behold, two men were talking with him, Moses and Elijah, who appeared in glory and spoke of his departure, which he was about to accomplish at Jerusalem. Now Peter and those who were with him were heavy with sleep, but when they became fully awake they saw his glory and the two men who stood with him. And as the men were parting from him, Peter said to Jesus, "Master, it is good that we are here. Let us make three tents, one for you and one for Moses and one for Elijah"—not knowing what he said. As he was saying these things, a cloud came and overshadowed them, and they were afraid as they entered the cloud. And a voice came out of the cloud, saying, "This is my Son, my Chosen One; listen to him!" And when the voice had spoken, Jesus was found alone. And they kept silent and told no one in those days anything of what they had seen.

Reflect:

What was the purpose of the transfiguration?

Imagine what Jesus faced. He knew the cross lay ahead; he knew his friends did not understand. Judging from what he prayed in the garden of Gethsemane, he knew the cross would be an excruciating place of submission. On that mountain, his Father met him with encouragement. The transfiguration was, in part, a moment of clarity. He experienced his full glory as the Son, heard his Father's blessing, and received strength from two faithful men of the past as they discussed what lay ahead.

God met the depth of his Son's human need on that mountain.

The transfiguration is a gift to God's people as well. It reminds us that Jesus has always been the Son of God, never merely just a man. The transfiguration allows us to look past all that seems to be going on and see what is true. Jesus Christ is the eternal Son who shares the Father's glory. And Jesus Christ came to die for our sins.

Years later, Peter told the story of being on the holy mountain. He said the three disciples were "eyewitnesses of his majesty" (2 Peter 1:16) and that they saw his glory and heard the voice from heaven proclaiming Jesus as the beloved Son of God.

But we also know these three disciples couldn't hold on to this vision. They came down from the mountain, bickered among themselves, deserted Christ when he was arrested, and despaired when he was crucified. Aware of his own weak and fickle nature, Peter wrote that what we really need is not a vision, but to pay attention to Scripture, the only thing that will sustain us in a dark world.

As you pray, hold in your mind the glory of the risen Christ. His reign will one day bring the shalom we long for. Ask God for the faithfulness to read the Scriptures and follow Jesus day by day. Affirm your commitment to a life of reading and heeding the Word of God. Then close your prayers with these words from Peter:

Pray:

We weren't, you know, just wishing on a star when we laid the facts out before you regarding the powerful return of our Master, Jesus Christ. We were there for the preview! We saw it with our own eyes: Jesus resplendent with light from God the Father as the voice of Majestic Glory spoke: "This is my Son, marked by my love, focus of all my delight." We were there on the holy mountain with him. We heard the voice out of heaven with our very own ears. We couldn't be more sure of what we saw and heard—God's glory, God's voice. The prophetic Word was confirmed to us. You'll do well to keep focusing on it. It's the one light you have in a dark time as you wait for daybreak and the rising of the Morning Star in your hearts. Amen.

(2 Peter 1:16–19 MSG)

Ordinary Time Day 38
SALLY BREEDLOVE

Read: *Luke 9:37–43*

> On the next day, when they had come down from the mountain, a great crowd met him. And behold, a man from the crowd cried out, "Teacher, I beg you to look at my son, for he is my only child. And behold, a spirit seizes him, and he suddenly cries out. It convulses him so that he foams at the mouth, and shatters him, and will hardly leave him. And I begged your disciples to cast it out, but they could not." Jesus answered, "O faithless and twisted generation, how long am I to be with you and bear with you? Bring your son here." While he was coming, the demon threw him to the ground and convulsed him. But Jesus rebuked the unclean spirit and healed the boy, and gave him back to his father. And all were astonished at the majesty of God.

Reflect:

Matthew, Mark, and Luke all described the story of the transfiguration. Each one followed it with the story of the demon-possessed boy, his desperate father, and the disciples' inadequacy to handle the situation at the foot of the mountain.

Perhaps we need these stories side by side if we are to survive our world. From a mountaintop, a proclamation was made: Jesus is the Son of God whose glory is so brilliant, it blinds. And Jesus is the one who would die.

Meanwhile, down in the valley, the world is helpless in the face of evil's destructive power. But Jesus entered our broken world. He was not simply the Glorified One adored by all of heaven. He was not simply our "future Savior."

Jesus was also the Lord who entered into the argument taking place at the foot of the mountain. Jesus was the one who paid attention to the father's needs and asked him to tell the story of his son's sickness. And Jesus was the one who looked at his disciples and sighed, "*You don't have to be faithless and twisted as you live in this world!*"

Faithless people quit turning to Jesus. They don't count on him; they don't listen to him. They go their own way and try to make life work on their own terms.

Twisted people are no longer "true." Twistedness makes something become useless, like a twisted ruler, a twisted nail, or a twisted tire. Twisted things were designed for good purposes, but they are out of alignment. They make things worse, not better.

In his grace, Christ comes to faithless and twisted people like the disciples—like us—to heal them and to love them.

As you consider this story, what do you most want to hold in your heart as you pray? Do you feel anguish for someone you love who cannot find healing? Do you despair as you see the arguing and ineffectiveness all around you? Are you bound by evil and sin? Do you fear you are being destroyed by your own choices and by what other people have done to you?

In Mark's version of this story, the father cried out: "I believe; help my unbelief!" (Mark 9:24). In your own words, call out to Jesus with whatever faith you have. He will supply the rest.

Pray:

Almighty God, whose Son took upon himself the afflictions of your people: Regard with your tender compassion those suffering from anxiety, depression, or mental illness; bear their sorrows and their cares; supply all their needs; help them to put their whole trust and confidence in you; and restore them to strength of mind and cheerfulness of spirit; through Jesus Christ our Lord. Amen.

(Anglican Church in North America Book of Common Prayer)

Ordinary Time Day 39

MADISON PERRY

Read: *Luke 9:46–50*

> An argument arose among them as to which of them was the
> greatest. But Jesus, knowing the reasoning of their hearts, took a
> child and put him by his side and said to them, "Whoever receives
> this child in my name receives me, and whoever receives me receives
> him who sent me. For he who is least among you all is the one who
> is great."
>
> John answered, "Master, we saw someone casting out demons
> in your name, and we tried to stop him, because he does not follow
> with us." But Jesus said to him, "Do not stop him, for the one who
> is not against you is for you."

Reflect:

A group of Jesus's disciples were arguing over a burning question. It was
obvious who the greatest of the whole group was—Jesus. But what about his
followers? Who was the greatest among them?

Jesus's followers were apparently multiplying far outside the boundaries of
their little group. A hierarchy seemed to be breaking out among them, as Peter
and John were chosen to hike with Jesus up the Mount of Transfiguration and
witness the glory of God. How could Jesus's disciples make sure their commitment to him wouldn't be overlooked in his coming kingdom?

Jesus's disciples did not trust that God would simply provide for them,
bless them, and fill them with boundless joy and contentment. No, there
had to be a secret, a way to get ahead and make sure things would go well for
them. They believed the blessings of God were scarce.

To teach them, Jesus introduced them to a young child. Jesus's disciples
wished that they had all been present to receive Moses and Elijah on the
Mount of Transfiguration. But would they be willing to receive a small child,
an image-bearer of the living God? The disciples wanted to understand the

secrets of heaven and earth and find the secret path to greatness. But would they learn the most difficult lesson of all, a lesson any child could teach them?

Jesus perceives the reasoning of our hearts. He knows the desires that haunt us and drive us. What has been driving you lately? What threatens to overtake you?

One of the greatest battles in the Christian life is allowing God to put you exactly where you need to be and trusting him to give you exactly what you need in order to gain infinite joy.

God's gifts are on a completely different magnitude from the paltry earnings and accumulations that characterize our days. Status in God's kingdom is unfathomable from an earthly perspective. Now is the time for our schemes and selfish ambitions to be unseated and for us to see that in loving one another we are receiving the greatest gift there is.

Call to mind God's promises to you. He will never leave you nor forsake you. He has made you for eternal life. Now tell God about the burdens you have been carrying, the tasks you have given yourself to make yourself great. Ask the Lord to help you to shoulder every load you have been given to carry. Now ask God whom he has called you to receive in love and ask him to give you the strength and courage to receive that person (or those people) in love.

Pray:

O God, the source of all holy desires, all good counsels, and all just works: Give to your servants that peace which the world cannot give, that our hearts may be set to obey your commandments, and that we, being defended from the fear of our enemies, may pass our time in rest and quietness; through the merits of Jesus Christ our Savior. Amen.

(Anglican Church in North America Book of Common Prayer)

Ordinary Time Day 40

SALLY BREEDLOVE

Read: *Luke 9:51; Philippians 3:12–14; & Hebrews 12:22–24*
When the days drew near for him to be taken up, he set his face to
go to Jerusalem.

Not that I have already obtained this or am already perfect, but I
press on to make it my own, because Christ Jesus has made me his
own. Brothers, I do not consider that I have made it my own. But
one thing I do: forgetting what lies behind and straining forward
to what lies ahead, I press on toward the goal for the prize of the
upward call of God in Christ Jesus.

But you have come to Mount Zion and to the city of the living
God, the heavenly Jerusalem, and to innumerable angels in festal
gathering, and to the assembly of the firstborn who are enrolled in
heaven, and to God, the judge of all, and to the spirits of the righteous made perfect, and to Jesus, the mediator of a new covenant.

Reflect:

The incarnation has made the invisible visible: God is present with us. We
don't have to make an arduous journey to find him. Christ and his kingdom
are here now. As his people, we are the temple of the living God. There's no
need to fear how things will turn out. The guaranteed ending of our story is
full joy, a joy that will increase as eternity unfolds.

At the same time, our life with God is a journey of walking toward and
working out what is already true. We are not passive recipients of God's grace.
God invites us to be active participants in his grace. Our faith is meant to
mirror Jesus's. He knew he was headed toward a premature death by crucifixion. He also knew he would be raised from the dead. His death was not

the abyss of unrecoverable despair. Yes, it had to be entered into, but he kept his eye on the joy that lay beyond.

As Christians, we know God is sovereign and his kingdom will prevail. But for now, along with the rest of the world, we have to walk out our faith, day by day.

As you pray, ask God to galvanize your courage. In prayer, remind yourself of the future you have in Jesus Christ. Often what stalls us on this journey is insisting that life will quickly work out on our own terms. Ask forgiveness for those stubborn places. Pray that your courage and hope will infect those around you who are discouraged.

Pray:

You, Lord, are patience, and pity, and sweetness, and love; therefore we sons of men are not consumed. You have exalted your mercy above all things, and have made our salvation, not our punishment, your glory; so that there, where sin abounded, not death, but grace superabounded. . . . Blessed Savior! Many waters could not quench your love, nor no pit overwhelm it. But, though the streams of your blood were coursing through darkness, grave, and hell, yet by these your conflicts, and seemingly hazards, did you arise triumphant, and therein made us victorious. Amen.

(George Herbert)

Ordinary Time Day 41
MADISON PERRY

Read: *Luke 9:57–62*

> As they were going along the road, someone said to him, "I will
> follow you wherever you go." And Jesus said to him, "Foxes have
> holes, and birds of the air have nests, but the Son of Man has
> nowhere to lay his head." To another he said, "Follow me." But he
> said, "Lord, let me first go and bury my father." And Jesus said to
> him, "Leave the dead to bury their own dead. But as for you, go and
> proclaim the kingdom of God." Yet another said, "I will follow you,
> Lord, but let me first say farewell to those at my home." Jesus said
> to him, "No one who puts his hand to the plow and looks back is fit
> for the kingdom of God."

Reflect:

Jesus had given Israel the chance to encounter him and follow him. He had
opened to them a portion of the earth-shattering glories of the good news—
healing, wisdom, justice, and life. And then he turned his face toward Jerusalem.

When Jesus first called his followers, he was an unknown itinerant, a man
from the wilderness possessing no human authority.

But by the power and authority of the Holy Spirit, he built a reputation
and a large following. At the beginning of his public ministry, people joined
him out of curiosity, personal ambition, or utter desperation. But as his rejec-
tion and crucifixion loomed large, it would become obvious that the way of
Jesus was inextricably bound to death. There would be no path forward for
Israel, the known world, or the entire cosmos that failed to reckon with our
sin and death. The time for casual following was over.

What brings you to Jesus? Do you come out of routine or habit? Do you
come to him in utter desperation? Regardless, what are you prepared to give
up for the life Jesus has for you?

The Gospels lead us on a journey. Most often we begin following Jesus at the most appealing level. It is only when we are farther down the road that we discern what it means to choose to follow him to the end.

Mercifully, by the time we make the choice to follow Jesus, we probably see through all the other petty agendas and temporary fixes that would threaten our loyalty to him. Other peoples' perceptions are ultimately nothing compared to the eternal love of the triune God. Following Christ might not have initially threatened our old routines and relationships, but in the end, Jesus is all that matters. The entirety of our lives pales in comparison to the weight of glory present in the face of Jesus Christ.

There was no way forward for Jesus that did not involve suffering for our sins. There is no moving forward for us in him that does not involve laying down everything and allowing him to direct our paths. Rest assured: He will be with you to the end of your earthly days, and forever after that.

Come to Jesus and offer him everything. Ask him to help you see through any lies or idols that would distract you from discipleship to him. In that place of surrender, ask him for eternal life and for the patience to wait for his kingdom to come on earth as it is in heaven.

Pray:

Almighty God, whose most dear Son went not up to joy but first he suffered pain, and entered not into glory before he was crucified: Mercifully grant that we, walking in the way of the Cross, may find it none other than the way of life and peace; through Jesus Christ your Son our Lord. Amen.

(Anglican Church in North America Book of Common Prayer)

6th Sunday of Ordinary Time
KARI WEST

Read: *Psalm 10:1–2, 7–9, 12–18*

Why, O Lord, do you stand far away?
> Why do you hide yourself in times of trouble?

In arrogance the wicked hotly pursue the poor;
> let them be caught in the schemes that they have devised....

His mouth is filled with cursing and deceit and oppression;
> under his tongue are mischief and iniquity.

He sits in ambush in the villages;
> in hiding places he murders the innocent.

His eyes stealthily watch for the helpless;
> he lurks in ambush like a lion in his thicket;

he lurks that he may seize the poor;
> he seizes the poor when he draws him into his net....

Arise, O Lord; O God, lift up your hand;
> forget not the afflicted.

Why does the wicked renounce God
> and say in his heart, "You will not call to account"?

But you do see, for you note mischief and vexation,
> that you may take it into your hands;

to you the helpless commits himself;
> you have been the helper of the fatherless.

Break the arm of the wicked and evildoer;
> call his wickedness to account till you find none.

The Lord is king forever and ever;
> the nations perish from his land.

O Lord, you hear the desire of the afflicted;
> you will strengthen their heart; you will incline your ear

to do justice to the fatherless and the oppressed,
> so that man who is of the earth may strike terror no more.

Reflect:

The psalmist used God's character as his argument to beg God to act.

Why? In this psalm, we learn the wicked were killing the innocent. They lurked like lions to attack the vulnerable. They deceived, they scoffed, and they used and abused others. They treated God's beloved image-bearers as trash to be discarded at their whim. They believed God would not demand an account; they lived as though God did not see or care.

The psalmist didn't cave in to despair when faced with this grim reality. Instead, he took these experiences to God and demanded that God not be silent. He even asked why God was far away and why he hid (v. 1). We understand his questions—God sometimes appears distant in our own lives.

But the psalmist ultimately refused to give in to his doubts. He continued to petition God for his action, and he gave us this anchoring image of our Father: God himself sees each wrong and each grief. God is not far away, even when circumstances suggest it. He sees each moment of injustice, of abuse, of trouble, and of pain. He sees, and he takes it into his own hands. He helps the weak, the vulnerable, the fatherless, and the widow.

It can be hard to believe in God's tender care for the vulnerable. It was hard for the psalmist to believe, and it is hard for us today. And yet, the end of this psalm will hold true. God will listen to and strengthen his people; he will work justice for the oppressed. Evil will not have the last word. Our God is King forever.

Come before the Lord with honesty. Do you believe he is silent or far off? Do you believe nothing in the world will ever change? Pray this psalm to the Lord and ask for his action. Thank him for the justice done at the cross, pray for a heart of humility, and ask that his name would be glorified in all the earth. Pray that his kingdom would come and that his perfect will would be done.

Pray:

You, Lord, hear the desire of the afflicted; you encourage them, and you listen to their cry, defending the fatherless and the oppressed, so that mere earthly mortals will never again strike terror. Amen.

(Adapted from Psalm 10:17–18)

Ordinary Time Day 43
KARI WEST

Read: *Romans 1:1–7*

> Paul, a servant of Christ Jesus, called to be an apostle, set apart
> for the gospel of God, which he promised beforehand through
> his prophets in the holy Scriptures, concerning his Son, who was
> descended from David according to the flesh and was declared to be
> the Son of God in power according to the Spirit of holiness by his
> resurrection from the dead, Jesus Christ our Lord, through whom
> we have received grace and apostleship to bring about the obedience
> of faith for the sake of his name among all the nations, including
> you who are called to belong to Jesus Christ,
>
> To all those in Rome who are loved by God and called to be
> saints:
>
> Grace to you and peace from God our Father and the Lord Jesus
> Christ.

Reflect:

What comes to mind when you think about the gospel? Is it primarily an intellectual concept, a list of theological ideas, a rubric for moral living, or a half-remembered story from your churched childhood?

Do you think of the gospel as what God has done for us?

This long-promised reality of the Son of God clothing himself in humanity, living perfectly, dying sacrificially, and resurrecting in power—it was all done by God so we could belong to him. We who hated him, we who ran from him, we who had nothing to offer to our Creator God, we who would die in our miserable rebellion—now we are the friends of God.

Why did Christ live, die, and return again to life? Paul knew: Christ lived, died, and was resurrected so that God could give us grace and peace.

God removed every barrier that stood between us so that we could be his own.

As you pray, meditate on this passage and ask the Spirit to reveal the deep, personal, and intimate love of your Father for you in these words.

You are his, and he has moved heaven and earth to make it so. Rejoice!

Pray:

For this reason I bow my knees before the Father, from whom every family in heaven and on earth is named, that according to the riches of his glory he may grant you to be strengthened with power through his Spirit in your inner being, so that Christ may dwell in your hearts through faith—that you, being rooted and grounded in love, may have strength to comprehend with all the saints what is the breadth and length and height and depth, and to know the love of Christ that surpasses knowledge, that you may be filled with all the fullness of God.

Now to him who is able to do far more abundantly than all that we ask or think, according to the power at work within us, to him be glory in the church and in Christ Jesus throughout all generations, forever and ever. Amen.

(Ephesians 3:14–21)

Ordinary Time Day 44

WILLA KANE

Read: *Romans 4:19–25*

> He did not weaken in faith when he considered his own body, which was as good as dead (since he was about a hundred years old), or when he considered the barrenness of Sarah's womb. No unbelief made him waver concerning the promise of God, but he grew strong in his faith as he gave glory to God, fully convinced that God was able to do what he had promised. That is why his faith was "counted to him as righteousness." But the words "it was counted to him" were not written for his sake alone, but for ours also. It will be counted to us who believe in him who raised from the dead Jesus our Lord, who was delivered up for our trespasses and raised for our justification.

Reflect:

People all over the world and all throughout the ages have seen the whole course of their lives change in incredible ways when they trusted God's promises.

Abraham believed the unbelievable: A hundred-year-old man with an infertile wife would have a son, and his descendants would be as many as the stars in the night sky. Noah built an ark when there was no sign of rain. Moses led the Israelites out of bondage through the Red Sea with the Egyptian army in hot pursuit. The young girl Mary accepted her role as the mother of God's Son.

More than seven thousand promises from God to humanity are recorded in the Bible. How can we, like Abraham, be "fully convinced" that God is able to do whatever he promises? We only have to look back at the history of Israel and know, "None of the good promises the LORD had made to the house of Israel failed. Everything was fulfilled" (Joshua 21:45 CSB).

During each season, even in the long, hard, uncertain days, remember and believe. Today, embrace these assurances of God:

- "As far as the east is from the west, so far does he remove our transgressions from us" (Psalm 103:12).
- "And I will give you a new heart, and a new spirit I will put within you. And I will remove the heart of stone from your flesh and give you a heart of flesh" (Ezekiel 36:26).
- "It is the LORD who goes before you. He will be with you; he will not leave you or forsake you. Do not fear or be dismayed" (Deutcronomy 31:8).
- "I have said these things to you, that in me you may have peace. In the world you will have tribulation. But take heart; I have overcome the world" (John 16:33).

Our God is a promise maker and a promise keeper, unchanging, faithful, strong, true, and sovereign. As we hold to God's promises, he gives us strength to persevere, trust to overcome fear, and hope to claim a brighter future.

Will you build your life on his words rather than the shifting foundations of this world? As you pray, remember these promises from the Lord. Tell God that you want to build your life on his Word. Pray for your friends who need to be reminded that God is faithful. Then praise God for his faithfulness! God will keep his promises and complete what he has already begun.

Pray:

O merciful God, grant us the grace we need to trust in your promises and build our lives around your Word. Holy Spirit, increase our faith and help our unbelief. We ask this, trusting in the good and powerful name of Christ, in whose blood we are covered, in whose righteousness we are clothed, now and for eternity. Amen.

Ordinary Time Day 45

MARY RACHEL BOYD

Read: *Romans 6:5–14*

For if we have been united with him in a death like his, we shall certainly be united with him in a resurrection like his. We know that our old self was crucified with him in order that the body of sin might be brought to nothing, so that we would no longer be enslaved to sin. For one who has died has been set free from sin. Now if we have died with Christ, we believe that we will also live with him. We know that Christ, being raised from the dead, will never die again; death no longer has dominion over him. For the death he died he died to sin, once for all, but the life he lives he lives to God. So you must also consider yourselves dead to sin and alive to God in Christ Jesus.

Let not sin therefore reign in your mortal body, to make you obey its passions. Do not present your members to sin as instruments for unrighteousness, but present yourselves to God as those who have been brought from death to life, and your members to God as instruments for righteousness. For sin will have no dominion over you, since you are not under law but under grace.

Reflect:

How very great a cost Christ paid when he willingly shed his blood for all of us.

Christ's death was not only pain and suffering on behalf of his own body. It was also taking physically on himself the intensity and anguish of everyone else's death. The result? We are no longer enslaved to sin. We are free. God will not change his mind. The death of his Son instituted and finalized our freedom from the dominion of evil. We have been made alive, and we are now invited to consider ourselves "dead to sin and alive to God in Christ Jesus" (v. 11).

Read again this incredible word from Paul: "For sin will have no dominion over you, since you are not under law but under grace" (v. 14). Do you wake every morning rejoicing in this great news? Do you give thanks to God for the grace that now covers every part of you?

As you pray, thank your Father that because of Jesus's shed blood on the cross, he is able to offer you forgiveness, freedom, and life. Ask him to show you what it means for you personally to live into this new life.

Pray:

We give thanks to you, Father, for your holy name which you made to dwell in our hearts. Thank you for the knowledge, faith, and immortality which you made known to us through Jesus your Son. To you be glory forever.

You, Lord Almighty, created all things for your name's sake, and gave people food and drink for their enjoyment, that they might give thanks to you. And you have blessed us with spiritual food and drink and eternal light through your Son.

Above all we give thanks to you that you are mighty. To you be glory forever. Amen.

(The Didache)

Ordinary Time Day 46

KARI WEST

Read: *1 Corinthians 1:1–9*

> Paul, called by the will of God to be an apostle of Christ Jesus, and our brother Sosthenes,
>
> To the church of God that is in Corinth, to those sanctified in Christ Jesus, called to be saints together with all those who in every place call upon the name of our Lord Jesus Christ, both their Lord and ours:
>
> Grace to you and peace from God our Father and the Lord Jesus Christ.
>
> I give thanks to my God always for you because of the grace of God that was given you in Christ Jesus, that in every way you were enriched in him in all speech and all knowledge—even as the testimony about Christ was confirmed among you—so that you are not lacking in any gift, as you wait for the revealing of our Lord Jesus Christ, who will sustain you to the end, guiltless in the day of our Lord Jesus Christ. God is faithful, by whom you were called into the fellowship of his Son, Jesus Christ our Lord.

Reflect:

After this introduction, Paul went on to address the issue of divisions within the church at Corinth. What a timely topic for our day. We live in a world rife with contempt and fracture along every conceivable fault line, both in our culture at large and in our churches.

But first Paul took the time to remind the Corinthian believers who they were in Jesus, what Jesus had done and would continue to do in them, and what they could expect at the end of days.

Before urging unity, Paul drew the church's gaze back to the Savior who had sanctified them, who had given them the blessed name of his holy people, and who had enriched them in every way. Sustained love for one another can only come out of a deep-rooted hope in the person and work of Jesus. Christ has given us all we need for life and godliness. Christ has made us holy, and he will keep drawing us into holiness. Christ will pour faith into our souls, enabling us to stand firm to the end.

We can wait eagerly for Christ to be revealed in fullness; we can hope in our future blameless state before the judgment seat of God; we can know friendship with God.

Are you weary of the divisions all around you? Are you exhausted from relational fractures? True unity between brothers and sisters in the Lord will flow from hearts of faith and trust in God. Remember your identity—you are loved and called by God, created for and joined to his family.

As you read these verses, pray that the Holy Spirit will give you a deeper understanding of God's love for you, Christ's work for you, and your own calling to build up others in love. Ask the Spirit to bring you to repentance and change where you have despised a brother or sister. Plead for the strength to live peaceably and humbly.

Pray:

O God the Father of our Lord Jesus Christ, our only Savior, the Prince of Peace: Give us grace to take to heart the grave dangers we are in through our many divisions. Deliver your Church from all enmity and prejudice, and everything that hinders us from godly union. As there is one Body and one Spirit, one hope of our calling, one Lord, one Faith, one Baptism, one God and Father of us all, so make us all to be of one heart and of one mind, united in one holy bond of truth and peace, of faith and love, that with one voice we may give you praise; through Jesus Christ our Lord, who lives and reigns with you and the Holy Spirit, one God in everlasting glory. Amen.

(Anglican Church in North America Book of Common Prayer)

Ordinary Time Day 47

KARI WEST

Read: *1 Corinthians 1:26–31*

For consider your calling, brothers: not many of you were wise according to worldly standards, not many were powerful, not many were of noble birth. But God chose what is foolish in the world to shame the wise; God chose what is weak in the world to shame the strong; God chose what is low and despised in the world, even things that are not, to bring to nothing things that are, so that no human being might boast in the presence of God. And because of him you are in Christ Jesus, who became to us wisdom from God, righteousness and sanctification and redemption, so that, as it is written, "Let the one who boasts, boast in the Lord."

Reflect:

Pride is a poison; self-reliance, an abyss. As we come before God's throne, all the things we put so much credence in—our own intellects, our social posturing, our physical, political, or economic strength—are shown to be inconsequential at best and a hindrance at worst. God looks to the humble.

We idolize ourselves, our success, our status, and our positions of power and prestige. But God in his mercy warns us away from this trap of lauding such trivialities.

Paul reminded us: *See those whom the world forgets, those the world considers foolish, weak, lowly, and beyond notice or care? God chooses to accomplish his glorious purposes through such people.*

God's power will flow through those who acknowledge their desperate need for him. If we are wrapped up in arrogance and fixated on our human achievements, then we will miss our chance to be caught up in the greater story God is telling on the earth.

Do you hunger for humility? Do you seek out those in your community who could teach you about dependence? Do you honor and follow leaders—in the church, in your workplace, and in the political sphere—who model graciousness and lack hubris?

As you pray, confess pride. Plead for a right understanding of yourself that will lead to humility and dependence. Trust that God will answer and bless. Ask the Holy Spirit to reveal how you might gather people around you who will encourage dependence on the Lord. Ask for the courage to honor leaders in every sphere of life who display humility. Refuse to throw your lot in with those steeped in arrogance.

Be at peace. As we live into holy habits of confession and repentance, God will grant us what we most deeply need—reliance on and conformity to his Son, the one who is our righteousness, our holiness, and our redemption.

Pray:

Father, please give us this mind among ourselves
which is ours in Christ Jesus,
who, though he was in the form of God,
did not count equality with God a thing to be grasped,
but emptied himself, by taking the form of a servant,
being born in the likeness of men.
And being found in human form,
he humbled himself by becoming obedient to the point of death,
even death on a cross.
Therefore, God has highly exalted him
and bestowed on him the name that is above every name,
so that at the name of Jesus every knee should bow,
in heaven and on earth and under the earth,
and every tongue confess that Jesus Christ is Lord
to the glory of God the Father. Amen.

(Adapted from Philippians 2:6–11)

Ordinary Time Day 48

KARI WEST

Read: *1 Corinthians 3:1–4, 16–23*

But I, brothers, could not address you as spiritual people, but as people of the flesh, as infants in Christ. I fed you with milk, not solid food, for you were not ready for it. And even now you are not yet ready, for you are still of the flesh. For while there is jealousy and strife among you, are you not of the flesh and behaving only in a human way? For when one says, "I follow Paul," and another, "I follow Apollos," are you not being merely human?...

Do you not know that you are God's temple and that God's Spirit dwells in you? If anyone destroys God's temple, God will destroy him. For God's temple is holy, and you are that temple.

Let no one deceive himself. If anyone among you thinks that he is wise in this age, let him become a fool that he may become wise. For the wisdom of this world is folly with God. For it is written, "He catches the wise in their craftiness," and again, "The Lord knows the thoughts of the wise, that they are futile." So let no one boast in men. For all things are yours, whether Paul or Apollos or Cephas or the world or life or death or the present or the future—all are yours, and you are Christ's, and Christ is God's.

Reflect:

"Are you not acting like mere humans?" (v. 3 NIV).

At first glance, Paul's accusation against the Corinthians seems to be strange and puzzling. Aren't we all human beings? What's the problem with acting like one?

We find a clue to what Paul meant in the word *mere.* Paul was jealous for the Corinthians to catch the grand vision of how God was working in his people. They were not merely individual human beings any longer, trapped in the pettiness and anguish of self-worship and self-aggrandizement. The bogs of pride no longer smothered their hearts, corrupted their desires, or thwarted their ability to worship the right things in the right order. They had been freed!

But freed for what? The answer the same for the Corinthians then as it is for us today: to be God's temple, together with our new family of fellow believers. We are freed to become the place where God dwells.

Do you treasure God's presence in the midst of his church? Is it your deep desire? Do you see it as the best, the most precious reality? It's better than receiving honor from other people, better than one's political party staying in or stepping into power, better than any crisis ending, better than our economy thriving, and better than stability in our country and our homes.

God is forming us together into his holy temple, a place for the Spirit of God to dwell. There is something profoundly sacred about the church and the relationships between the blood-bought brothers and sisters of Christ. How we need eyes of faith to see what God is working in his people by his Spirit. We are his temple.

And those who persist in jealousy, rivalry, and arrogance damage that holy dwelling place of God. We can build up the temple in humility, or we can tear it apart with pride.

As you pray, ask the Spirit to reveal the depth of the beauty of his work in and through his church. Confess pride and plead for greater humility. Meditate on the glory of our identity and our end: We will one day be fully knit together as the dwelling place of God.

Pray:

Father, make us into a humble people. Enable us to hold the right things sacred. Deepen our imaginations to grasp the glory of your work in our midst. Give us your peace and your love. Amen.

7th Sunday of Ordinary Time

MADISON PERRY

Read: *Psalm 14*

> The fool says in his heart, "There is no God."
>> They are corrupt, they do abominable deeds;
>> there is none who does good.
> The LORD looks down from heaven on the children of man,
>> to see if there are any who understand,
>> who seek after God.
> They have all turned aside; together they have become corrupt;
>> there is none who does good,
>> not even one.
> Have they no knowledge, all the evildoers
>> who eat up my people as they eat bread
>> and do not call upon the LORD?
> There they are in great terror,
>> for God is with the generation of the righteous.
> You would shame the plans of the poor,
>> but the LORD is his refuge.
> Oh, that salvation for Israel would come out of Zion!
>> When the LORD restores the fortunes of his people,
>> let Jacob rejoice, let Israel be glad.

Reflect:

The psalmist diagnosed his day's woes, and they were summed up in the heart of the fool. The fool turned aside to corruption, disregarded God, and preyed on others.

This reflects Scripture's deep truth that creation went awry because God's people failed to worship their King. Adam and Eve were appointed to govern the garden, but they disregarded God's law and sought to overthrow him, sending the cosmos into a tailspin. And humanity's revolt was at its worst when the masses came together to demand the crucifixion of the one who could tame nature and put all wrongs to right.

The psalmist's prayer was not a quiet spiritual moment or a time to ignore the world's obvious disarray. No, the psalmist brought up the ruin of this world epitomized by evil people. Amazingly, he saw himself implicated in it all. For under heaven, "there is none who does good, not even one" (v. 3). When you see the darkness tearing this world apart, do you link it with the heart? Do you admit the darkness in your own heart?

And yet the psalmist was not absolutely crushed by the darkness. Hundreds of years before Christ, he wrote this: "Oh, that salvation for Israel would come out of Zion! When the LORD restores the fortunes of his people, let Jacob rejoice, let Israel be glad" (v. 7).

Indeed, salvation has come out of Zion. God found one who was righteous, Jesus of Nazareth, and our Savior bore the weight of our betrayal. Our fortunes have been restored and we have peace with God. We hail a resurrected King.

But we are still in the midst of brokenness. As you pray, join the psalmist in raging against the evil at work in this world. Do not neglect your place in it. Pay attention to those who have suffered. Then turn to the cross of Jesus Christ. Jesus died and rose so that we might all have life. This darkness is already passing, for we have seen the salvation of our Lord. Be joyful in this season. We know how our story will end.

Pray:

Blessed are you, O Lord, the God of our fathers, Creator of the changes of day and night, who gives rest to the weary, renews the strength of those who are spent, and bestows on us occasions of song in the evening. As you have protected us in the day that is past, so be with us in the coming night; keep us from every sin, every evil, and every fear; for you are our light and salvation, and the strength of our life. To you be glory for endless ages. Amen.

Ordinary Time Day 50
SALLY BREEDLOVE

Read: *1 Corinthians 4:20–5:1, 6–13*

For the kingdom of God does not consist in talk but in power. What do you wish? Shall I come to you with a rod, or with love in a spirit of gentleness? It is actually reported that there is sexual immorality among you, and of a kind that is not tolerated even among pagans, for a man has his father's wife….

Your boasting is not good. Do you not know that a little leaven leavens the whole lump? Cleanse out the old leaven that you may be a new lump, as you really are unleavened. For Christ, our Passover lamb, has been sacrificed. Let us therefore celebrate the festival, not with the old leaven, the leaven of malice and evil, but with the unleavened bread of sincerity and truth.

I wrote to you in my letter not to associate with sexually immoral people—not at all meaning the sexually immoral of this world, or the greedy and swindlers, or idolaters, since then you would need to go out of the world. But now I am writing to you not to associate with anyone who bears the name of brother if he is guilty of sexual immorality or greed, or is an idolater, reviler, drunkard, or swindler—not even to eat with such a one. For what have I to do with judging outsiders? Is it not those inside the church whom you are to judge? God judges those outside. "Purge the evil person from among you."

Reflect:

It's easy to focus on the parts of Scripture that fit our views and values. We want a God who is soft on our comfortable sins but ruthlessly opposed to the sins we despise. But when we read the Bible without editing out the parts we don't like, we are confronted by God individually. His holiness is a blazing fire of purity. His generosity and compassion make our virtue-signaling embarrassingly self-congratulatory, and his directness in calling what is evil, evil, silences our secret hope that other people's sins are worse than ours.

Christians today are deeply divided over the issue of practical godliness. Is godliness about protecting life? Is it a traditional view of gender and sexuality? Is it about prioritizing economic and racial justice? Embracing all forms of inclusiveness?

We divide into camps. We take our view of God's agenda into our politics, and the divisive spirit of our political world becomes the spirit of our local church. We judge each other's faith; we turn friends and family into enemies.

Paul ended 1 Corinthians 4 with this: "The kingdom of God does not consist in talk but in power" (v. 20). What did he mean by power? Perhaps he meant the power of a thoroughly godly life?

Next Paul underscored the grace Christians have received: "You really are [already] unleavened" (v. 7)! Paul defined the implications of an unleavened life of godliness: keeping sex within the bond of covenant marriage; turning from malice and evil; rejecting greed and not taking advantage of others; stopping derogatory talk about others; renouncing addictions; laying down idols that imprison us; loving those outside the faith, even when they live lives antithetical to God; and calling other Christians to join us in pursuing wholehearted holiness.

As you pray, ask God to reveal where you need to repent. Commit yourself to a greater godliness. Ask him to give you compassion for this world. Ask him to make you like his Son Jesus. A life of power is a life of ongoing godliness, and godliness makes visible the kingdom of God.

Pray:

Lord, Jesus, Master Carpenter of Nazareth, through hard wood and sharp nails of the Cross, you wrought our full salvation. Wield well your carpenter's tools in us, your workshop, that we who come to you rough-hewn may be fashioned into truer beauty by your hand; who with the Father and the Holy Spirit live and reign, one God, world without end. Amen.

(Anglican Church in North America Book of Common Prayer)

Ordinary Time Day 51

SALLY BREEDLOVE

Read: *1 Corinthians 6:1–13, 18–20*

When one of you has a grievance against another, does he dare go to law before the unrighteous instead of the saints? Or do you not know that the saints will judge the world? And if the world is to be judged by you, are you incompetent to try trivial cases? Do you not know that we are to judge angels? How much more, then, matters pertaining to this life! So if you have such cases, why do you lay them before those who have no standing in the church? I say this to your shame. Can it be that there is no one among you wise enough to settle a dispute between the brothers, but brother goes to law against brother, and that before unbelievers? To have lawsuits at all with one another is already a defeat for you. Why not rather suffer wrong? Why not rather be defrauded? But you yourselves wrong and defraud—even your own brothers!

Or do you not know that the unrighteous will not inherit the kingdom of God? Do not be deceived: neither the sexually immoral, nor idolaters, nor adulterers, nor men who practice homosexuality, nor thieves, nor the greedy, nor drunkards, nor revilers, nor swindlers will inherit the kingdom of God. And such were some of you. But you were washed, you were sanctified, you were justified in the name of the Lord Jesus Christ and by the Spirit of our God.

"All things are lawful for me," but not all things are helpful. "All things are lawful for me," but I will not be dominated by anything. "Food is meant for the stomach and the stomach for food"—and God will destroy both one and the other. The body is not meant for sexual immorality, but for the Lord, and the Lord for the body.... Flee from sexual immorality. Every other sin a person commits is outside the body, but the sexually immoral person sins against his own body. Or do you not know that your body is a temple of the Holy Spirit within you, whom you have from God? You are not your own, for you were bought with a price. So glorify God in your body.

Reflect:

Paul's stance toward the Corinthian church was fierce. Imagine having a preacher or teacher you admire confront you about the lawsuit you filed, your sex life, how much you think about winning at all costs, how much you drink, or how often you get angry. You, like many of us, would flinch and put up your defenses. You would likely flinch now if you let Paul's words sink in deeply.

What was his point? Was Paul the behavior inspector and corrector? In truth, he did hold all of God's people to the highest imaginable standard, namely, the standard of becoming like Christ, of being "little Christs" in this dark world.

But Paul's heart was for our well-being, freedom, and joy—not to shame us or merely improve our ethics. We will one day inherit God's kingdom in all its fullness. In this life we are being prepared for that future. Our daily choices—who we are becoming by way of our desires and habits—really matter.

But here is the key: Paul insisted that God has already made us holy. God wants us to live into the person he has already made us to be in Christ and live into the gift of a clean heart. We don't have to manufacture our own goodness. God invites us to live in sync with who we already are!

God desires an intimate friendship with us. We belong to him. He wants us to be free, not enslaved to lesser choices.

As you pray, consider the dignity and privilege that God has heaped on you. Lift your heart, your choices, and your thoughts up to him. Let God's Word give you hope so that you can choose a life of holiness, freedom, and joy.

Pray:

O Holy Spirit, beloved of my soul, I adore you. Enlighten me, guide me, strengthen me, console me. Tell me what I should do; give me your orders. I promise to submit myself to all that you desire of me and to accept all that you permit to happen to me. Let me only know your will. Amen.

(Joseph Mercier)

Ordinary Time Day 52

SALLY BREEDLOVE

Read: *1 Corinthians 7:32–38*

> I want you to be free from anxieties. The unmarried man is anxious about the things of the Lord, how to please the Lord. But the married man is anxious about worldly things, how to please his wife, and his interests are divided. And the unmarried or betrothed woman is anxious about the things of the Lord, how to be holy in body and spirit. But the married woman is anxious about worldly things, how to please her husband. I say this for your own benefit, not to lay any restraint upon you, but to promote good order and to secure your undivided devotion to the Lord.
>
> If anyone thinks that he is not behaving properly toward his betrothed, if his passions are strong, and it has to be, let him do as he wishes: let them marry—it is no sin. But whoever is firmly established in his heart, being under no necessity but having his desire under control, and has determined this in his heart, to keep her as his betrothed, he will do well. So then he who marries his betrothed does well, and he who refrains from marriage will do even better.

Reflect:

First Corinthians 7 is an interesting and confusing chapter. When we sit with the whole chapter, we may wonder what Paul meant. Did he see marriage as a less worthy choice and lifelong singleness and devotion to Christ as a better choice, for all time and for all people?

Despite our confusion, parts of chapter 7 are straightforward and perhaps troubling in their implications. Notice if you find yourself resisting one of the places where his meaning is clear.

Marriage is a relationship of mutuality, not one of submission and domination. Singleness with self-control is a gift some people are given. The covenant that binds two people together is sacred and should not be lightly disregarded. Contentment with one's place in life is a good thing. This world won't last forever.

Our world wants to control the discussion about marriage. Perhaps you feel your own pushback to Paul's words. How you see marriage and how you live as a married or an unmarried person has real consequences. Your framework is either a road to well-being and peace or a road to disharmony, confusion, and pain. Paul said that living into God's truth about marriage and singleness leads to a less anxious and less complicated life—a kind of life that frees one to pay attention to God and his kingdom.

As you pray, sit with your own story of married life or singleness. How do you long for God to free you from anxiety and confusion? How is God inviting you to a life of following after him?

Pray:

Merciful Savior, you loved Martha and Mary and Lazarus, hallowing their home with your sacred presence: Bless our homes, we pray, that your love may rest upon us, and that your presence may dwell with us. May we all grow in grace and in the knowledge of you, our Lord and Savior. Teach us to love one another as you have commanded. Help us to bear one another's burdens in fulfillment of your law, O blessed Jesus, who with the Father and the Holy Spirit live and reign, one God, for ever and ever. Amen.

(Anglican Church in North America Book of Common Prayer)

Ordinary Time Day 53

SALLY BREEDLOVE

Read: *1 Corinthians 8*

Now concerning food offered to idols: we know that "all of us possess knowledge." This "knowledge" puffs up, but love builds up. If anyone imagines that he knows something, he does not yet know as he ought to know. But if anyone loves God, he is known by God.

Therefore, as to the eating of food offered to idols, we know that "an idol has no real existence," and that "there is no God but one." For although there may be so-called gods in heaven or on earth—as indeed there are many "gods" and many "lords"—yet for us there is one God, the Father, from whom are all things and for whom we exist, and one Lord, Jesus Christ, through whom are all things and through whom we exist.

However, not all possess this knowledge. But some, through former association with idols, eat food as really offered to an idol, and their conscience, being weak, is defiled. Food will not commend us to God. We are no worse off if we do not eat, and no better off if we do. But take care that this right of yours does not somehow become a stumbling block to the weak. For if anyone sees you who have knowledge eating in an idol's temple, will he not be encouraged, if his conscience is weak, to eat food offered to idols? And so by your knowledge this weak person is destroyed, the brother for whom Christ died. Thus, sinning against your brothers and wounding their conscience when it is weak, you sin against Christ. Therefore, if food makes my brother stumble, I will never eat meat, lest I make my brother stumble.

Reflect:

One hears a passage like this and wants answers to the obvious questions: "How much freedom do I have to follow my own conscience? Does another person have the right to shape my choices? What if I disagree with that person? Do I have to make my life accommodate that individual?"

We all have places where we disagree with another Christian's choices or freedoms. So what do we do? Put our energy into convincing the person that our perspective is right? Why do we keep on arguing when we know from experience that arguments about who is "more right" rarely solve anything? All the facts and knowledge we amass only move us further apart. We live in a world that is fracturing into a million pieces because of such fights.

We need to listen to the first three verses in this chapter. Paul told us that when an issue matters deeply to people, knowledge rarely solves a disagreement. Love is the builder of people and relationships. Humility, not perfect knowledge, keeps us connected to God. Admitting that God knows us at the core of our beings keeps us honest. We matter because of God's love for us, not because of our rightness.

Is there an ongoing broken relationship in your life right now? Ask God how he is inviting you into love, into humility, and into being known. Lay down your need to be right. See those around you as full recipients, just like you are, of the mercy of God. Be at peace. God loves you miraculously and mercifully, but not because you are right about everything. Submit to being loved, and therefore embrace God's call to love.

Pray:

Almighty and everliving God, we are taught by your holy Word to offer prayers and supplications and to give thanks for all people. We humbly ask you mercifully to receive our prayers. Inspire continually the universal Church with the spirit of truth, unity, and concord; and grant that all who confess your holy Name may agree in the truth of your holy Word, and live in unity and godly love. Amen.

(Anglican Church in North America Book of Common Prayer)

Ordinary Time Day 54

SALLY BREEDLOVE

Read: *1 Corinthians 9:19–27*

For though I am free from all, I have made myself a servant to all, that I might win more of them. To the Jews I became as a Jew, in order to win Jews. To those under the law I became as one under the law (though not being myself under the law) that I might win those under the law. To those outside the law I became as one outside the law (not being outside the law of God but under the law of Christ) that I might win those outside the law. To the weak I became weak, that I might win the weak. I have become all things to all people, that by all means I might save some. I do it all for the sake of the gospel, that I may share with them in its blessings.

Do you not know that in a race all the runners run, but only one receives the prize? So run that you may obtain it. Every athlete exercises self-control in all things. They do it to receive a perishable wreath, but we an imperishable. So I do not run aimlessly; I do not box as one beating the air. But I discipline my body and keep it under control, lest after preaching to others I myself should be disqualified.

Reflect:

Ordinary Time lasts quite a long time in the church year. Each day offers us an opportunity to throw our lots in with Jesus's. It is so easy to think, *Nothing ever changes. I have the same problems, disappointments, and heartaches I have always carried.*

But when we read Paul's words, we see a man who wasn't bound by the drudgery of day after day. He was free, and he used his freedom to fully participate in living for Jesus and loving this world—each day! He was committed to living well and to making it to the finish line of his life without flagging. He wanted to hear the "Well done" of Jesus at the end of his days.

What do you want? An easy life, a safe life, a successful life, or a life where you are seen and appreciated? Paul said he wanted to live the gospel, not just know about it. He wanted to enter the world to serve as Jesus did. He wanted to understand people's lives and perspectives so he could speak the truth of Jesus in ways that made sense to them.

The atmosphere of Paul's soul was electric with anticipation. He was excited about the life he had chosen, as excited as an athlete before a championship game.

Our world can be so dreary, broken, complicated, and empty. What if you were to choose to enter the world around you and live into the fullness of your life in Christ? What if you were to decide to build a deep friendship with someone who doesn't yet know Jesus? What if you were to spend real time seeking to understand and enjoy this person? What if you were to pray that your words and your life might become a bridge to bring the person to Jesus?

As you pray, ask for the desire to join in God's gospel work. Ask him to bring someone to mind whom you could befriend. Be the gospel to that person. Pray.

Pray:

Almighty God our Savior, you desire that none should perish, and you have taught us through your Son that there is great joy in heaven over every sinner who repents: Grant that our hearts may ache for a lost and broken world. May your Holy Spirit work through our words, deeds, and prayers, that the lost may be found and the dead made alive, and that all your redeemed may rejoice around your throne; through Jesus Christ our Lord. Amen.

(Anglican Church in North America Book of Common Prayer)

Ordinary Time Day 55
SALLY BREEDLOVE

Read: *1 Corinthians 10:11–13, 31*

Now these things happened to them as an example, but they were written down for our instruction, on whom the end of the ages has come. Therefore let anyone who thinks that he stands take heed lest he fall. No temptation has overtaken you that is not common to man. God is faithful, and he will not let you be tempted beyond your ability, but with the temptation he will also provide the way of escape, that you may be able to endure it....

So, whether you eat or drink, or whatever you do, do all to the glory of God.

Reflect:

Paul loved the Corinthian church. He spent more time with these believers (and with the church in Ephesus) than with believers in any other place. Paul knew this church, warts and all, but he never walked away from them in disgust. He wrote four letters we know of (two of which are in the Bible) to help teach them and disciple them.

Paul longed for the people of Corinth to follow Jesus wholeheartedly. He longed for them to become true disciples, not casual yes-people to the gospel.

Chapter by chapter in 1 Corinthians, Paul called out the sin of the Corinthian church and brought up the controversies and arguments that plagued them. He did not want them to be discouraged, as 1 Corinthians 10 makes clear. Their situation was not hopeless. The trials they faced, like the trials we face, are universally present in all human existence. Neither we nor they have been uniquely singled out for pain or difficulty.

Life is hard. Perhaps it would help to place our distress in perspective if we were to accept that reality. As Acts 14:22 declares, "Through many tribulations we must enter the kingdom of God."

But God's faithfulness is far bigger than the difficulty of life. Paul wrote that in every temptation, God offers us grace to escape the pressure to give in, and grace to endure until the temptation passes.

Is there a place in your life right now where you feel pushed beyond your ability to endure? Confess that to God, and as you pray, thank him for the truth that he is so much larger than your weariness and temptation. God is faithful; he will help you. He will give you endurance. As you end your prayer time, reenter your life as one who knows that God will be faithful.

Pray:

Dear Lord and Savior Jesus Christ: I hold up all my weakness to your strength, my failure to your faithfulness, my sinfulness to your perfection, my loneliness to your compassion, my little pains to your great agony on the Cross. I pray that you will cleanse me, strengthen me, guide me, so that in all ways my life may be lived as you would have it lived, without cowardice and for you alone. Show me how to live in true humility, true contrition, and true love. Amen.

(Anglican Church in North America Book of Common Prayer)

8th Sunday of Ordinary Time
KARI WEST

Read: *Psalm 15*

> O LORD, who shall sojourn in your tent?
> > Who shall dwell on your holy hill?
> He who walks blamelessly and does what is right
> > and speaks truth in his heart;
> who does not slander with his tongue
> > and does no evil to his neighbor,
> > nor takes up a reproach against his friend;
> in whose eyes a vile person is despised,
> > but who honors those who fear the LORD;
> who swears to his own hurt and does not change;
> who does not put out his money at interest
> > and does not take a bribe against the innocent.
> He who does these things shall never be moved.

Reflect:

"O LORD, who shall sojourn in your tent?"

Is the opening question of this psalm one that you ask? Is it the reason you seek to live a godly life? The psalmist wasn't interested in the best way to get by in life. He was not seeking the right steps to make it to the top of a social, professional, or religious ladder. He was not seeking the character traits needed to be successful and healthy. No, he asked a much deeper, much more profound, and much more interesting question than that: How can we live near God?

God is who we were made for and who we need; God is the source of life; God is the fountain of joy; God is the wellspring of everlasting delight. Our souls were intricately crafted to know the unknowable riches of God. How can we draw near to him?

Pause and reflect. How often is being close to God your true desire? What is revealed by the choices you make for your life? What do you spend your time and energy pursuing?

The psalmist listed manifold qualities of godliness: living blamelessly, practicing righteousness, acknowledging truth, actively loving others, honoring goodness, and being honest.

But the first and most important quality? Asking that first question. Knowing that the goal of life is a relationship with the mysterious, everlasting, almighty God, the lover of your soul.

As you pray, ask to know afresh that you were made for life with God. Pray for the reminder that life apart from him is ultimate misery. Thank Christ that he has lived the only perfect life and died so that we might become the righteousness of God in him. Ask for strength to walk in a manner pleasing to him.

Pray:

Bring us, O Lord God, at our last awakening
into the house and gate of heaven,
to enter into that gate and dwell in that house,
where there shall be no darkness nor dazzling,
but one equal light;
no noise nor silence, but one equal music;
no fears nor hopes, but one equal possession;
no ends nor beginnings, but one equal eternity:
in the habitations of thy majesty and glory,
world without end.
Amen.

(John Donne)

Ordinary Time Day 57
SALLY BREEDLOVE

Read: *1 Corinthians 10:23–11:1*

"All things are lawful," but not all things are helpful. "All things are lawful," but not all things build up. Let no one seek his own good, but the good of his neighbor. Eat whatever is sold in the meat market without raising any question on the ground of conscience. For "the earth is the Lord's, and the fullness thereof." If one of the unbelievers invites you to dinner and you are disposed to go, eat whatever is set before you without raising any question on the ground of conscience. But if someone says to you, "This has been offered in sacrifice," then do not eat it, for the sake of the one who informed you, and for the sake of conscience—I do not mean your conscience, but his. For why should my liberty be determined by someone else's conscience? If I partake with thankfulness, why am I denounced because of that for which I give thanks?

So, whether you eat or drink, or whatever you do, do all to the glory of God. Give no offense to Jews or to Greeks or to the church of God, just as I try to please everyone in everything I do, not seeking my own advantage, but that of many, that they may be saved.

Be imitators of me, as I am of Christ.

Reflect:

Paul's instructions to the Corinthian church rang clear and strong. Paul encouraged them to imitate him, inasmuch as he imitated Christ.

But what does it look like to imitate Jesus?

- To imitate Jesus is to follow Jesus.
- To imitate Jesus is to know the Gospels in such a way that the stories about him shape your mind and your imagination. Only then will you know what imitation looks like in the everyday situations of your own life.

126

- To imitate Jesus is to find wise and godly Christians and then pattern your life after theirs.
- To imitate Jesus is to choose to love across all the lines that divide you from others.
- To imitate Jesus is to be an unrecognized servant.
- To imitate Jesus is to be willing to lay down your life for the sake of others.
- To imitate Jesus is to care more for the Father's approval than for the approval of anyone else.
- To imitate Jesus is to live a holy life.
- To imitate Jesus is to be willing to oppose the greed and hypocrisy of religiosity.
- To imitate Jesus is to spend time with the Father.
- To imitate Jesus is to know the Scriptures.

What statements of your own can you add to this list? As you pray, ask God where he is particularly inviting you to imitate Jesus. Then take up that invitation, day by day.

Pray:

Gracious and holy Father, please give me intellect to understand you, reason to discern you, diligence to seek you, wisdom to find you, a spirit to know you, a heart to meditate upon you, ears to hear you, eyes to see you, a tongue to proclaim you, a way of life pleasing to you, patience to wait for you, and perseverance to look for you. Grant me a perfect end, your holy presence, a blessed resurrection, and life everlasting. Amen.

(Benedict of Nursia)

Ordinary Time Day 58

KARI WEST

Read: *1 Corinthians 13*

If I speak in the tongues of men and of angels, but have not love,
I am a noisy gong or a clanging cymbal. And if I have prophetic
powers, and understand all mysteries and all knowledge, and if I
have all faith, so as to remove mountains, but have not love, I am
nothing. If I give away all I have, and if I deliver up my body to be
burned, but have not love, I gain nothing.

Love is patient and kind; love does not envy or boast; it is not
arrogant or rude. It does not insist on its own way; it is not irritable
or resentful; it does not rejoice at wrongdoing, but rejoices with
the truth. Love bears all things, believes all things, hopes all things,
endures all things.

Love never ends. As for prophecies, they will pass away; as for
tongues, they will cease; as for knowledge, it will pass away. For we
know in part and we prophesy in part, but when the perfect comes,
the partial will pass away. When I was a child, I spoke like a child, I
thought like a child, I reasoned like a child. When I became a man,
I gave up childish ways. For now we see in a mirror dimly, but then
face to face. Now I know in part; then I shall know fully, even as I
have been fully known.

So now faith, hope, and love abide, these three; but the greatest
of these is love.

Reflect:

Paul knew what it meant to be considered a paradigm of virtue. People would
have commended his wisdom, his faith, and his prophetic voice. He knew
the cost of following Jesus; he was well acquainted with suffering.

Yet Paul also knew the source of real power. Without love, he insisted,
all our efforts are smoke and ash. They will amount to nothing. More than
that, without love, we ourselves become nothing—like chaff driven before
the wind.

Paul's words may resonate in uncomfortable ways, if we are paying attention. Have we truly considered his message? Do we really believe these famous verses? He insisted that love—not accomplishments, to-do lists, resumes, or feats of "godliness"—is the measure of our humanity.

That is a terrifying reality to consider. As we read Paul's many descriptions of love, we see how short we fall of this all-important eternal virtue. We'd rather measure ourselves by our smaller accomplishments or by check marks of godliness. How can anyone love as Paul described it?

Thank God that love is both the measure and the means of our humanity. We are pulled into this utterly impossible but deeply good calling by the powerful love of Jesus, the one who knows each of us fully.

Read Paul's description of love again, but this time, substitute the name of Jesus—the full and final manifestation of love.

Jesus is patient, *Jesus* is kind. *Jesus* does not envy, *Jesus* does not boast, *Jesus* is not proud. *Jesus* does not dishonor others, *Jesus* is not self-seeking, *Jesus* is not easily angered, *Jesus* keeps no record of wrongs. *Jesus* does not delight in evil but rejoices with the truth. *Jesus* always protects, always trusts, always hopes, always perseveres. *Jesus* never fails.

As you pray, rest in the perfect and perfecting love of your Savior. Ask him for greater obedience to heed this great call of love.

Pray:

May the love of Christ henceforth constrain us to live no longer to ourselves, but to him who died for us. May we more and more consider ourselves not as our own, but as bought with a price, and may we use the blessings that you have given us in your fear and love, with gratitude to you the giver of them all. Amen.

(William Wilberforce)

Ordinary Time Day 59

KARI WEST

Read: *1 Corinthians 15:1–11*

Now I would remind you, brothers, of the gospel I preached to you, which you received, in which you stand, and by which you are being saved, if you hold fast to the word I preached to you—unless you believed in vain.

For I delivered to you as of first importance what I also received: that Christ died for our sins in accordance with the Scriptures, that he was buried, that he was raised on the third day in accordance with the Scriptures, and that he appeared to Cephas, then to the twelve. Then he appeared to more than five hundred brothers at one time, most of whom are still alive, though some have fallen asleep. Then he appeared to James, then to all the apostles. Last of all, as to one untimely born, he appeared also to me. For I am the least of the apostles, unworthy to be called an apostle, because I persecuted the church of God. But by the grace of God I am what I am, and his grace toward me was not in vain. On the contrary, I worked harder than any of them, though it was not I, but the grace of God that is with me. Whether then it was I or they, so we preach and so you believed.

Reflect:

Christ died for our sins; Christ was buried; Christ rose from death to reign in life. If we lose this central story, we lose everything.

By this gospel, we are saved. Christ's death has bought us peace with God and ushered us into his family. His resurrection has inaugurated the coming kingdom and secured his final, full victory over the cosmos.

This resurrected Christ appeared to multitudes—many of whom were still alive when Paul was writing. This resurrected Christ appeared to Paul himself and wrought an incredible transformation in his life—from hating and persecuting the church to pouring himself out for its good. And yet despite their proximity to the resurrection, the Corinthian believers were in danger of losing their focus. We, too, need to take care that we do not lose sight of the death and resurrection of Jesus.

Paul wanted this central truth to sink into the Christians at Corinth, and it should still resonate with us today: Embrace the resurrection! In this gospel, we find fresh power for life and godliness, as Paul did. Through this gospel, we learn that Christ will make all things new.

As you pray, remember the one in whose name you come before the Father. Praise him for his sacrificial death, praise him for his victory over all lesser powers, praise him for breaking the curse of death, praise him for his current reign, and praise him for his promised restoration of all things.

Hail our risen and reigning Lord and Savior Jesus Christ, God over all. As you end your time of prayer, rejoice in the truth of these words in the presence of your heavenly Father:

Pray:
Death and darkness, get you packing.
Nothing now to man is lacking.
All your triumphs now are ended,
And what Adam marred is mended.
Graves are beds now for the weary,
Death a nap to wake more merry.
Amen.

(From *"Easter Hymn,"* Henry Vaughan)

Ordinary Time Day 60
MADISON PERRY

Read: *2 Corinthians 3:7–18*

Now if the ministry of death, carved in letters on stone, came with such glory that the Israelites could not gaze at Moses' face because of its glory, which was being brought to an end, will not the ministry of the Spirit have even more glory? For if there was glory in the ministry of condemnation, the ministry of righteousness must far exceed it in glory. Indeed, in this case, what once had glory has come to have no glory at all, because of the glory that surpasses it. For if what was being brought to an end came with glory, much more will what is permanent have glory.

Since we have such a hope, we are very bold, not like Moses, who would put a veil over his face so that the Israelites might not gaze at the outcome of what was being brought to an end. But their minds were hardened. For to this day, when they read the old covenant, that same veil remains unlifted, because only through Christ is it taken away. Yes, to this day whenever Moses is read a veil lies over their hearts. But when one turns to the Lord, the veil is removed. Now the Lord is the Spirit, and where the Spirit of the Lord is, there is freedom. And we all, with unveiled face, beholding the glory of the Lord, are being transformed into the same image from one degree of glory to another. For this comes from the Lord who is the Spirit.

Reflect:

Thank the Lord for the gift of his Word! It is challenging, foreign, and so unlike the thoughts our world teaches us to think. It is very likely that you did not wake up this morning thinking about Moses and Israel or about Jesus and the outpouring of the Holy Spirit.

But for Paul, the Christian life was not a onetime spiritual event, a single mountaintop experience that he could leave behind and keep going on as before. Paul wrote here about being among those who "with unveiled face" are "beholding the glory of the Lord" (v. 18).

What would it look like for you to contemplate the Lord's glory? Can you squeeze it onto your list of priorities?

"But when one turns to the Lord," verse 16 tells us, "the veil is removed." Paul instructed us about the crucial first step—we must turn to the Lord. We must take our eyes off other things and look to the Lord. This can happen only if we are willing to look upon something that may shatter us, reconfigure our priorities, threaten our identities, and endow us with an exalted hope. Are you willing to abandon yourself in order to find yourself?

Let us contemplate the Lord. Praise the Lord, the Creator of heaven and earth. Praise the Lord, in whose hands are the caverns of the earth. The heights of the hills are his also. The stars run their courses according to his paths and do his bidding. Praise the Lord, who chose Israel to be his people. Praise the Lord, who offers discipline to those he loves, and who will never leave us or forsake us. Praise the Lord, born of the young girl Mary, born to die and conquer death. Praise the Lord, whose Spirit guides us today and into eternity. He will transform us in his glory.

Pray:

Lord, forgive us for our dull minds and dull hearts. Thank you for refreshing us in your Word and restoring to us the joy of our salvation. In every way that we do not honor you, correct us as a gentle and loving Father. In every way that we can serve you, equip us, call us, and accompany us by the power and presence of your Holy Spirit, through Jesus Christ our Lord. Amen.

Ordinary Time Day 61
MADISON PERRY

Read: *2 Corinthians 4:6–12*

For God, who said, "Let light shine out of darkness," has shone in our hearts to give the light of the knowledge of the glory of God in the face of Jesus Christ.

But we have this treasure in jars of clay, to show that the surpassing power belongs to God and not to us. We are afflicted in every way, but not crushed; perplexed, but not driven to despair; persecuted, but not forsaken; struck down, but not destroyed; always carrying in the body the death of Jesus, so that the life of Jesus may also be manifested in our bodies. For we who live are always being given over to death for Jesus' sake, so that the life of Jesus also may be manifested in our mortal flesh. So death is at work in us, but life in you.

Reflect:

The gospel promises us extravagant things. God puts within his people the light of the knowledge of the glory of God in the face of Jesus Christ. We bear great treasure and are filled to overflowing with the life of Jesus.

But in truth, the gospel is not manifested in our creaturely strength and passing fleshly glory, but in our very weakness. This is the great contradiction of our everyday lives as we embrace the way of Christ, where we at once take up our crosses and also know life and rest. Glorious ruins are we, afflicted and perplexed vessels of the living God. Saint Paul proclaimed without despair, "We always carry around in our body the death of Jesus" (2 Corinthians 4:10 NIV), revealing his resurrection life.

Have you given up? Is there any part of your life that you have surrendered to death, to the realm of utter pointlessness, to suffering and despair?

Come to Jesus now for rest. Name your burdens and ask him to share in them. Ask for the strength to continue to struggle. Finally, ask for the privilege of beholding the light of the knowledge of the glory of God, a glimpse of God's beauty far beyond anything this world could ever offer.

Pray:

For all from whom God's face is hidden—by extremity of suffering, by unbelief, by loss of faith, by wickedness of men. For all righteous and faithful men, who are tempted to cast away faith or to lose confidence in God. For all who are perplexed by the darkness of divine ways, not knowing why they are afflicted. For all who are burdened and troubled for the evil and suffering permitted by God to exist. Lord, hear our prayer. Amen.

(Henry Wotherspoon)

Ordinary Time Day 62
MADISON PERRY

Read: *2 Corinthians 5:16–21*

From now on, therefore, we regard no one according to the flesh. Even though we once regarded Christ according to the flesh, we regard him thus no longer. Therefore, if anyone is in Christ, he is a new creation. The old has passed away; behold, the new has come. All this is from God, who through Christ reconciled us to himself and gave us the ministry of reconciliation; that is, in Christ God was reconciling the world to himself, not counting their trespasses against them, and entrusting to us the message of reconciliation. Therefore, we are ambassadors for Christ, God making his appeal through us. We implore you on behalf of Christ, be reconciled to God. For our sake he made him to be sin who knew no sin, so that in him we might become the righteousness of God.

Reflect:

In this age of self-improvement, we are urged to take up the task of self-creation, of fashioning ourselves according to our own (inevitably shallow) vision of what is good and beautiful. In an age like ours, Paul's celebration of a "new creation" (v. 17) might sound like an invitation to finally become the people we want to be.

However, Paul's words do not fit well into a universe built to exalt people. He had in mind not the passing glory of the flesh but the eternal and resplendent glory of the living God.

To be a new creation is to be born anew, not only as true sons and daughters of the King but also as ambassadors for Christ and ministers of reconciliation. Ever since the beginning of evil's war against our Lord, creation has become polluted by sin and alienated from God. God's holiness will not abide sin.

The task that falls to us is to enter into Christ's reconciliation of heaven and earth by offering this world to God so that he might make it righteous.

Our hope is that every square inch of creation will be filled with the presence of God, becoming a new and transfigured creation. And the first offering that we make is ourselves. As God cleanses us and renews our hearts, we become the firstfruits of his new creation.

God's restoration is cosmic; his renewal will be all-encompassing. Offer your heart and your life to God. Give him permission to renew you, to lift you out of hopelessness and rebellion and into new life. Ask him to give you a truer picture of his heart for the reconciling of all things to himself. Ask him how your life can reflect his heart. Glorify him. It won't be long before this reconciliation is fully accomplished.

Pray:

Lord, I am your poor creature, you have in your mercy begun a blessed work in me, and where you have begun, you have said you will make an end. When you created the world you did not leave it till all was done; and when you created man you made an end. Now, I ask you, perfect the new creature in my soul. As you have begun to enlighten my understanding and direct my affections to the best things, so I commit my soul unto you for further guidance and direction to full happiness. Amen.

(Richard Sibbes)

9th Sunday of Ordinary Time

MADISON PERRY

Read: *Psalm 23*

    The LORD is my shepherd; I shall not want.
        He makes me lie down in green pastures.
    He leads me beside still waters.
        He restores my soul.
    He leads me in paths of righteousness
        for his name's sake.
    Even though I walk through the valley of the shadow of death,
        I will fear no evil,
    for you are with me;
        your rod and your staff,
        they comfort me.
    You prepare a table before me
        in the presence of my enemies;
    you anoint my head with oil;
        my cup overflows.
    Surely goodness and mercy shall follow me
        all the days of my life,
    and I shall dwell in the house of the LORD
        forever.

Reflect:

Psalm 23 opens for us a vista of blessing, but in order to fully embrace it we must cede control of our lives. When we pray Psalm 23, we center ourselves on God's ways and God's leading. To pray this psalm, we must acknowledge that we are but sheep.

Throughout the Gospels, Jesus and his disciples proclaimed that the kingdom of God was near. It is good news for us that the kingdom of God is near because within it we can be mere sheep who receive rest, sustenance, and protection.

Yet this psalm doesn't promise a pain-free existence. It guides us from verdant pasture through the shadow of death, from God's comfort and salvation to a table set in the midst of our enemies. But ultimately, we will receive these promises: We will be anointed with the Holy Spirit, our cup of life will overflow, goodness and mercy will follow us all the days of our life, and we will dwell in the house of the Lord forever.

Begin your prayers in humility, as a sheep looking to your Shepherd. Acknowledge your dependence on his hand. Ask that Christ's will would be done in your life, now and forever. Finally, let your requests give way to hope, thank God for his salvation, and express your wish to dwell in his house forever.

Pray:

My God, set right the broken spring. Restore to me the joy of your salvation. You have given me back my freedom; give me back my wings. Take away the weariness, the jadedness, that follow the hour of struggle. Heal the shrinking of the sinew that succeeds the angel's blessing. Remove the paralysis that lingers after the sorrow itself has fled. When I stand beside the fountains of living water, wipe away past tears from my eyes. Amen.

(George Matheson)

Ordinary Time Day 64

MADISON PERRY

Read: *2 Corinthians 6:1–13*

Working together with him, then, we appeal to you not to receive the grace of God in vain. For he says,

"In a favorable time I listened to you,
and in a day of salvation I have helped you."

Behold, now is the favorable time; behold, now is the day of salvation. We put no obstacle in anyone's way, so that no fault may be found with our ministry, but as servants of God we commend ourselves in every way: by great endurance, in afflictions, hardships, calamities, beatings, imprisonments, riots, labors, sleepless nights, hunger; by purity, knowledge, patience, kindness, the Holy Spirit, genuine love; by truthful speech, and the power of God; with the weapons of righteousness for the right hand and for the left; through honor and dishonor, through slander and praise. We are treated as impostors, and yet are true; as unknown, and yet well known; as dying, and behold, we live; as punished, and yet not killed; as sorrowful, yet always rejoicing; as poor, yet making many rich; as having nothing, yet possessing everything.

We have spoken freely to you, Corinthians; our heart is wide open. You are not restricted by us, but you are restricted in your own affections. In return (I speak as to children) widen your hearts also.

Reflect:

Open wide your heart to God and his people. Do not let yourself be restrained in your affection. If you harbor in yourself love of riches, a vain desire for glory, the nagging impulse toward sloth, or the bitter, consuming darkness of despair, then listen to the heart of Christ in the words of Paul. Unbind your affections and receive Christ, as today is the day of salvation.

Reread the middle portion of our passage:

Behold, now is the favorable time; behold, now is the day of salvation. We put no obstacle in anyone's way, so that no fault may be found with our ministry, but as servants of God we commend ourselves in every way: by great endurance, in afflictions, hardships, calamities, beatings, imprisonments, riots, labors, sleepless nights, hunger; by purity, knowledge, patience, kindness, the Holy Spirit, genuine love; by truthful speech, and the power of God; with the weapons of righteousness for the right hand and for the left; through honor and dishonor, through slander and praise. We are treated as impostors, and yet are true; as unknown, and yet well known; as dying, and behold, we live; as punished, and yet not killed; as sorrowful, yet always rejoicing; as poor, yet making many rich; as having nothing, yet possessing everything.

Let God's goodness sink in. If your heart rejoices, read it again. Praise the Lord for his salvation!

Pray:

O you whose chosen dwelling is the heart that longs for your presence and humbly seeks your face: we come to you as the day declines and the shadows of evening fall: Deepen within us every feeling of shame and sorrow for the wrong we have done, for the good we have left undone; and strengthen every desire to amend our lives according to your holy will. Restore us to the joy of your salvation; bind up that which is broken; rekindle the sacred fire; give light to our minds, strength to our wills, and rest to our souls; according to your loving kindness in Jesus Christ our Lord. Amen.

(John Hunter)

Ordinary Time Day 65

SALLY BREEDLOVE

Read: *2 Corinthians 6:16 & Revelation 21:3*

What agreement has the temple of God with idols? For we are the temple of the living God; as God said,

> "I will make my dwelling among them and walk among them,
>   and I will be their God,
>   and they shall be my people."

And I heard a loud voice from the throne saying, "Behold, the dwelling place of God is with man. He will dwell with them, and they will be his people, and God himself will be with them as their God."

Reflect:

Does your life these days feel like a steep climb or a long journey with no clear destination?

God's chosen people knew that reality. Three times each year, they journeyed to Jerusalem for religious festivals. The road was long, and the incline grew sharp as they neared the Holy City.

At its highest point, Jerusalem is twenty-five hundred feet above sea level, while just twenty-two miles to the east lies the Dead Sea, the lowest point on earth. The Israelites sang songs along the way, and we know them today as the Psalms of Ascent.

Theirs was not only a physical journey; it was also a spiritual one. The road to Jerusalem was a steep climb, but the people completed the journey because they needed to worship their God in his temple. The magnificent temple built by Solomon was where the very Spirit of God dwelt in the holy of holies.

Maybe today you feel as if you climb and climb, yet you make no progress. Perhaps you're exhausted by the hills you're forced to walk over during a challenging season. But even now, there is good news for you.

Although we face physical climbs in a fallen world, we do not face a spiritual one. In a miraculous change of address, God's Spirit has moved from a temple built by craftsmen on a hill in Jerusalem to hearts reclaimed through the blood of Christ.

We no longer face a journey of ascent. Instead, our Lord Jesus descended to the earth, lived among us, and died a criminal's death to pay for sins not his own. He came to us. He conquered death. Then he ascended to the throne to sit at the right hand of the Father and sent his Spirit to live in those who receive his free gift of salvation.

Paul exhorted the Corinthians, "Do you not know that you are God's temple and that God's Spirit dwells in you?" (1 Corinthians 3:16).

Pause to soak in this great and joyful truth. The God of the universe has sent the Spirit of his Son Jesus Christ to reside in your heart. Celebrate the blessing that you, built together with other believers, are the temple of our living Lord. Thank him for this extraordinary gift and choose to walk forward in this reality.

Pray:

O Christ, thank you for descending to earth and redeeming your people so that we could forever know your nearness. Even in the midst of our exhaustion, give us grace to hold on to that truth and to hope in the promise of full and unbroken friendship with you. Amen.

Ordinary Time Day 66
MADISON PERRY

Read: *2 Corinthians 6:16–7:1*

What agreement has the temple of God with idols? For we are the temple of the living God; as God said,

> "I will make my dwelling among them and walk among them,
>   and I will be their God,
>   and they shall be my people.
> Therefore go out from their midst,
>   and be separate from them, says the Lord,
> and touch no unclean thing;
>   then I will welcome you,
> and I will be a father to you,
>   and you shall be sons and daughters to me,
> says the Lord Almighty."

Since we have these promises, beloved, let us cleanse ourselves from every defilement of body and spirit, bringing holiness to completion in the fear of God.

Reflect:

Hear God's promises: "I will make my dwelling among them and walk among them, and I will be their God …. I will welcome you, and I will be a father to you" (vv. 16, 17–18).

Paul exhorted his readers to live into the full completion of these promises. Just as Jesus often urged his disciples, Paul asked his friends to be ready for the time when God's holiness was revealed in full.

We who know Christ have been given his Holy Spirit to dwell in us. But we who have been restrained by sin for so long too often abandon the call to holiness. We walk in darkness instead of in the light.

Do you desire the completion of holiness in your own life? God's desire is not to use you but to complete you. And he will never abandon you to anything less than what is best for you.

God's holiness is not austere and lifeless. It is the fullness of his life brought to bear on creation, the intense and complete indwelling of his mercy, joy, and justice. To know God's life is to know both his all-embracing love and his swift and lifesaving intolerance of evil.

Meditate on God's promises. Thank him for his infinite mercy and unstoppable love. Then ask him for the grace and strength to walk in a manner worthy of your call in Christ.

Pray:

Almighty and ever living God, let your fatherly hand ever be upon us; let your Holy Spirit ever be with us, and so lead us in the knowledge of and obedience to your Holy Word, that we may faithfully serve you in this life and joyfully dwell with you in the life to come; through Jesus Christ our Lord. Amen.

(Adapted from Anglican Church in North America Book of Common Prayer)

Ordinary Time Day 67
MADISON PERRY

Read: *2 Corinthians 8:1–9*

> We want you to know, brothers, about the grace of God that has been given among the churches of Macedonia, for in a severe test of affliction, their abundance of joy and their extreme poverty have overflowed in a wealth of generosity on their part. For they gave according to their means, as I can testify, and beyond their means, of their own accord, begging us earnestly for the favor of taking part in the relief of the saints—and this, not as we expected, but they gave themselves first to the Lord and then by the will of God to us. Accordingly, we urged Titus that as he had started, so he should complete among you this act of grace. But as you excel in everything—in faith, in speech, in knowledge, in all earnestness, and in our love for you—see that you excel in this act of grace also.
>
> I say this not as a command, but to prove by the earnestness of others that your love also is genuine. For you know the grace of our Lord Jesus Christ, that though he was rich, yet for your sake he became poor, so that you by his poverty might become rich.

Reflect:

"But as you excel in everything—in faith, in speech, in knowledge, in all earnestness, and in our love for you—see that you excel in this act of grace also" (v. 7).

Paul asked the Corinthians to examine whether or not they were generous. It can be easy for a Christian to think or say, "What I do with my resources isn't *spiritual* enough to think deeply about."

To counter that idea, let's notice how Paul understood giving. He wrote about giving as an act of grace. Every area and segment of our lives—from words, to deeds, to wallets—is a place where God's grace can dwell and his salvation can be made known. Pity the person who is only partially baptized, who has held himself or herself back from a complete and full-body immersion in God's grace!

When we give to someone else, in that very act God is present in his grace, freeing us on the one hand and blessing someone else with his bounty on the other. We give because of love for God, and we give to someone made in the image of God. Here we declare our freedom from greed, insecurity, and pride. Thanks be to the Lord for providing us people to whom to give and an opportunity to know and experience his love and his grace through giving!

Are there places in your life where you do not yet know the fullness of salvation? Could one of these be your wallet? What else comes to mind?

Come and lay it all down at the foot of the cross. Ask that God will make his grace known to you in every moment and in every act and that as you live, your thoughts, words, and deeds will glorify him. Thank him for his salvation, and rest in the peace that you are eternally provided for beyond measure.

Pray:

Lord Jesus Christ, you stretched out your arms of love on the hard wood of the cross that everyone might come within the reach of your saving embrace: So clothe us in your Spirit that we, reaching forth our hands in love, may bring those who do not know you to the knowledge and love of you; for the honor of your Name. Amen.

(Anglican Church in North America Book of Common Prayer)

Ordinary Time Day 68
KARI WEST

Read: *2 Corinthians 9:10–15*

He who supplies seed to the sower and bread for food will supply and multiply your seed for sowing and increase the harvest of your righteousness. You will be enriched in every way to be generous in every way, which through us will produce thanksgiving to God. For the ministry of this service is not only supplying the needs of the saints but is also overflowing in many thanksgivings to God. By their approval of this service, they will glorify God because of your submission that comes from your confession of the gospel of Christ, and the generosity of your contribution for them and for all others, while they long for you and pray for you, because of the surpassing grace of God upon you. Thanks be to God for his inexpressible gift!

Reflect:

We often live with a mindset of scarcity and conservation. With only a limited amount of time, money, and abilities, we have to act accordingly, doling out those resources carefully within clearly defined parameters.

But in this passage, we come face-to-face with an abundant, limitless God—the great farmer who desires to produce massive stores of righteousness within his people. Paul was not trying to nickel-and-dime the Corinthians; he was not trying to guilt or coerce them into giving up a bit of their hard-earned limited incomes so the church could stay out of the red each month.

Instead, Paul was inviting them into a deeper, more powerful, more abundant way of living. He encouraged them, *"Give cheerfully, knowing that our plentiful God is more than able to provide for you out of his infinite hidden storehouses."*

More than that, as we respond to God with free and openhanded generosity, he will produce a lavish harvest of godliness and increased generosity within our hearts. And if that isn't enough, God will use our generosity to yield yet another harvest as it meets the needs of other believers, producing thankfulness in their hearts toward God and deep affection for his body, the church.

As you pray, pause and meditate on this vision of our boundless, generous God. He overflows with grace and mercy, and he is ready to produce great harvests of righteousness in his people. Ask him to reveal one way you could grow in cheerful generosity. See that way as an invitation to this great dance of giving and receiving life in his name.

Pray:

Teach us, O God, to use the world, without abusing it, and to receive the things needful for the body, without losing our part in your love, which is better than life itself. Whatever we have of this world, O may we have the same with your leave and love; sanctified to us by the Word of God and by prayer, and by the right improvement therof to your glory. And whatever we want of worldly things, leave us not destitute of the things that accompany salvation; but adorn our souls with such graces of your Holy Spirit, that we may adorn the doctrine of God our Savior in all things. Amen.

(John Wesley)

Ordinary Time Day 69

KARI WEST

Read: *Matthew 4:23–25*

And he went throughout all Galilee, teaching in their synagogues
and proclaiming the gospel of the kingdom and healing every
disease and every affliction among the people. So his fame spread
throughout all Syria, and they brought him all the sick, those
afflicted with various diseases and pains, those oppressed by demons,
those having seizures, and paralytics, and he healed them. And great
crowds followed him from Galilee and the Decapolis, and from
Jerusalem and Judea, and from beyond the Jordan.

Reflect:

The Gospels give us picture after picture of the words and works of Jesus. He
taught about God's kingdom wherever he went, and he met people's needs
with miracle after miracle. Yet in these few brief verses, Matthew offered us a
rich, succinct encapsulation of the heart of Christ's public ministry. It's as if
Matthew wanted us to see what Jesus was about before he got into the details
of his narrative.

Take a few moments and reflect on the description of Christ's actions.

He proclaimed the good news of the kingdom, and he healed every
disease and every sickness. Let that realization sink in. Every disease. Every
sickness. What must it have been like in Galilee in those days with demons
cast aside, lame men walking, pain erased, and death cheated?

Why so much healing? That question has many right answers, but one vital
answer is this: Christ was setting up signposts all over Galilee. Why eradicate
pain? Because pain is an interloper. Why reverse paralysis? Because human beings
were meant to dance in joy for the glory of God. Why cast out demons? Because
Satan is defeated. Why heal? Because life will trample death.

Christ will restore the cosmos. He will rule his good kingdom. He will.

The work is already under way. Perhaps Matthew, in these short verses, gave us a foretaste of Christ's cosmic undoing of all the world's brokenness and sin.

As you pray, meditate on the works of Christ, culminating in his death and resurrection. Hope in his redemption, his return, and his restoration. Look for the signs that his kingdom is breaking in today.

Pray:

Above all, long-expected Messiah, do come! Your ancient people who despised you once are waiting for you in your second coming, and we, the Gentiles, who knew you not, neither regarded you, we too, are watching for your advent. Make no tarrying, O Jesus! May your feet soon stand again on Olivet! . . . Earth travails for your coming. The whole creation groans in pain together until now. Your own expect you; we are longing till we are weary for your coming. Come quickly, Lord Jesus, come quickly. Amen and Amen.

(Charles Spurgeon)

10th Sunday of Ordinary Time
ELIZABETH GATEWOOD

Read: *Psalm 27:1–6*

The LORD is my light and my salvation;
      whom shall I fear?
The LORD is the stronghold of my life;
      of whom shall I be afraid?
When evildoers assail me
      to eat up my flesh,
my adversaries and foes,
      it is they who stumble and fall.
Though an army encamp against me,
      my heart shall not fear;
though war arise against me,
      yet I will be confident.
One thing have I asked of the LORD,
      that will I seek after:
that I may dwell in the house of the LORD
      all the days of my life,
to gaze upon the beauty of the LORD
      and to inquire in his temple.
For he will hide me in his shelter
      in the day of trouble;
he will conceal me under the cover of his tent;
      he will lift me high upon a rock.
And now my head shall be lifted up
      above my enemies all around me,
and I will offer in his tent
      sacrifices with shouts of joy;
I will sing and make melody to the LORD.

Reflect:

Who was God to this psalmist? Reread verse 5: "For he will hide me in his shelter in the day of trouble; he will conceal me under the cover of his tent; he will lift me high upon a rock."

God is a strong building, a fortress. The psalmist invited us to build our lives under the sheltering protection of God's presence. When we learn to inhabit spaces bounded by his grace, we find rest and shelter. We find protection from the enemy. God is our sheltering place, not because he replaces an earthly sheltering place and certainly not because he gives us permission to ignore those who need a sheltering roof over their heads. God is our sheltering place because his protection is fundamental to our human needs, both spiritual and physical.

God is also the host, welcoming us to a grand house. We find our protection and refuge in him; he invites us to dwell close to him. Israel's story was one of exodus, exile, and then return to the land. For much of their existence, the Israelites yearned and pressed toward home. Their tents, the tabernacle, and ultimately the temple did not neatly meet their spiritual hunger for finding a refuge in God.

Jesus continues to invite people to take refuge in the sheltering God even as he renews their bodies. And in a magnificent though mystifying twist, when we are in relationship with this refuge God, our bodies become his house—the temple of the Holy Spirit.

As you come to pray, ask yourself these questions: How do I experience the refuge that God provides? Do I identify it more with a personal sheltering in God or more with a corporate participation in worship at the church, his house? Thank the Lord for his sheltering presence and ask for deeper trust in him.

Pray:

Sheltering God, who invites us into your house and your very presence, what does it look like to take refuge in you? We are so comfortable and secure that we hardly notice the need for shelter in you until we feel the world unraveling. Then we crawl toward you, questioning you instead of simply taking refuge. Calm us with your presence. Welcome us into your house with its gloriously warm hearth and table set for all. Help us to surrender our lives to become your dwelling and our bodies to be filled by your Holy Spirit. Amen.

Ordinary Time Day 71
BILL BOYD

Read: *Matthew 5:1–11, 17–20*

Seeing the crowds, he went up on the mountain, and when he sat down, his disciples came to him.

And he opened his mouth and taught them, saying:

"Blessed are the poor in spirit, for theirs is the kingdom of heaven.

"Blessed are those who mourn, for they shall be comforted.

"Blessed are the meek, for they shall inherit the earth.

"Blessed are those who hunger and thirst for righteousness, for they shall be satisfied.

"Blessed are the merciful, for they shall receive mercy.

"Blessed are the pure in heart, for they shall see God.

"Blessed are the peacemakers, for they shall be called sons of God.

"Blessed are those who are persecuted for righteousness' sake, for theirs is the kingdom of heaven.

"Blessed are you when others revile you and persecute you and utter all kinds of evil against you falsely on my account. . . .

"Do not think that I have come to abolish the Law or the Prophets; I have not come to abolish them but to fulfill them. For truly, I say to you, until heaven and earth pass away, not an iota, not a dot, will pass from the Law until all is accomplished. Therefore whoever relaxes one of the least of these commandments and teaches others to do the same will be called least in the kingdom of heaven, but whoever does them and teaches them will be called great in the kingdom of heaven. For I tell you, unless your righteousness exceeds that of the scribes and Pharisees, you will never enter the kingdom of heaven."

Reflect:

Again and again in our lives with the Lord, we must reorient ourselves to how very different life in the kingdom of God is from life lived outside of God's kingdom and his rule.

A life with Jesus demands that we understand that "Christianity" is not a creed or set of morals or a religion. No, a life with Jesus is a life in which we live as citizens of the kingdom that he has inaugurated, and that kingdom is alive in the midst of the rebellious and broken world we also inhabit.

The kingdom does not begin at some later date. It is *now*. It is a kingdom that transcends the worldly boundaries between heaven and earth. It is a kingdom that places us in our proper place, beholden to the triune God who is Love.

Reread these verses from Matthew. Listen as honestly as you can to Jesus's words about blessedness in God's kingdom. As you pray, ask yourself, *Am I submitting my thinking, my life, and my heart to these words from my King? Or have I fallen into the service of another king?*

Then thank God for the ways his kingdom can calm your fears, ease your striving, and clarify your sense of what matters in life.

Pray:

Almighty God, from whom all thoughts of truth and peace proceed: Kindle, we pray, in the hearts of all people the true love of peace, and guide with your pure and peaceable wisdom those who take counsel for the nations of the earth; that in tranquility your kingdom may go forward, till the earth is filled with the knowledge of your love; through Jesus Christ our Lord. Amen.

(Anglican Church in North America Book of Common Prayer)

Ordinary Time Day 72
WILLA KANE

Read: *Matthew 5:3*

"Blessed are the poor in spirit, for theirs is the kingdom of heaven."

Reflect:

The beatitudes describe a life God blesses. They are not a qualification for salvation—not things to *do* but a way to *be*.

It's fitting that this first beatitude deals with the quality of our hearts. It begins a spiritual sequence that leads us down, step by step, and then up into life in God's kingdom.

There is no entry into this kingdom apart from the poverty of spirit that comes from humility. We must go down in order to go up. How are we to understand this in a world that tells us self-sufficiency, self-confidence, and self-expression are imperative for a successful life?

We have only to look at a holy God and imagine standing before him to understand how small and insignificant we are.

We have only to look at Jesus and contemplate the cross, where he died for us to turn the tables on our worldly pride, the sin behind all sin.

When we are right-sized and pride is forced to flee, there is room in our hearts for God's Spirit to fill us.

As you pray, contemplate a holy God. Be honest about the pride that infects your heart.

Lift your eyes to the one who wears a crown in heaven because he wore a crown of thorns on earth. This Jesus, who hung on the cross for you, welcomes you into his kingdom, the kingdom of heaven. In true humility, enter in.

Battling pride is a daily chore, something to be fought in the power of the Spirit by acknowledging your need for God and expressing gratitude to him.

Pride wilts in a thankful heart, and humility flourishes in the soil of spiritual disciplines: Prayer and the study of God's Word lead to worship.

As *The Message*'s version of Matthew 5:3 tells us, "You're blessed when you're at the end of your rope. With less of you there is more of God and his rule."

You may feel as if you're at the end of your rope. In God's economy, that's a good place to be. Less of you, more of God. Poor in spirit, rich in the kingdom of heaven. Rejoice.

Pray:

Father God, I yearn for poverty of spirit so your kingdom can be my forever home. I abhor and turn from pride that closes the door to life with you. Help me in all my doings to put down sin; humble my pride. Right-size my life so that you might be glorified; in Jesus's name. Amen.

Ordinary Time Day 73
WILLA KANE

Read: *Matthew 5:4*
"Blessed are those who mourn, for they shall be comforted."

Reflect:

In a season of sadness, we know what it is to mourn and to long for comfort. As Jesus leads us to the next stepping-stone toward life in his kingdom, he invites us to mourn not just the things that are broken in our world but also what is broken at the center of our hearts.

In the first beatitude, we see that those who are poor in spirit are invited into life in God's kingdom. If poverty of spirit is about understanding God's holiness and humankind's sinfulness, then this second beatitude is about feeling the pain that sinful brokenness brings.

If we let this pain touch us, it will break our hearts just as it breaks the heart of Jesus. Blessedly, as we come to him in sorrow, he comes to us as Comforter. He gives us his Spirit. And his Spirit knows us intimately, so he knows how to comfort each one of us. It's a provision of grace we can hardly take in.

Listen to Jesus's promise: "And I will pray the Father, and he shall give you another Comforter, that he may abide with you for ever" (John 14:16 KJV).

The word *comfort* means "to strengthen greatly." In your weakness, in your sadness, open yourself to the comfort, strength, and power of Christ. The apostle Paul embraced this divine exchange offered by the Lord:

> But he said to me, "My grace is sufficient for you, for my power is
> made perfect in weakness." Therefore I will boast all the more gladly
> of my weaknesses, so that the power of Christ may rest upon me.
> For the sake of Christ, then, I am content with weaknesses, insults,
> hardships, persecutions, and calamities. For when I am weak, then
> I am strong. (2 Corinthians 12:9–10)

A diagnosis of terminal illness causes us to mourn. The diagnosis of sin should do no less. Sin infects and destroys; even the small sins in our lives, left unchecked, will germinate, grow, and multiply. Only the gospel can deal with our sin effectively.

As you pray, pause to consider your moral bankruptcy before the Lord. Let this reality travel down from your mind and settle in your heart. Mourn it. Push back against a world that tells us grieving sin is repressive and restrictive. Press back against a culture that says, "Don't worry! Be happy."

Jesus didn't just mourn sin; he also conquered it. And he invites us into this upside-down kingdom where those who truly mourn sin will be blessed with the comfort he himself gives.

Listen to these promises from Scripture. Rejoice and embrace them for yourself and those you love: "This is my comfort in my affliction, that your promise gives me life" (Psalm 119:50). "Sing for joy, O heavens, and exult, O earth; break forth, O mountains, into singing! For the LORD has comforted his people and will have compassion on his afflicted" (Isaiah 49:13).

End your prayer time with thanksgiving. Our Lord does not leave us as mourners.

Pray:

Father, we confess our sin to you. We confess that we have far to go in our journey of sanctification. Please forgive us things done and things left undone; forgive us our thoughts, words, and deeds of darkness. Let us know the depth of our sin. And now, Father, strengthen us with your grace and comfort. Let us once again embrace the cross as our place of full and free forgiveness. Give us fresh amazement and gratitude; let us walk in the light of the gospel; for Jesus's sake and in his name. Amen.

Ordinary Time Day 74
WILLA KANE

Read: *Matthew 5:5*
"Blessed are the meek, for they shall inherit the earth."

Reflect:

Here, again, is another step toward the life God blesses: meekness. We move from poverty of spirit to godly mourning and then to repentance. Repentance cleanses our hearts so we can be meek.

This is Christ's upside-down kingdom: poverty instead of riches, mourning instead of happiness, meekness instead of control.

The wisdom of the world says that meekness is weakness. But in Jesus's world, the word *meekness* describes what it is like for a wild stallion to be brought into submission by his master. The horse doesn't lose strength as it is tamed, but it learns to wait patiently for direction. Picture a Thoroughbred, perfectly still until his master gently urges him forward. Imagine yourself, in meekness, looking to the Father, your eyes, heart, and mind focused on him, waiting for a gentle word, a gentle pressure. Meekness does not diminish us. It allows us to forget ourselves as we focus on God.

Look at the world around you. It seems that nothing is given; everything must be seized, asserted, and won. The way to get ahead is to take what you can when you can, to always be ready to define yourself and defend yourself. Fortune favors the bold.

Now consider Jesus who entered Jerusalem, not triumphantly on a stallion, but humbly on a donkey. Consider this Jesus who was falsely accused, convicted, and humiliated, but uttered not a word of defense.

Though he is meek, he still promised an inheritance to those who follow his example. An inheritance cannot be purchased. It's a gift, something we could never earn or deserve.

In meekness, bow before the Lord and receive the inheritance he has planned for you with a thankful heart. When Jesus returns to set up his kingdom on earth, it is the meek who will be there with him. Rejoice.

Pray:

I am no longer my own, but thine. Put me to what thou wilt, rank me with whom thou wilt. Put me to doing, put me to suffering. Let me be employed by thee or laid aside for thee, exalted for thee or brought low for thee. Let me be full, let me be empty. Let me have all things, let me have nothing. I freely and heartily yield all things to thy pleasure and disposal. And now, O glorious and blessed God, Father, Son, and Holy Spirit, thou art mine, and I am thine. So be it. And the covenant which I have made on earth, let it be ratified in heaven. Amen.

(John Wesley)

Ordinary Time Day 75
WILLA KANE

Read: *Matthew 5:6*
> "Blessed are those who hunger and thirst for righteousness, for they shall be satisfied."

Reflect:

We are praying the beatitudes in order, as each one builds on the last.

The first four deal with humanity's relationship with God. When we recognize our emptiness without him, we mourn. As we repent of our pride, we become meek.

Once we are emptied of self and the counterfeits the world has on offer, we notice a chasm inside our hearts that cries to be filled. We're hungry and thirsty for something, for someone who will satisfy our longings.

What are we searching for?

The prophet Isaiah spoke about the remedy we need: "Come, everyone who thirsts, come to the waters; and he who has no money, come, buy and eat! Come, buy wine and milk without money and without price" (Isaiah 55:1).

The remedy is Jesus, who proclaimed blessing on those who hunger and thirst for righteousness. Righteousness—a right relationship with God—is what we need. It comes from being united to Christ through his body and blood, which was freely given in sacrifice for us. Not a righteousness of our own but the righteousness of Jesus credited to accounts bankrupted by sin.

Come now, emptied of yourself, to Jesus. Pray to receive this bread of life and living water. Seek satisfaction in him alone.

Hungering and thirsting for righteousness restores our relationship with God and flows out to restored relationships with others. As we become more like Christ, we yearn for righteousness in the whole human family—for freedom, equality, justice, integrity, and honor.

As you pray, consider the broken relationships and institutions around you. How can you, empowered by the Spirit of Christ, be an agent of love? How can you work for justice where there is corruption, freedom where there is captivity, or integrity and honor where there is moral bankruptcy?

Our hunger and thirst are unable to be satisfied by anything in this world. They point us instead to another world, the one we were made for: God's kingdom, the kingdom of heaven.

Pray:
O God, teach me the happy art
of attending to things temporal
with a mind on things eternal.
Send me forth to have compassion.
Help me to walk as Jesus walked,
my only Savior and perfect model,
his mind my inward guest,
his meekness my covering garb.
Let my happy place be among the poor in spirit,
my delight in the gentle ranks of the meek.
Let me always esteem others better than myself
and find in true humility
an heirdom to two worlds.
Amen.

(From *The Valley of Vision*)

Ordinary Time Day 76
SALLY BREEDLOVE

Read: *Matthew 5:7*
"Blessed are the merciful, for they shall receive mercy."

Reflect:

With this fifth beatitude, Jesus continued to turn presumptions upside down. A life blessed by God, he said, is a life where we offer and receive mercy.

Jesus could have said, "Blessed are those who forgive, for they will know forgiveness." But instead he said, "Blessed are the merciful." Why? Two parables can help answer this question.

In the parable about the sinner and the Pharisee (Luke 18), the sinner stood far off, undone by his sin. He cried out for mercy, not forgiveness. The Pharisee, however, was full of contempt and firmly believed he was better than the sinner.

In another parable (Luke 10), the good Samaritan turned away from the personal prejudices he might have felt toward the Jews. He rescued a badly wounded Jew lying on the roadside. He didn't ask the injured man what he'd done wrong. He cleaned and wrapped up his wounds, took the man to an inn, and paid for his care.

As the lawyer who had questioned Jesus admitted, the Samaritan was the only one in the story who extended mercy. Mercy cuts through contempt and judgment and invites us to offer forgiveness, kindness, help, and generosity.

What is it like for you when contempt, judgment, and a desire to even the score rise up in you? What is it like for you when you wonder why people can't get their lives together or agree with your beliefs? What is it like for you when someone sins against you?

At the cross, every judgment God could make about each of us is swallowed up by the mercy of God. If we let God's mercy settle deep in our souls, we will realize that to withhold mercy is to contradict all we say we believe.

Amazingly, the more mercy we offer to others, the more we will understand God's mercy in our lives.

Our world knows so little of mercy. Across racial, economic, and political lines, we fire the artillery of contempt and judgment. Will we confess our sin and humble ourselves?

As you pray, ask yourself if you really believe you need mercy. Repent of your pride and your contempt toward others. Thank God for the places in your own story where mercy has triumphed. Then speak to God about the ways you judge others or withhold forgiveness and compassion. Ask God to pour out his mercy through you to a particular person with whom you struggle.

Pray:

Almighty God, you have not dealt with us according to our sins, nor rewarded us according to our iniquities; grant that we, who for our evil deeds deserve to be punished, by the might of your grace may mercifully be relieved; through our Lord and Savior Jesus Christ, who lives and reigns with you and the Holy Spirit, one God, for ever and ever. Amen.

(Anglican Church in North America Book of Common Prayer)

11th Sunday of Ordinary Time
MADISON PERRY

Read: *Psalm 29*

> Ascribe to the LORD, O heavenly beings,
>> ascribe to the LORD glory and strength.
> Ascribe to the LORD the glory due his name;
>> worship the LORD in the splendor of holiness.
> The voice of the LORD is over the waters;
>> the God of glory thunders,
>> the LORD, over many waters.
> The voice of the LORD is powerful;
>> the voice of the LORD is full of majesty.
> The voice of the LORD breaks the cedars;
>> the LORD breaks the cedars of Lebanon.
> He makes Lebanon to skip like a calf,
>> and Sirion like a young wild ox.
> The voice of the LORD flashes forth flames of fire.
> The voice of the LORD shakes the wilderness;
>> the LORD shakes the wilderness of Kadesh.
> The voice of the LORD makes the deer give birth
>> and strips the forests bare,
>> and in his temple all cry, "Glory!"
> The LORD sits enthroned over the flood;
>> the LORD sits enthroned as king forever.
> May the LORD give strength to his people!
>> May the LORD bless his people with peace!

Reflect:

At every moment of your life, you can live firmly ensconced in God's kingdom. Here you are in exile. But at the same time, you play and pray in the throne room of the heavenly King. Your place has been secured by the death and resurrection of our Savior.

The Lord will surely watch over you and keep you. Now you see only the start of an eternal adventure. Perhaps in this season, it feels as if you are treading backward. Maybe your work feels fruitless, or perhaps you are in an extended season of sickness. Maybe you cannot help but sense the deep pain of the world.

Regardless of your circumstances, on a much deeper level, there is forward movement. God is renewing you, redeeming you, and saving you to the uttermost.

Let this moment do its work in you. Receive your season as a gift. Turn your eyes upward to your Father and King. In his kingdom, the limits of the present age are shattered. You may feel hemmed in here, but in God's kingdom all things are possible. He will hold you fast.

Pray:

Keep watch, dear Lord, with those who work, or watch, or weep this night, and give your angels charge over those who sleep. Tend the sick, Lord Christ; give rest to the weary, bless the dying, soothe the suffering, pity the afflicted, shield the joyous; and all for your love's sake. Amen.

(Anglican Church in North America Book of Common Prayer)

Ordinary Time Day 78
SALLY BREEDLOVE

Read: *Matthew 5:8*

"Blessed are the pure in heart, for they shall see God."

Reflect:

In Matthew 5:8, Jesus declared that a happy life is one where our purified hearts allow us to see God.

Is seeing God your highest good? We live in a flattened world that tells us that other things should be our highest good instead. And granted, many of our ideals are good things. We might long for happier relationships, social justice, adherence to good doctrine, a moral leader, the end of racial tensions, or a better job. The list goes on. But these longings never reach the core of what we need.

We were made for God. David, a man of great ability and passion, wasn't controlled by a hunger for political power, the respect of his family, his own safety, or even his desire to build the temple. He confessed his core longing in Psalm 27:4: "I'm asking GOD for one thing, only one thing: To live with him in his house my whole life long. I'll contemplate his beauty; I'll study at his feet" (MSG).

As we rightly lament a world that is so very broken, it is good for us to pause and realize that nothing in this world will ever be enough. We were made for God, and yet we, too, are broken.

So what does it mean to have a pure heart? Ponder the following questions:

- A pure heart is a cleansed heart (Psalm 51). Is there a sin or sin pattern you need to confess to God?
- A pure heart is an undivided heart. In the parable of the seed and the sower (Matthew 13), we read about the things that stifle growth. The cares of this world, the deceitfulness of riches, and the desire for

other things can fill our hearts and choke out God's good for our life. What keeps your heart divided?

The only path to God is Jesus Christ. His Spirit is our guide; the hedgerows of faithfulness to Scripture and a life of doing justice, loving mercy, and walking humbly with God keep us on the path.

As you pray, examine your own heart. Don't fall into endless introspection or self-condemnation. Listen for the Holy Spirit's voice. He will point out what is amiss and will invite you into life.

Pray:

O God, by whom the meek are guided in judgment, and light rises up in darkness for the godly: Grant us, in all our doubts and uncertainties, the grace to ask what you would have us do, that the Spirit of wisdom may save us from all false choices; that in your light we may see light, and in your straight path we may not stumble; through Jesus Christ our Lord. Amen.

(Anglican Church in North America Book of Common Prayer)

Ordinary Time Day 79

SALLY BREEDLOVE

Read: *Matthew 5:9*

"Blessed are the peacemakers, for they shall be called sons of God."

Reflect:

Peacemaking: the costliest of endeavors. At Christ's birth, angels joyfully proclaimed this baby would bring peace. But they didn't disclose the cost of that peace.

Paul did. He announced in Colossians 1:20, "All the broken and dislocated pieces of the universe—people and things, animals and atoms—get properly fixed and fit together in vibrant harmonies, all because of his death, his blood that poured down from the cross" (MSG).

The death of Jesus secured peace. And now, God gives us the work of offering peace to the broken and dislocated places in our world.

What price must we pay? The beatitudes show us the way: a reformed heart, humility to admit our own brokenness, grief as we consider the world's pain and our own complicity in it, surrender to not being in charge, hunger for transformation, submission to living by mercy, and the priority of an unpolluted heart over self-interest.

This costly peace with God reshapes us so that the civil war simmering in our hearts is brought under God's kingship. If we insist on locating all that is "wrong with the world" outside of ourselves, we will blame a particular group of people for the brokenness we see. We will not make peace; we will feed conflict.

Learning peace with God and with ourselves frees us to join the work of reconciliation. To make peace, we offer the gospel of Jesus. There is no other path to shalom.

But we are also called to live by the ways of Jesus if we want to be peacemakers. The ways Jesus brought shalom into this world should unsettle all of us. He overturned tables in the temple where profits were made by the elite class. He cared for the outcast Syrophoenician woman. He refused to settle an inheritance dispute between brothers. He submitted to Pilate's cowardice and the Sanhedrin's murderous hatred. He never spoke against Roman oppression. He refused to conform to the status quo.

If we want to imitate Jesus's peacemaking in our world, we must learn from him. If we do so, we will come to look like what we really are: children of the heavenly Father.

Pray for those you know who are broken by the lack of peace in our world. Ask our Lord what needs to happen in you and how you need to be changed so you, too, can become a peacemaker.

Pray:

O God, you made us in your own image, and you have redeemed us through your Son Jesus Christ: Look with compassion on the whole human family; take away the arrogance and hatred which infect our hearts; break down the walls that separate us; unite us in bonds of love; and work through our struggle and confusion to accomplish your purposes on earth; that, in your good time, all nations and races may serve you in harmony around your heavenly throne; through Jesus Christ our Lord. Amen.

(Anglican Church in North America Book of Common Prayer)

Ordinary Time Day 80

SALLY BREEDLOVE

Read: *Matthew 5:10–12*

"Blessed are those who are persecuted for righteousness' sake, for theirs is the kingdom of heaven.

"Blessed are you when others revile you and persecute you and utter all kinds of evil against you falsely on my account. Rejoice and be glad, for your reward is great in heaven, for so they persecuted the prophets who were before you."

Reflect:

Most of us can agree that the preceding beatitudes in Matthew 5 make sense. More humility to admit our own weakness, more sadness for the broken places in the world and in our own lives, less grasping, more compassion, and more doing our best to help people get along—these are ideals we can embrace.

But how can the happy life be one of persecution, slander, and exclusion? It's natural to feel resistance to this truth.

Jesus raised the stakes in verse 11: "Blessed are *you* when others revile you and persecute you." He shifted from talk of a coming kingdom and spoke directly to his listeners. His clarity is unmistakable. If we fully align with Jesus, we will likely end up being opposed and persecuted. When it happens, we will have a great reason to be happy.

This "blessing" seems absurd and scary.

But we must remember: God's people have always been opposed by the world and its systems. At times we may live in harmony, but eventually each one of us has to decide which kingdom has our loyalty. If we stand with Christ, we will never be fully accepted or favored by the world.

This choice is not easy, and it can be costly. Christians in the early church were given a test: Throw a pinch of incense on a Roman altar fire and say aloud, "Caesar is Lord." Then they were free to worship any other god. Defiance meant persecution or even death.

Is our day any different? In many places, religious persecution is sometimes deadly; however, persecution can also be legal, social, educational, or economic harassment or exclusion. It's easy to want to give in. But Jesus encourages us: *Resist going along with the world. Stay in solidarity with me. Endure. I have a reward for you.*

As you pray, ask the Lord to make your character above reproach. Ask him to give you an enduring heart of loyalty toward him. Ask for yourself and others true godliness, courage, steadfast faith, and endurance. Receive the following Scripture as a benediction from your heavenly Father.

Pray:

You're blessed when your commitment to God provokes persecution. The persecution drives you even deeper into God's kingdom. Not only that—count yourselves blessed every time people put you down or throw you out or speak lies about you to discredit me. What it means is that the truth is too close for comfort and they are uncomfortable. You can be glad when that happens— give a cheer, even!— for though they don't like it, *I* do! And all heaven applauds. And know that you are in good company. My prophets and witnesses have always gotten into this kind of trouble. Amen.

(Matthew 5:10–12 MSG)

Ordinary Time Day 81
SALLY BREEDLOVE

Read: *Matthew 5:13*

"You are the salt of the earth, but if salt has lost its taste, how shall its saltiness be restored? It is no longer good for anything except to be thrown out and trampled under people's feet."

Reflect:

The Sermon on the Mount was a panoramic teaching. Like the best of guides pointing out the mountain ranges before a long hike, Christ offered a sweeping view of life in God's kingdom. He showed us the mountains of blessedness this life offers, and he paused to warn us that we would encounter persecution. Then he reminded of us who we are, not how hard we need to work to become something. He said two simple things: You are salt. You are light.

What's so good about being salt?

Jesus's listeners heard three things when he said, "You are the salt of the earth": You are valuable, you are beneficial, and you are essential.

In the ancient world, salt was precious. Sometimes Roman soldiers were paid in salt. Our word *salary* comes from the same root word. Salt was even exchanged measure for measure for gold along some ancient trade routes. God instructed the Jews to add salt to their offerings in worship as an additional sacrifice.

Salt was and is also useful. It is antiseptic, preserving meat and vegetables from rot. Salt brings out the best flavor. Without salt, eating would only be a duty, something we'd do to assuage hunger and stay alive, but with little pleasure.

Finally, salt is vital. If your body loses too much salt, you die.

Jesus asserted our essential value by calling us salt, but in the same word, he gave us purpose: Penetrate the world you live in. Change it by your presence. Don't be concerned that you are so small and the world is so large. It takes only a little salt to change things. Your value is in your saltiness, not in becoming like the world you live in.

Be present. Be an agent of change.

We live in a deteriorating, infected, and dying culture. Are we willing to be shaken up and poured out for the sake of others? Will we bring practical benefit, joy, and true healing to people around us?

As you pray, ask that God's people will become healing, joy, and life to this world. Pray that day by day you will move toward others as a good gift of salt.

Pray:

Almighty God, whose Son our Savior Jesus Christ is the light of the world: Grant that your people, illumined by your Word and Sacraments, may shine with the radiance of Christ's glory, that he may be known, worshiped, and obeyed to the ends of the earth; through Jesus Christ our Lord, who with you and the Holy Spirit lives and reigns, one God, now and for ever. Amen.

(Anglican Church in North America Book of Common Prayer)

Ordinary Time Day 82

SALLY BREEDLOVE

Read: *Matthew 5:14–16*

> "You are the light of the world. A city set on a hill cannot be hidden.
> Nor do people light a lamp and put it under a basket, but on a
> stand, and it gives light to all in the house. In the same way, let your
> light shine before others, so that they may see your good works and
> give glory to your Father who is in heaven."

Reflect:

We are accustomed to believing we have to do things right or do significant things in order to matter. But Jesus broke into our misguided sense of
ourselves when he called us salt and light. His sermon was clear: Our first
calling is to be a certain kind of person—aware of our need and our brokenness, generous, hungry for God, mercy-filled, pure of heart, peacemaking,
and willing to be misunderstood and even hated. But that way of being is not
a checklist for behavior. It's a call to respond to the mercy of God, the one
who knows us fully and loves us completely.

As the rest of Matthew 5–7 unfolds, we learn how kingdom people are
to live practically. But first Christ emphasized our worth to him. He declared
to us, *You are the salt of the earth; you are the light of the cosmos* (in the Greek,
the word isn't *world*, but *cosmos*).

It's as if Christ was saying, *You are useful, essential. You bring goodness. You
make things better. Through you, people around you have an opportunity to see
God's glory.* We can so easily believe that God expects too much from us. But
didn't Christ command us, "Be the salt; be the light"?

He has said that you are the salt and that you are the light. Will you
choose to believe such outrageous things about yourself?

Yesterday, we considered the gifts that salt can bring. Today let's ask a
different question: What would we be like if we were to take Christ at his
word and believe we are light?

As we close, take a moment to reflect and hold your own heart up to God. Ponder the following questions and then close in prayer.

- Do you seek to find your own light, or are you content to reflect the light of Christ?
- Do you trust Christ that the "stand" he puts you on is the best place for your light to shine? Or do you insist on making a platform for yourself?
- Are you committed to a life of doing good, and will you seek to do that good so that God is seen, or do you need to be seen?
- Will you ask God to deal with the dark places in your own life and heart so that light spills out to those around you?

Pray:

Jesus, you are the light of the world; in you is no darkness at all. May I walk with you so that your light shines in me and through me. Father, make me fully a child of the light; for Christ's sake. Amen.

Ordinary Time Day 83
KARI WEST

Read: *Matthew 7:7–11*

> "Ask, and it will be given to you; seek, and you will find; knock, and it will be opened to you. For everyone who asks receives, and the one who seeks finds, and to the one who knocks it will be opened. Or which one of you, if his son asks him for bread, will give him a stone? Or if he asks for a fish, will give him a serpent? If you then, who are evil, know how to give good gifts to your children, how much more will your Father who is in heaven give good things to those who ask him!"

Reflect:

In yesterday's reflection, we were reminded that God sees us as the light of the world. Today's passage encourages us to trust the goodness and graciousness of God. This confidence in the love of God should move us to ask, to seek, to knock—to pray.

God cares for us with the rich, abiding, all-encompassing love of a father. The human love of a parent for a child is just the barest hint and echo of the kind of love that God possesses for all those who trust in his name. Jesus put it bluntly, "If you then, who are evil, know how to give good gifts to your children, how much more will your Father who is in heaven give good things to those who ask him!" (v. 11).

Human parents are inevitably and permanently imperfect. But if we comprehend any goodness and provision in the way parents care for their kids, let that lead us to meditate on the length, width, height, and depth of the love of our heavenly Father. His love far surpasses any human love just as a tsunami surpasses a ripple in the water.

As you pray, contemplate the depth of the Father's love for you. Let his love drive you to seek, to ask, to knock—to know more of him at all costs. Jesus promised that your Father in heaven will "give good things to those who ask him" (v. 11). Do not hesitate to tell your Father what you need today. Trust in his deep goodness to meet you where you are.

Pray:

Compose our spirits to a quiet and steady dependence on your good providence, that we may take no thought for our life, nor be anxious for anything, but by prayer and supplication, with thanksgiving, still make known our requests to you our God. And help us to pray always and not faint; in everything to give thanks, and offer up the sacrifice of praise continually; to rejoice in hope of your glory; to possess our souls in patience; and to learn in whatsoever state we are, there to be content. Amen.

(John Wesley)

12th Sunday of Ordinary Time
KARI WEST

Read: *Psalm 73:1–7, 21–28*

Truly God is good to Israel,
   to those who are pure in heart.
But as for me, my feet had almost stumbled,
   my steps had nearly slipped.
For I was envious of the arrogant
   when I saw the prosperity of the wicked.
For they have no pangs until death;
   their bodies are fat and sleek.
They are not in trouble as others are;
   they are not stricken like the rest of mankind.
Therefore pride is their necklace;
   violence covers them as a garment.
Their eyes swell out through fatness;
   their hearts overflow with follies....
When my soul was embittered,
   when I was pricked in heart,
I was brutish and ignorant;
   I was like a beast toward you.
Nevertheless, I am continually with you;
   you hold my right hand.
You guide me with your counsel,
   and afterward you will receive me to glory.
Whom have I in heaven but you?
   And there is nothing on earth that I desire besides you.
My flesh and my heart may fail,
   but God is the strength of my heart and my portion forever.
For behold, those who are far from you shall perish;
   you put an end to everyone who is unfaithful to you.
But for me it is good to be near God;
   I have made the Lord GOD my refuge,
   that I may tell of all your works.

Reflect:

Asaph, the author of this psalm, immediately drew his audience into the narrative. In the opening verses, Asaph recounted his observations of the wicked. He saw a vicious pattern that had cut through the centuries—we recognize it even today. Arrogant, ruthless individuals amassed wealth and power and then wielded those instruments to oppress the poor and the downtrodden. They were opposed to God and openly mocked him; they cloaked themselves in pride and violence. Despite their evil, they seemed to live privileged, comfortable, and carefree lives.

Asaph envied such people. He wanted the ease of their lives for himself. He wanted the wealth, the prestige, and perhaps the lack of conscience. He had spent his life trying to honor God, but what did he have to show for it? Punishment by the wicked and daily affliction. If we are honest, we will admit that we feel like Asaph.

But Asaph could perceive only one small part of the story. His envy had so corroded his heart that he forgot who it was who had held his right hand—the God of all heaven and earth, the God of justice, mercy, grace, and glory. He forgot that God had not finished his great work of justice on the earth. And he forgot that—in the midst of all the anguish and confusion of a world undone by evil—God is always present, always guiding, and always strengthening his people. He will be our portion forever, and he will bring us to glory.

Ask God to search your heart and reveal any unclean way within you. Confess if you, like Asaph, are envying the wicked and questioning whether God will do what he has promised to do. Ask for fresh conviction of God's all-sufficiency to bring about his purposes, restore his world, and be a strong refuge for his people. Ask for patience and for peace.

Pray:

Father, make my heart like a weaned child with its mother. Let me trust you, hope in you, and await your return, come what may. Amen.

Ordinary Time Day 85

SALLY BREEDLOVE

Read: *Malachi 4:4–6*

"Remember the law of my servant Moses, the statutes and rules that I
commanded him at Horeb for all Israel.

"Behold, I will send you Elijah the prophet before the great and
awesome day of the LORD comes. And he will turn the hearts of
fathers to their children and the hearts of children to their fathers,
lest I come and strike the land with a decree of utter destruction."

Reflect:

What would we see if we were to really behold our children?

Jesus saw children as a gift. He said they're the example of what it means
to trust God. He liked being around them.

As many children as adults were resurrected throughout Scripture. That's
something worth pondering.

The book of Proverbs insists that the work of adults is to teach children
to be wise. But in order to teach their children wisdom, parents must first
pursue wisdom for themselves.

The *Shema*, the heart of what it means to follow after God according to
the Old Testament, gives parents clear marching orders. Parents must diligently teach their children to love God and to know his Word:

"Hear, O Israel: The LORD our God, the LORD is one. You shall love
the LORD your God with all your heart and with all your soul and
with all your might. And these words that I command you today
shall be on your heart. You shall teach them diligently to your children, and shall talk of them when you sit in your house, and when
you walk by the way, and when you lie down, and when you rise."
(Deuteronomy 6:4–7)

Pray for yourself. How have you been called to grow up? No one comes close to being perfect. You may be weighed down with a sense of your inadequacies and failures. Will you receive God's mercy and accept how human you are? Even as a parent, you are God's child. Let him father you.

Your heart may ache for your broken, messy family. Pray for those you love and for your own heart.

If you are a grandparent, a neighbor, an aunt or uncle, or a friend, ask God to show you how you can support a particular child. Pray for children who are isolated, in danger, unhappy, or facing neglect and need. Pray the Lord gives you some way you can encourage others to seek him.

Pray:

O Lord, Jesus taught us to love one another and showed us what love is. For those of us who are living with family and friends, please give us an extra measure of love for the people who share our homes. May the heart of parents be turned to their children and away from hollow ambitions. May spouses be given patience and affection for each other. For those of us who are living alone, help us to be patient and to remain in prayer. Please give those who are lonely friendship with other people and, above all, the companionship of your Son by the power of the Holy Spirit. Join us all together into the body of Christ; let us receive the words you spoke to your Son at the river Jordan—we are beloved by you. Amen.

Ordinary Time Day 86
WILLA KANE

Read: *1 Thessalonians 1:2–10*

We give thanks to God always for all of you, constantly mentioning you in our prayers, remembering before our God and Father your work of faith and labor of love and steadfastness of hope in our Lord Jesus Christ. For we know, brothers, loved by God, that he has chosen you, because our gospel came to you not only in word, but also in power and in the Holy Spirit and with full conviction. You know what kind of men we proved to be among you for your sake. And you became imitators of us and of the Lord, for you received the word in much affliction, with the joy of the Holy Spirit, so that you became an example to all the believers in Macedonia and in Achaia. For not only has the word of the Lord sounded forth from you in Macedonia and Achaia, but your faith in God has gone forth everywhere, so that we need not say anything. For they themselves report concerning us the kind of reception we had among you, and how you turned to God from idols to serve the living and true God, and to wait for his Son from heaven, whom he raised from the dead, Jesus who delivers us from the wrath to come.

Reflect:

Perhaps for you, this season doesn't promise much joy. Perhaps it feels more like bleak midwinter, living in the minor key of a plaintive hymn. Are you experiencing another month of discord, peril, pain, or uncertainty? Do you wonder when, O Lord, it will end?

Some of us are isolated physically and emotionally. The news around us invites us to outrage, not joy; we are tempted to doubt, not trust.

Paul's message to a young church in Thessalonica was a message of hope for all of us, despite where we find ourselves. He reminded them—and now us, by extension—of who they were to God the Father. God's love is demonstrated in the life of Jesus the Son and poured into us by the presence of the Holy Spirit.

You are beloved and chosen to be his own by God the Father.

Beloved and *chosen*. Let these words saturate your very being.

Now turn to consider the gospel message that comes not just with words but with Holy Spirit power, to change us from the inside out. Jesus has saved us. Even now he lives in us and intercedes for us. He will come again to make all things new.

Abandon the god substitutes of your old life and make room for true God worship. Let joy invade and conquer your suffering. Christ, our rescuer, will come again in glory. Allow that hope to form a steely strength in your soul.

Pray that God would pour out his message through you to others, not just in words but also as a living display of Christ our Light and Redeemer.

Pause to ponder these divine truths. Hear God your Father call you his beloved. Thank him that he has chosen you to be his own. Receive his strength to endure dark days. Let the joy of who you are in Christ settle in your inmost being. Delight in the expectant hope of Christ's return. Let these realities transform the landscape of your heart.

Pray:

Grant us, Lord, not to be anxious about earthly things, but to love things heavenly; and even now, as we live among things that are passing away, to hold fast to those that shall endure; through Jesus Christ our Lord, who lives and reigns with you and the Holy Spirit, one God, for ever and ever. Amen.

(Anglican Church in North America Book of Common Prayer)

Ordinary Time Day 87

WILLA KANE

Read: *1 Thessalonians 2:4–13*

But just as we have been approved by God to be entrusted with the gospel, so we speak, not to please man, but to please God who tests our hearts. For we never came with words of flattery, as you know, nor with a pretext for greed—God is witness. Nor did we seek glory from people, whether from you or from others, though we could have made demands as apostles of Christ. But we were gentle among you, like a nursing mother taking care of her own children. So, being affectionately desirous of you, we were ready to share with you not only the gospel of God but also our own selves, because you had become very dear to us.

For you remember, brothers, our labor and toil: we worked night and day, that we might not be a burden to any of you, while we proclaimed to you the gospel of God. You are witnesses, and God also, how holy and righteous and blameless was our conduct toward you believers. For you know how, like a father with his children, we exhorted each one of you and encouraged you and charged you to walk in a manner worthy of God, who calls you into his own kingdom and glory.

And we also thank God constantly for this, that when you received the word of God, which you heard from us, you accepted it not as the word of men but as what it really is, the word of God, which is at work in you believers.

Reflect:

Paul used the imagery of family relationships to describe his love and care for this newly planted Thessalonian church. His message was personal. Paul the evangelist had been faithful to reach these converts. Paul the edifier was faithful to teach them. Eight times in these verses, Paul pointed them to God.

Paul himself was under God's authority. The result? He exuded humility like a little child. No demands, no impure motives, just unselfish love.

A mother's love intimately shares and cares; this love is exemplified in a mother feeding and caring for her own children. In some Bible translations, the image is one of a nursing mother on whom a child relies completely for nourishment. Love like this means opening your own life as you share the gospel.

A father's love leads, pleads, encourages, and urges children toward worthy living and a share in God's kingdom and glory. A father's love points to the Father through the Son, in the Spirit. Love like this is leadership in action. Love holds nothing back.

What is your own heart toward those around you who desperately need the good news of Christ? Does unselfish love describe the orientation of your heart toward those who believe but are fatigued or falling away during a difficult season?

Pause and pray. Who needs your time, your tender affection, and your intimate care? Who needs encouragement toward godly living? Who needs you to share your life with them?

The gospel is the only thing of value you can give away, over and over again, and still possess it in its entirety. It is the opposite of hoarding; it's a life of joyful generosity. How is this possible? Jesus, our source, never runs out and never runs dry. He is not a cistern but a fountain. He fed five thousand people with five loaves and had much to spare. He is the living water and the bread of life.

Come to the family table, feed on the Word of God, and then share its nourishment with others. Let the gospel change you—then give it away.

Pray:

Heavenly Father, replace hunger and thirst for things that pass away with a holy and insatiable desire for you and your Word. Fill us with a gospel that satisfies deep in our souls and overflows to a desperate waiting world. Give us your tenderness and love, and hearts of joyful generosity. Amen.

Ordinary Time Day 88
SALLY BREEDLOVE

Read: *1 Thessalonians 2:17–20 & 2 Corinthians 4:6*

But since we were torn away from you, brothers, for a short time, in person not in heart, we endeavored the more eagerly and with great desire to see you face to face, because we wanted to come to you—I, Paul, again and again—but Satan hindered us. For what is our hope or joy or crown of boasting before our Lord Jesus at his coming? Is it not you? For you are our glory and joy.

For God, who said, "Let light shine out of darkness," has shone in our hearts to give the light of the knowledge of the glory of God in the face of Jesus Christ.

Reflect:

Paul missed his friends in Thessalonica. Hearing they were doing well wasn't enough for him.

We long for embodied life with others and for tangible companionship. When someone dear to us dies, as the person's face grows dim in our minds, we grieve once again. It is not just the particulars of the person's appearance we long for; we could find that in a photo. What we long for is the person's *presence*.

In some mysterious way, we know that faces communicate the very presence of someone. Face and presence are inextricably linked. In the Old Testament, God is sometimes called "the Presence," and the Hebrew words for *presence* and *face* are the same. Moses met with God in person, face-to-face, as a friend meets with a friend (Exodus 33:11).

It is Ordinary Time. Christ has risen indeed. He was once again present with his friends. He ate, walked, and talked with them. He prepared breakfast for them. They saw his face, and he saw theirs. They experienced each other's presence.

Whom do you wish you could see face-to-face? Do you have family far away? A friend who has died? Or perhaps there is someone from whom you are estranged and you long to see this individual in person and make things right.

We long for in-person connection. Receive that longing as a gift. You were made for it. Pour out your heart to God today. Tell him the ones you long to see. Pray for those people.

Then pause again. One day you will see Jesus face-to-face, as Paul declared in 1 Corinthians 13:12. Death does not have the final word. Sit in awe with the truth that Christ was indeed raised from the dead and that one day we, too, will have new bodies. Pray for your longing for the full presence of Jesus so that your longing for that day will grow within you.

Pray:

O Lord Jesus Christ, we rejoice in your victory over death! You live and reign, and by the power of the Holy Spirit you are with each of us. By your Spirit, we are together with those who are united in you. Please be present with those who are living alone or are cut off from loved ones. For those who carry great burdens, join them in carrying those yokes and bring them peace. We live in your resurrection world. As the old fades away, may we see your new creation. Father, may we catch glimpses of the face of your Son Jesus and know his presence in our hearts. Amen.

Ordinary Time Day 89
WILLA KANE

Read: *1 Thessalonians 3:1–8*

Therefore when we could bear it no longer, we were willing to be left behind at Athens alone, and we sent Timothy, our brother and God's coworker in the gospel of Christ, to establish and exhort you in your faith, that no one be moved by these afflictions. For you yourselves know that we are destined for this. For when we were with you, we kept telling you beforehand that we were to suffer affliction, just as it has come to pass, and just as you know. For this reason, when I could bear it no longer, I sent to learn about your faith, for fear that somehow the tempter had tempted you and our labor would be in vain.

But now that Timothy has come to us from you, and has brought us the good news of your faith and love and reported that you always remember us kindly and long to see us, as we long to see you—for this reason, brothers, in all our distress and affliction we have been comforted about you through your faith. For now we live, if you are standing fast in the Lord.

Reflect:

In our passage, Paul wrote to a young church about suffering. Unable to return to them himself, he sent Timothy to them so that he could be "cheering [them] on so [they] wouldn't be discouraged by these hard times" (v. 2 MSG).

Our times are hard, and many of us are discouraged. What can we learn from Paul's message? How are we to suffer well in this season?

Suffering shouldn't come as a surprise. We must remember that it is a promised part of our calling. In Paul's words, "we are destined for such troubles" (v. 3 NLT), so we must be on guard. Satan, the tempter, loves nothing more than to use hard times to weaken our faith and draw our eyes away from Jesus and onto our circumstances.

If suffering is our destiny, how do we receive it? We must stand firm in the Lord, in faith, and in his promises. We can stand firm in Christ because he is our Rock.

With a quiet heart, ponder these verses:

- I waited patiently for the LORD; he inclined to me and heard my cry. He drew me up from the pit of destruction, out of the miry bog, and set my feet upon a rock, making my steps secure (Psalm 40:1–2).
- You keep him in perfect peace whose mind is stayed on you, because he trusts in you. Trust in the LORD forever, for the LORD GOD is an everlasting rock (Isaiah 26:3–4).
- From the end of the earth I call to you when my heart is faint. Lead me to the rock that is higher than I, for you have been my refuge, a strong tower against the enemy (Psalm 61:2–3).

Wait patiently, train your mind on Jesus, and let him be a rock and refuge—a tower of strength against the enemy. This kind of waiting is active, steady, and expectant.

As you turn to him in prayer, stand firm in the Lord. He is your strength.

Pray:

Most loving Father, you will us to give thanks for all things, to dread nothing but the loss of you, and to cast all our care on the One who cares for us. Preserve us from faithless fears and worldly anxieties, and grant that no clouds of this mortal life may hide from us the light of that love which is immortal, and which you have manifested unto us in your Son, Jesus Christ our Lord. Amen.

(Anglican Church in North America Book of Common Prayer)

Ordinary Time Day 90
WILLA KANE

Read: *1 Thessalonians 4:1–12*

Finally, then, brothers, we ask and urge you in the Lord Jesus, that as you received from us how you ought to walk and to please God, just as you are doing, that you do so more and more. For you know what instructions we gave you through the Lord Jesus. For this is the will of God, your sanctification: that you abstain from sexual immorality; that each one of you know how to control his own body in holiness and honor, not in the passion of lust like the Gentiles who do not know God; that no one transgress and wrong his brother in this matter, because the Lord is an avenger in all these things, as we told you beforehand and solemnly warned you. For God has not called us for impurity, but in holiness. Therefore whoever disregards this, disregards not man but God, who gives his Holy Spirit to you.

Now concerning brotherly love you have no need for anyone to write to you, for you yourselves have been taught by God to love one another, for that indeed is what you are doing to all the brothers throughout Macedonia. But we urge you, brothers, to do this more and more, and to aspire to live quietly, and to mind your own affairs, and to work with your hands, as we instructed you, so that you may walk properly before outsiders and be dependent on no one.

Reflect:

The Christian life is intended to be lived from the inside out. God himself designed our bodies as a temple for the Holy Spirit—Christ is in us as we walk this earth and learn his ways.

Paul's letter to the Thessalonians urges us to live this kind of life: a life of purity, holiness, and dignity. Sit with his words for a moment. Do they describe the way you're living—beautiful and holy from the inside out? Or do you struggle with disorder in your thought life, your sex life, your work life, or your family life?

Where is your life unkempt? When hearts are disordered, relationships are too. Life feels like a mess, not a beautiful dance.

Running roughshod over others is easy to excuse when times are hard. Wearing emotions on one's sleeve, using words lit by short fuses, selfishly dismissing the concerns of others—this is not the way to live a life of love.

Pause to examine your heart by looking at your excuses. What do they reveal? "I'd be more patient if only …"; "My thought life would be purer if only …"; "I wouldn't say this or do that if only …"; "I'd be more generous or loving if only …"; "My life would be more beautiful if only …"

Pray. Confess to the Lord the things in your heart that are disordered and disheveled. Lay these things at the cross, at the feet of Christ.

God's gift to you is the Holy Spirit. As he indwells you, his job is to transform—to bring purity, holiness, and beauty to your inmost being.

Receive this gift. Don't reject it. Invite the Spirit in and be transformed.

Pray:

Holy Spirit, breath of God and fire of love, I cannot pray without your aid: Kindle in me the fire of your love, and illumine me with your light; that with a steadfast will and holy thoughts I may approach the Father in spirit and in truth; through Jesus Christ my Lord, who reigns with you and the Father in eternal union. Amen.

(Anglican Church in North America Book of Common Prayer)

13th Sunday of Ordinary Time

KARI WEST

Read: *Psalm 78:19–32*

> They spoke against God, saying,
> > "Can God spread a table in the wilderness?
> He struck the rock so that water gushed out
> > and streams overflowed.
> Can he also give bread
> > or provide meat for his people?"
> Therefore, when the LORD heard, he was full of wrath;
> > a fire was kindled against Jacob;
> > his anger rose against Israel,
> because they did not believe in God
> > and did not trust his saving power.
> Yet he commanded the skies above
> > and opened the doors of heaven,
> and he rained down on them manna to eat
> > and gave them the grain of heaven.
> Man ate of the bread of the angels;
> > he sent them food in abundance.
> He caused the east wind to blow in the heavens,
> > and by his power he led out the south wind;
> he rained meat on them like dust,
> > winged birds like the sand of the seas;
> he let them fall in the midst of their camp,
> > all around their dwellings.
> And they ate and were well filled,
> > for he gave them what they craved.
> But before they had satisfied their craving,
> > while the food was still in their mouths,
> the anger of God rose against them,
> > and he killed the strongest of them
> > and laid low the young men of Israel.
> In spite of all this, they still sinned;
> > despite his wonders, they did not believe.

Reflect:

"Despite his wonders, they did not believe" (v. 32): How quickly the Israelites came to distrust the God who had rescued them from slavery and who had provided for their needs through miracles.

And though he continued to care for them by giving them bread from heaven and causing meat to rain down like dust, he also struck down some of the people because they distrusted his faithfulness and disregarded his power.

We may be quick to flinch because of the way God judged his people in this passage. We may wonder if God overreacted. We may think he was too harsh. But what if our gut response reveals our numbness to the severity of sin? What if a story like this one is meant to awaken us to the reality that God is holy and just as well as merciful and loving? Distrust of the Father matters; disregard for his laws matters; our flattering tongues and deceitful hearts matter.

For such things, the bread of heaven was broken.

Ask the Lord to reveal where your heart is more controlled by our culture's attitudes than by his character as revealed in Scripture. Thank him that this passage is not the end of the story, but that in the fullness of time, God sent better bread from heaven, broken for the healing of the world. Praise the Father that his justice was perfectly satisfied in Jesus. Ask for a soft heart that confesses that sin is heinous, Christ is beautiful, the Spirit is powerful, and the Father is trustworthy.

Pray:

O God, whose thunder shakes the sky,
Whose eye this atom globe surveys,
To thee, my only rock, I fly,
Thy mercy in thy justice praise.
Amen.

(from "The Resignation," Thomas Chatterton)

Ordinary Time Day 92
WILLA KANE

Read: *1 Thessalonians 4:13–5:11*

But we do not want you to be uninformed, brothers, about those who are asleep, that you may not grieve as others do who have no hope. For since we believe that Jesus died and rose again, even so, through Jesus, God will bring with him those who have fallen asleep. For this we declare to you by a word from the Lord, that we who are alive, who are left until the coming of the Lord, will not precede those who have fallen asleep. For the Lord himself will descend from heaven with a cry of command, with the voice of an archangel, and with the sound of the trumpet of God. And the dead in Christ will rise first. Then we who are alive, who are left, will be caught up together with them in the clouds to meet the Lord in the air, and so we will always be with the Lord. Therefore encourage one another with these words.

Now concerning the times and the seasons, brothers, you have no need to have anything written to you. For you yourselves are fully aware that the day of the Lord will come like a thief in the night. While people are saying, "There is peace and security," then sudden destruction will come upon them as labor pains come upon a pregnant woman, and they will not escape. But you are not in darkness, brothers, for that day to surprise you like a thief. For you are all children of light, children of the day. We are not of the night or of the darkness. So then let us not sleep, as others do, but let us keep awake and be sober. For those who sleep, sleep at night, and those who get drunk, are drunk at night. But since we belong to the day, let us be sober, having put on the breastplate of faith and love, and for a helmet the hope of salvation. For God has not destined us for wrath, but to obtain salvation through our Lord Jesus Christ, who died for us so that whether we are awake or asleep we might live with him. Therefore encourage one another and build one another up, just as you are doing.

Reflect:

We live tethered in tension. We're told that Jesus reigns, but we know that the world is broken and that our lives are messy. A virulent enemy stalks and steals. Turmoil and isolation dominate; unity feels shaky and unsustainable; conflict and uncertainty linger. The question lurks: What if death has the final say?

Against a backdrop of confusion and despair, Paul declared to the Thessalonians and to us that there is hope. We are children of the day, not of the dark, so we can have confidence that all those who believe the gospel will be caught up together to meet Christ when he returns. We can hope in this ultimate encouragement: We will be with the Lord forever.

Against a backdrop of stark loneliness, we have an amazing encouragement from God: A time will come when there will be a spectacular family reunion with the Master. It's not a date on the calendar but a deep assurance in our hearts. Jesus will return, he will gather us to himself, and we will be together with him forever.

Pause to consider this, to be encouraged—and even delighted—as you receive this promise. Imagine eternity with Christ and the family of God.

This is such good news that we cannot—must not—keep it to ourselves. We are told to build each other up and reassure one another with these words. Whom do you know who is still in darkness? Who is discouraged? Who is in despair?

As you pray, ask the Lord to send you as an encourager with this great good news—the best news of all: "He died for us so that, whether we are awake or asleep, we may live together with him" (1 Thessalonians 5:10 NIV).

Pray:

O God, thank you that new birth in Christ gives way to life eternal. Send me with your message of hope and peace as an encourager into a world that is lost and dying; in Jesus's name and for your glory. Amen.

Ordinary Time Day 93
WILLA KANE

Read: *1 Thessalonians 5:12–24*

We ask you, brothers, to respect those who labor among you and are over you in the Lord and admonish you, and to esteem them very highly in love because of their work. Be at peace among yourselves. And we urge you, brothers, admonish the idle, encourage the fainthearted, help the weak, be patient with them all. See that no one repays anyone evil for evil, but always seek to do good to one another and to everyone. Rejoice always, pray without ceasing, give thanks in all circumstances; for this is the will of God in Christ Jesus for you. Do not quench the Spirit. Do not despise prophecies, but test everything; hold fast what is good. Abstain from every form of evil.

Now may the God of peace himself sanctify you completely, and may your whole spirit and soul and body be kept blameless at the coming of our Lord Jesus Christ. He who calls you is faithful; he will surely do it.

Reflect:

Paul ended this first letter to the Thessalonians with a litany of to-dos—like a parent to a child who was leaving home. Remember this! Don't forget that! Do this! He gave seventeen practical instructions about living as believers.

Even halfway through, the list feels onerous and impossible: Honor your leaders and overwhelm them with love. Get along among yourselves, warn freeloaders, and encourage stragglers. Be patient and attentive. Don't snap, but look for the best in others and do your best to bring it out. Be cheerful and thank God no matter what. Pray all the time. Don't suppress the Spirit or discount prophecies. Don't be gullible. Keep the good and throw out the evil.

These instructions *were* onerous and impossible—until Paul delivered the most encouraging words that believers in Christ could hear: The one who calls you is faithful, and he will do it.

He will do it. He will make you holy and whole. He will put you together—spirit, soul, and body. He will fit you for the return of Christ.

As you pray, thank him for his faithfulness, for his perfect plan to forgive, redeem, and restore you, and for the assurance that he himself will do the work to sanctify you completely.

Pray:

Blessed Lord Jesus,

No human mind could conceive or invent the gospel.

Acting in eternal grace,

thou art both its messenger and its message,

lived out on earth through infinite compassion,

applying thy life to insult, injury, death,

that I might be redeemed, ransomed, freed.

Blessed be thou, O Father,

for contriving this way;

Eternal thanks to thee,

O Lamb of God,

for opening this way;

Praise everlasting to thee,

O Holy Spirit,

for applying this way to my heart.

Glorious Trinity,

impress the gospel on my soul.

Amen.

(From *The Valley of Vision*)

Ordinary Time Day 94

KARI WEST

Read: *2 Thessalonians 1:3–12*

> We ought always to give thanks to God for you, brothers, as is right, because your faith is growing abundantly, and the love of every one of you for one another is increasing. Therefore we ourselves boast about you in the churches of God for your steadfastness and faith in all your persecutions and in the afflictions that you are enduring.
>
> This is evidence of the righteous judgment of God, that you may be considered worthy of the kingdom of God, for which you are also suffering—since indeed God considers it just to repay with affliction those who afflict you, and to grant relief to you who are afflicted as well as to us, when the Lord Jesus is revealed from heaven with his mighty angels in flaming fire, inflicting vengeance on those who do not know God and on those who do not obey the gospel of our Lord Jesus. They will suffer the punishment of eternal destruction, away from the presence of the Lord and from the glory of his might, when he comes on that day to be glorified in his saints, and to be marveled at among all who have believed, because our testimony to you was believed. To this end we always pray for you, that our God may make you worthy of his calling and may fulfill every resolve for good and every work of faith by his power, so that the name of our Lord Jesus may be glorified in you, and you in him, according to the grace of our God and the Lord Jesus Christ.

Reflect:

We are almost halfway through Ordinary Time, which may feel like the least remarkable liturgical season. But when we commit to this daily walk with God through the year, we are not simply plodding along with no hope of a final destination. We are headed toward a magnificent culmination, a future moment when Christ will be revealed as the mighty, just, and splendid King of the cosmos.

This is the hope that Paul held out to the Thessalonians and to us: Remember that you are in the middle of the grand narrative of redemption.

Remember that your King reigns now but that his majesty, justice, perfection, and rule will be revealed and enacted in fullness on that final dawn.

It will be a glorious day—but not for everyone. For some, it will be a reckoning. Paul didn't mince words: Christ will come in judgment against those who persist in evil and who refuse the path of obedience and trust. He will fulfill all justice on the earth.

How does that sit with you? Does it make you angry, or confused, or hopeful? Allow yourself time to process the emotions that arise from this picture of the coming judgment. And then ask the Holy Spirit for fresh awareness of those who need to hear about this just and grand God.

Thank him that he will reveal himself in fullness and that he will bring perfect rule to the earth. Praise him that we will one day have our deepest heart's desire met—to marvel at and behold our King of glory.

Pray:

O God and Father of all, whom the whole heavens adore: Let the whole earth also worship you, all nations obey you, all tongues confess and bless you, and men, women, and children everywhere love you and serve you in peace; through Jesus Christ our Lord. Amen.

(Anglican Church in North America Book of Common Prayer)

Ordinary Time Day 95

KARI WEST

Read: *2 Thessalonians 2:13–17*

> But we ought always to give thanks to God for you, brothers
> beloved by the Lord, because God chose you as the firstfruits to be
> saved, through sanctification by the Spirit and belief in the truth.
> To this he called you through our gospel, so that you may obtain
> the glory of our Lord Jesus Christ. So then, brothers, stand firm
> and hold to the traditions that you were taught by us, either by our
> spoken word or by our letter.
>
> Now may our Lord Jesus Christ himself, and God our Father,
> who loved us and gave us eternal comfort and good hope through
> grace, comfort your hearts and establish them in every good work
> and word.

Reflect:

How often do you slow down and let the words of Scripture seep into your
soul? Do you believe that the Word of the Lord is sweeter than honey? We
are quick to read marvelous truths such as the ones found in this passage and
then move on to something else. We don't often sit and savor. Hear the Word
of the Lord now:

- *"beloved by the Lord"* (v. 13): You are his beloved, joined to his family.
- *"God chose you"* (v. 13): You have been seen, singled out, and cared for
  by the Almighty.
- *"saved, through sanctification by the Spirit"* (v. 13): Your salvation is
  not your own doing. It is the gift of God.
- *"That you may obtain the glory of our Lord Jesus Christ"* (v. 14): Your
  story will be fulfilled in a marvelous way.
- *"eternal comfort and good hope through grace"* (v. 16): God has lavished
  unending encouragement and good hope upon you.

Sit and savor. Meditate in a quiet place. Ask the Holy Spirit which truth you need to receive most today. Ask him to plant it deep within your soul.

May God encourage your heart and strengthen you in every good deed and word.

Pray:

Grant, Almighty God, that as you have given us once for all your only begotten Son to rule us, and have by your good pleasure consecrated him a king over us, that we may be perpetually safe and secure under his hand against all the attempts of the Devil and of the whole world—O grant that we may suffer ourselves to be ruled by his authority, and so conduct ourselves, that he himself may ever continue to watch for our safety; as you have committed us to him, that he may be the guardian of our salvation, so also suffer us neither to turn aside nor to fall, but preserve us ever in his service, until we at length be gathered into that blessed and everlasting kingdom, which has been procured for us by the blood of your only Son. Amen.

(John Calvin)

Ordinary Time Day 96
MADISON PERRY

Read: *2 Thessalonians 2:16–3:5, 16*

Now may our Lord Jesus Christ himself, and God our Father, who loved us and gave us eternal comfort and good hope through grace, comfort your hearts and establish them in every good work and word.

Finally, brothers, pray for us, that the word of the Lord may speed ahead and be honored, as happened among you, and that we may be delivered from wicked and evil men. For not all have faith. But the Lord is faithful. He will establish you and guard you against the evil one. And we have confidence in the Lord about you, that you are doing and will do the things that we command. May the Lord direct your hearts to the love of God and to the steadfastness of Christ. . . .

Now may the Lord of peace himself give you peace at all times in every way. The Lord be with you all.

Reflect:

The internet increasingly consumes time and space in the conversations around us. Your inbox is likely cluttered with missives from pastors, politicians, academic leaders, and businesses. But this glut of information is radically different from the communication that flows through the Scriptures.

Paul's goal, in his letters to the Thessalonians, was to encourage his younger brothers and sisters in Christ. These letters were written to a community he loved dearly, who had received the gospel in joy and become his family through faith. They were now enduring persecution, and many had been killed. How did Paul respond to such suffering?

Paul reminded the Thessalonians of God's love, which had given them eternal salvation and could bring comfort and consolation. He asked for their prayers for the ministry of the gospel. He reminded them of the hope they had been given in Christ. They could be hopeful that just as God's grace prevailed over Jesus's death and led to his resurrection, so grace would prevail over their own suffering and deaths.

What did hope look like on the ground? Paul wrote of being established in work and word. He encouraged his friends to continue doing their daily work and speaking their regular words, even in the midst of trials and tribulation. He prayed that peace would be with them "at all times in every way" (v. 16).

You may find yourself lacking hope. Perhaps you have never encountered the hard places in life as you are now. You have tried to live and plan well, but nothing you have done has provided the protection or stability you crave.

Yet you, too, can be hopeful. Our hope is not that our legacies will outlast every sea change. Our hope has nothing to do with our competence or calculations; it isn't derived from the greatness of our cities or the wisdom of our experts. Our hope is built on Jesus's blood and righteousness. The salvation of our God will prevail, even if it is with us now as only a whisper or a prayer.

When faced with impossible challenges, we can continue our daily work. We can go on caring for others and ourselves, praying, keeping the flowers watered, making the next meal, and doing the dishes. We do our daily work because of the eternally significant work God is doing through it. He is establishing us and sinking our roots ever deeper into his grace and love. He is glorifying himself and creating quiet testimonies of his beauty that will lead others home as well.

Pray against despair. Pray for relief for those who suffer. Ask God if there are others who face hopelessness. Be willing to tell them of your cause for hope. Trust that God is at work and surrender yourself to him anew.

Pray:

Lord Jesus Christ and God our Father, you who have loved us and given us everlasting consolation and good hope by grace; please comfort our hearts and establish us in every good work and word. Our Lord of peace, please give us peace always in every way. Lord, be with us. Amen.

(Adapted from *2 Thessalonians 2:16, 3:16*)

Ordinary Time Day 97

MADISON PERRY

Read: *Luke 10:25–37*

> And behold, a lawyer stood up to put him to the test, saying, "Teacher, what shall I do to inherit eternal life?" He said to him, "What is written in the Law? How do you read it?" And he answered, "You shall love the Lord your God with all your heart and with all your soul and with all your strength and with all your mind, and your neighbor as yourself." And he said to him, "You have answered correctly; do this, and you will live."
>
> But he, desiring to justify himself, said to Jesus, "And who is my neighbor?" Jesus replied, "A man was going down from Jerusalem to Jericho, and he fell among robbers, who stripped him and beat him and departed, leaving him half dead. Now by chance a priest was going down that road, and when he saw him he passed by on the other side. So likewise a Levite, when he came to the place and saw him, passed by on the other side. But a Samaritan, as he journeyed, came to where he was, and when he saw him, he had compassion. He went to him and bound up his wounds, pouring on oil and wine. Then he set him on his own animal and brought him to an inn and took care of him. And the next day he took out two denarii and gave them to the innkeeper, saying, 'Take care of him, and whatever more you spend, I will repay you when I come back.' Which of these three, do you think, proved to be a neighbor to the man who fell among the robbers?" He said, "The one who showed him mercy." And Jesus said to him, "You go, and do likewise."

Reflect:

"What shall I do to inherit eternal life?" The parable of the good Samaritan follows on the heels of this decisively important question.

The lawyer wanted to discover the minimum requirement for attaining eternal life. Jesus responded that eternal life depends on a life marked by an active and overwhelming love for God and a corresponding love for our neighbor. These commandments are not satisfied with a onetime action; they urge us toward lives whose every thought and deed reflect God's love.

The lawyer's search wasn't satisfied. He asked, "Who is my neighbor?" In one sense, everyone is potentially our neighbor. There are simply too many people to care about.

Jesus responded with the story we have heard many times. The Samaritan rescued a half-dead ethnic enemy who had been passed over by religious leaders. He cleansed him, ministered to his needs, and brought him to safety.

The lawyer's question was about the outer limit of who we must care for. But Jesus posed a different question: "Which of these three, do you think, proved to be a neighbor to the man who fell among the robbers?" (v. 36). Who chose the privilege of being a neighbor?

Jesus pointed out that the Samaritan, in loving and caring for a stranger, gained a neighbor and exemplified the path of mercy that leads to eternal life.

Life apart from God is a life with no neighbors, with no one whom you love as you love yourself. But the grace-filled eternal life of God leads you to discover all kinds of neighbors. One path sees love as a scarce resource and strangers as potential burdens; the other path sees love as a place to experience eternal life, where strangers are opportunities to wisely but extravagantly model God's love.

Take time to praise the Lord for his neighborly love for you. He has also drawn near to you as a neighbor would. Ask God which people are the neighbors whom you have been called to love. Ask God to help you see his image in them. Ask God to give you the strength and generosity to care for them. Thank him for the magnificent gift of eternal life.

Pray:

Set us free, loving Father, from the bondage of our sins, and in your goodness and mercy give us the liberty of that abundant life which you have made known to us in our Savior Jesus Christ; who lives and reigns with you, in the unity of the Holy Spirit, one God, now and for ever. Amen.

(Anglican Church in North America Book of Common Prayer)

14th Sunday of Ordinary Time
KARI WEST

Read: *Psalm 84:1–11*

> How lovely is your dwelling place,
>   O Lord of hosts!
> My soul longs, yes, faints
>   for the courts of the Lord;
> my heart and flesh sing for joy
>   to the living God.
> Even the sparrow finds a home,
>   and the swallow a nest for herself,
>   where she may lay her young,
> at your altars, O Lord of hosts,
>   my King and my God.
> Blessed are those who dwell in your house,
>   ever singing your praise!   *Selah*
> Blessed are those whose strength is in you,
>   in whose heart are the highways to Zion.
> As they go through the Valley of Baca
>   they make it a place of springs;
>   the early rain also covers it with pools.
> They go from strength to strength;
>   each one appears before God in Zion.
> O Lord God of hosts, hear my prayer;
>   give ear, O God of Jacob!   *Selah*
> Behold our shield, O God;
>   look on the face of your anointed!
> For a day in your courts is better
>   than a thousand elsewhere.
> I would rather be a doorkeeper in the house of my God
>   than dwell in the tents of wickedness.
> For the Lord God is a sun and shield;
>   the Lord bestows favor and honor.

Reflect:

The aim of our hearts will determine the beauty and depth of our lives.

Here the psalmist caught a vision of the glorious dwelling place of God—unparalleled in its beauty, its solace, and its strengthening power. God's dwelling is so lovely, and the psalmist yearned for it so deeply that he said it would be better to spend just one day there than a thousand days in any other place.

Those who have hearts set on pilgrimage are empowered from on high to live faithfully. The psalmist declared that those who have set their affections on God go from strength to strength. More than that, they can pass through the Valley of Baca, or Valley of Weeping, and even their tears will be turned into a spring. Even their sorrows will bear fruit in season, and nothing will be wasted, nothing ultimately lost.

God makes all things possible. God is our sun and shield.

Do you long for your life to reflect his power, his light, his strength, and his comfort? The truth is that God's dwelling place is now within you and within the gathered and scattered church.

As you pray, ask him to give you this all-consuming vision of his presence. Ask for greater faith to trust that one day in the Lord's presence is truly better than a thousand elsewhere. Contemplate the glorious dwelling of God.

Pray:

O God, grant that we may desire you, and desiring you seek you, and seeking you find you, and finding you be satisfied in you for ever. Amen.

(Francis Xavier)

Ordinary Time Day 99
MADISON PERRY

Read: *Luke 10:38–42*

> Now as they went on their way, Jesus entered a village. And a woman named Martha welcomed him into her house. And she had a sister called Mary, who sat at the Lord's feet and listened to his teaching. But Martha was distracted with much serving. And she went up to him and said, "Lord, do you not care that my sister has left me to serve alone? Tell her then to help me." But the Lord answered her, "Martha, Martha, you are anxious and troubled about many things, but one thing is necessary. Mary has chosen the good portion, which will not be taken away from her."

Reflect:

Consider the famous story of Mary and Martha, which follows the parable of the good Samaritan. In the story of these sisters, we see what happens when service becomes a distraction.

Martha hosted Jesus at her house. She worked as hard as she could, scurrying about, absorbed in her preparations. Her sister, Mary, sat at Jesus's feet and listened to his teaching. Martha went to Jesus and demanded that he make Mary help her. Jesus ought to have pity on her; she had been left "to serve alone" (v. 40). Martha thought Mary was the cause of her problems, but Jesus saw the burdens she was carrying; she was "anxious and troubled about many things" (v. 41).

How many times are we driven by the unconscious goals and thoughts of our imaginations? We still carry the impulses bestowed on us by parents, friends, teachers, bosses, and family. We are haunted by contradictory impulses, all the while judging ourselves for failing to meet impossible standards.

When have you recently felt like Martha—anxious and troubled about many things? Note that Jesus didn't articulate Mary's issues. Instead, he cut to the heart of the matter: "One thing is necessary. Mary has chosen the good portion, which will not be taken away from her" (v. 42).

There is a path to clarity and single-minded devotion. But you have to choose it. Does that sound too easy? If you could choose the good, would you?

What if choosing the good meant sitting at Jesus's feet and listening to his Word? Would you choose it then? What if it meant giving up control? Would you still want it? What if it made you look silly or put you at odds with people you want to impress, or people who want you to be busy doing more tangible work?

Truly, we cannot escape diminishment. We will all die one day and will be forced to give up everything we have clung to. But this truth, this goodness, cannot be taken away.

Choose the good. Choose Christ. Hear him call your name in love. Listen to him direct your path. Choose the good; it will not be taken from you.

Pray:

Almighty and everlasting God, you govern all things both in heaven and on earth: Mercifully hear the supplications of your people, and in our time grant us your peace; through Jesus Christ our Lord, who lives and reigns with you and the Holy Spirit, one God, for ever and ever. Amen.

(Anglican Church in North America Book of Common Prayer)

Ordinary Time Day 100

MADISON PERRY

Read: *Luke 11:1–13*

Now Jesus was praying in a certain place, and when he finished, one of his disciples said to him, "Lord, teach us to pray, as John taught his disciples." And he said to them, "When you pray, say:

"Father, hallowed be your name.
Your kingdom come.
Give us each day our daily bread,
and forgive us our sins,
for we ourselves forgive everyone who is indebted to us.
And lead us not into temptation."

And he said to them, "Which of you who has a friend will go to him at midnight and say to him, 'Friend, lend me three loaves, for a friend of mine has arrived on a journey, and I have nothing to set before him'; and he will answer from within, 'Do not bother me; the door is now shut, and my children are with me in bed. I cannot get up and give you anything'? I tell you, though he will not get up and give him anything because he is his friend, yet because of his impudence he will rise and give him whatever he needs. And I tell you, ask, and it will be given to you; seek, and you will find; knock, and it will be opened to you. For everyone who asks receives, and the one who seeks finds, and to the one who knocks it will be opened. What father among you, if his son asks for a fish, will instead of a fish give him a serpent; or if he asks for an egg, will give him a scorpion? If you then, who are evil, know how to give good gifts to your children, how much more will the heavenly Father give the Holy Spirit to those who ask him!"

Reflect:

Jesus taught his friends to pray. First, he gave them a series of God-focused petitions. Then he invited them to ponder the nature of prayer itself to become the kind of people who pray frequently, without ceasing and without feeling embarrassed. As Jesus knows, we will never outgrow our dependence on God.

Why don't we know how to pray? Perhaps the real problem is that we don't want to keep asking God for things. Maybe, in our prideful state, we want God to give us enough to sustain us without our having to ask again, so that we don't have to continually drag ourselves before him.

Perhaps you think, *If only God could empower me to take care of myself and get what I want for myself.* But remember, God loves you so much that he will never make you autonomous. The only self-oriented request of Jesus's model prayer is for daily bread, just enough for the day.

What is the greatest thing we could ever ask God for? Jesus dares us to think bigger about God's generosity, which far exceeds our desires for glory, earthly wisdom, or material provision. God wants to give us his very self. Jesus himself would ultimately die and ascend so that he might send his Spirit, the Comforter, into our hearts.

It is good to be perpetually unsatisfied with all this world has to offer. That signifies that we should ask for something greater from God. Ask Jesus to fill your heart with his Spirit and bring you into communion with his Father. The triune God will never take his eyes off you. His strong arms will always shelter you; his love will be to you "better than wine" (Song of Solomon 1:2).

There is so much at stake in every prayer. Ask for the Holy Spirit and he will be given to you; seek and ye will find; knock and the door will be opened unto you. Choose what is good and it will never be taken from you.

Pray:

Our Father who art in heaven, hallowed be thy name. Thy kingdom come, thy will be done on earth as it is in heaven. Give us this day our daily bread, and forgive us our trespasses as we forgive those who trespass against us. And lead us not into temptation, but deliver us from evil. For thine is the kingdom, and the power, and the glory, forever and ever. Amen.

Ordinary Time Day 101

MADISON PERRY

Read: *Luke 11:33–36*

"No one after lighting a lamp puts it in a cellar or under a basket, but on a stand, so that those who enter may see the light. Your eye is the lamp of your body. When your eye is healthy, your whole body is full of light, but when it is bad, your body is full of darkness. Therefore be careful lest the light in you be darkness. If then your whole body is full of light, having no part dark, it will be wholly bright, as when a lamp with its rays gives you light."

Reflect:

It is easy to neglect Jesus's words—they are so counterintuitive that they can be hard to understand and even harder to live out. In truth, his thoughts are not our thoughts. But thankfully, as we meditate daily on his words, the truth we need from our God will become clearer.

Jesus spoke about eyes in an unexpected way. He called them "the lamp of [the] body" (v. 34). If our eye is healthy, so will our body be healthy. We will have no darkness at all within. But how are our eyes like lamps?

People in centuries past believed that our eyes help to form the world that we see. We don't just "take in" the world. Instead, we actively sort and filter reality according to the patterns we care about and understand. (In more familiar Christian language, we receive the world around us through the eyes of our heart.)

For example, when looking into a crowd for a familiar face, the eyes of our heart filter out unfamiliar faces until they focus on the person we love. In the same way, if we have dropped coins in the grass, the eyes of our heart help us skim over hundreds of green blades until we find what we have lost. The eyes of the heart help to create the world within which we live, and we see things through the lens of what we love. This is why two people can look out at the same scene and perceive it differently.

When we love the wrong things, our perspective is skewed. God's Word loses its central place in our hearts. We see the world through darkened eyes that fixate on what benefits us most and what we can most easily control.

Praise the Lord that we have had the opportunity of receiving his Word into our hearts. There is no greater privilege than to be saved from our darkened vision. Praise the Lord that he has rescued us with a light that is capable of displacing every darkness.

Consider the competing visions of value that you are tempted to embrace—greed, lust, pride, ambition, selfishness. Turn your eyes on Jesus and ask him to be the center of your vision.

Pray:

Be Thou my Vision, O Lord of my heart;
Naught be all else to me, save that Thou art;
Thou my best Thought, by day or by night,
Waking or sleeping, Thy presence my light.
Be Thou my Wisdom, and Thou my true Word;
I ever with Thee and Thou with me, Lord;
Thou my great Father, I Thy true son,
Thou in me dwelling, and I with Thee one.
Riches I heed not, nor man's empty praise,
Thou mine Inheritance, now and always;
Thou and Thou only, first in my heart,
High King of Heaven, my Treasure Thou art.
High King of Heaven, my victory won;
May I reach Heaven's joys, O bright Heav'n's Sun;
Heart of my own heart, whate'er befall,
Still be my Vision, O Ruler of all. Amen.

("Be Thou My Vision," translated by Mary E. Byrne)

Ordinary Time Day 102

MADISON PERRY

Read: *Luke 12:1–3*

> In the meantime, when so many thousands of the people had gathered together that they were trampling one another, he began to say to his disciples first, "Beware of the leaven of the Pharisees, which is hypocrisy. Nothing is covered up that will not be revealed, or hidden that will not be known. Therefore whatever you have said in the dark shall be heard in the light, and what you have whispered in private rooms shall be proclaimed on the housetops."

Reflect:

Imagine: A crowd of people have gathered around Jesus, thousands in such close proximity that they were nearly trampling one another. They were eager to catch a glimpse of the man who was rumored to be the new king of Israel, God's Chosen One who would free them and usher in a new age of judgment and prosperity.

In the background, politics and power were at work. Jesus had begun to encounter significant opposition from the Pharisees. The current leaders of Israel wanted to kill him. They claimed to worship Israel's God, but they were most interested in perpetuating their religious system and their position in the world. They were closed off to what God was doing in Jesus. They were a little bit of "leaven" that would corrupt the whole loaf.

But Jesus didn't say the Pharisees were simply bad leaders. Something specific about them was deadly and toxic. Jesus pulled no punches: "Beware of the leaven of the Pharisees, which is hypocrisy" (v. 1).

The Pharisees were different people in public than they were in private. They managed to appear respectful of Jesus in public, while they scoffed and plotted against him behind closed doors. They paraded around as God-fearing in public, but they were power-hungry in private.

O that they had the humility of Nicodemus! He was able to approach Jesus in private and their meeting transformed his life (John 3).

How can we take Jesus's warning to heart? We need to decide if we will seek Jesus earnestly with complete willingness to lay aside everything and follow him.

If Jesus were to approach you today as he did his first disciples, what would you do? Would you ask him to come back again in a month? What would you have to release or give up in order to be ready?

Our faith will never rise higher than our humility. There is no more courageous or truthful way to see ourselves than as people in complete need of Jesus. If we had eyes to see Jesus and to see ourselves clearly, then we would be more than ready to follow him at every moment. The humble faith that comes from submitting to Jesus would eventually leaven and pervade our whole lives.

Meet Jesus Christ in prayer. Humble yourself before him and thank him for his love. Express your willingness to follow him and ask him to lead you. Ask him if there is anything you need to leave behind or anyone you need to move toward in love.

Pray:

O Lord and Master of my life, give me not the spirit of sloth, despair, lust for power, and idle talk. But grant unto me, thy servant, a spirit of chastity, humility, patience, and love. Yea, O Lord and King, grant me to see mine own faults and not to judge my brother or sister. For you are blessed now and forever. Amen.

(Lenten Prayer of Saint Ephrem)

Ordinary Time Day 103

KARI WEST

Read: *Luke 12:4–7*

"I tell you, my friends, do not fear those who kill the body, and after
that have nothing more that they can do. But I will warn you whom
to fear: fear him who, after he has killed, has authority to cast into
hell. Yes, I tell you, fear him! Are not five sparrows sold for two
pennies? And not one of them is forgotten before God. Why, even
the hairs of your head are all numbered. Fear not; you are of more
value than many sparrows."

Reflect:

"Do not fear those who kill the body" (v. 4).

Christ gave this command as the shadow of Golgotha loomed large, as
those who would torture and kill the body of Jesus conspired behind closed
doors. The power of those who could kill the body would soon be on bloody
display on a hill outside Jerusalem.

In light of what was to come, Christ knew that his listeners needed a
reorientation of their fears. He urged them: *Don't fear people whose power ends
at death. Fear a holy God who has the power to cast souls into hell.* And then he
repeated himself: *Fear this powerful God!*

But Jesus didn't conclude his teaching there. He went on to say that this
God, the mighty Ruler of all, never forgets a sparrow. This God, who has all
of creation at his feet, knows the number of hairs on your head. Jesus offered
profound and seemingly contradictory instructions: *Fear God but be confident that you are of great value to the Father, so fear not.*

And because Jesus didn't fear those who kill the body—because he feared
a holy God who would cast unrepentant souls into hell, because he shared
his Father's deep love for his people who were lost in sin—he bled out on that
hill outside Jerusalem. So that we might fear God, and fear not.

As you pray, ponder the power, the holiness, and the love of God. Let
these truths make you brave in a world full of lesser realities.

Pray:

O you high and holy One that inhabits eternity, you are to be feared and loved by all your servants. All your works praise you, O God; and we especially give thanks unto you for your marvelous love in Christ Jesus, by whom you have reconciled the world to yourself. You have given us exceeding great and precious promises. You have sealed them with his blood. You have confirmed them by his resurrection and ascension, and the coming of the Holy Spirit. We thank you that you have given us so many happy opportunities of knowing the truth as it is in Jesus, even the mystery which was hid from ages and generations, but is now revealed to them that believe. Amen.

(John Wesley)

Ordinary Time Day 104

KARI WEST

Read: *Luke 12:8–12*

"And I tell you, everyone who acknowledges me before men, the Son of Man also will acknowledge before the angels of God, but the one who denies me before men will be denied before the angels of God. And everyone who speaks a word against the Son of Man will be forgiven, but the one who blasphemes against the Holy Spirit will not be forgiven. And when they bring you before the synagogues and the rulers and the authorities, do not be anxious about how you should defend yourself or what you should say, for the Holy Spirit will teach you in that very hour what you ought to say."

Reflect:

There is no solely private faith in Jesus. He does not give us the option of honoring him in solitude and denying him in public. Belief in Christ is an all-encompassing reality that spills over into our public personas, our daily conversations, and every aspect of our outward living.

Consider here the staggering reward that Jesus held out for faithful witness: He will acknowledge us before the angels of God. Even today he offers us a seal of approval and a banner of friendship. There is no better thing.

Yet here, too, we have a grave warning from Jesus—faith that doesn't overflow into public confession is not true faith. And those without true saving faith in Jesus cannot have his approval or his friendship.

Public faith doesn't mean perfect faith. We know from the story of Peter's denial that believers will falter and fail in their witness of the Lord. Christ offers forgiveness and restoration for us in all our failings, but let the warning find its mark. Jesus's words here must be allowed their full weight. Faith that consistently and publicly denies Christ isn't of the Spirit.

Jesus offered gracious encouragement after his words of warning. He promised that the Spirit would give us the words to speak "in that very hour" of our need (v. 12). We can rest in the reality that Christ will give us what we need to do the things he tells us to do. The Holy Spirit will be our teacher.

Reflect for a moment before you pray. Is your public persona an accurate and true reflection of your faith in Christ? Are there places where you need the Spirit to gently guide you toward a more integrated life? Confess your need for help in these areas. Pray for courage to follow Christ wherever he calls and to live an undivided life. Walk in obedience to Christ's commands.

Pray:

May the Word in us never be smothered with the cares of this life, so that we would become unfruitful. But help us to walk on the King's Highway, never turning aside to the right hand or the left, and led by the Spirit through the Straight Gate. Then all that we do will prosper, both now and at the time of judgment, in Christ Jesus our Lord, to whom be glory now and forever. Amen.

(Gregory Nazianzen)

15th Sunday of Ordinary Time
KARI WEST

Read: *Psalm 85*

> LORD, you were favorable to your land;
>   you restored the fortunes of Jacob.
> You forgave the iniquity of your people;
>   you covered all their sin.   *Selah*
> You withdrew all your wrath;
>   you turned from your hot anger.
> Restore us again, O God of our salvation,
>   and put away your indignation toward us!
> Will you be angry with us forever?
>   Will you prolong your anger to all generations?
> Will you not revive us again,
>   that your people may rejoice in you?
> Show us your steadfast love, O LORD,
>   and grant us your salvation.
> Let me hear what God the LORD will speak,
>   for he will speak peace to his people, to his saints;
>   but let them not turn back to folly.
> Surely his salvation is near to those who fear him,
>   that glory may dwell in our land.
> Steadfast love and faithfulness meet;
>   righteousness and peace kiss each other.
> Faithfulness springs up from the ground,
>   and righteousness looks down from the sky.
> Yes, the LORD will give what is good,
>   and our land will yield its increase.
> Righteousness will go before him
>   and make his footsteps a way.

Reflect:

Let this psalm be a rubric for your prayer.

Rehearse the past goodness of God. Remember how far he has flung your sin and rebellion from you. Speak out loud to him about his deep forgiveness. Thank him that at such a great cost, he set aside his wrath and turned from his anger. List the many ways you've seen God work in your life and in the lives of those in your community.

Plead the perfect sacrifice of Christ on your behalf. Ask him for restoration. Ask him for fresh, renewing power in your life and within your family and your church so that you may seek him more faithfully and rest in his goodness.

Listen to what God has said to you, and revel in his promises of peace, the nearness of his salvation, and the current and future dwelling of his glory here with us. Pray fervently that we would not fall into folly and sin but would walk in a way that honors the Holy Spirit within us.

Hope in the beautiful picture laid before us—love and faithfulness greet each other like old friends; righteousness and peace kiss; faithfulness springs forth like water from the depths of the earth; and righteousness peers down from the heavens. The land will yield a great and plentiful harvest. God walks the earth, and righteousness prepares the way.

God will always give what is good. Let your heart be at peace.

Pray:

Teach me, my God and King,
In all things Thee to see,
And what I do in anything
To do it as for Thee.
Amen.

(From "The Elixir," George Herbert)

Ordinary Time Day 106

KARI WEST

Read: *Luke 12:13–21*

> Someone in the crowd said to him, "Teacher, tell my brother to divide the inheritance with me." But he said to him, "Man, who made me a judge or arbitrator over you?" And he said to them, "Take care, and be on your guard against all covetousness, for one's life does not consist in the abundance of his possessions." And he told them a parable, saying, "The land of a rich man produced plentifully, and he thought to himself, 'What shall I do, for I have nowhere to store my crops?' And he said, 'I will do this: I will tear down my barns and build larger ones, and there I will store all my grain and my goods. And I will say to my soul, "Soul, you have ample goods laid up for many years; relax, eat, drink, be merry."' But God said to him, 'Fool! This night your soul is required of you, and the things you have prepared, whose will they be?' So is the one who lays up treasure for himself and is not rich toward God."

Reflect:

What is the posture of your heart when you hear a command from Jesus? Is it resentment? Dismissal? Weariness? Does it feel like just another task for your to-do list?

Will you pause and consider afresh who speaks these words to you, so that you can see them for their strange and lovely potency? Christ wove each of us together and designed the deepest intricacies of our beings. He knows what our hearts, minds, and bodies need so we can grow into full humanity. He wants us to regain the birthright that we lost in the garden. His commands are some of the most solemn secrets of our flourishing: Live like *this*, for I made the world and your soul like *this*.

In response to a question about an inheritance dispute, Jesus warned his listeners, "One's life does not consist in the abundance of his possessions" (v. 15). He told the story of a rich man who poured all his energy into safeguarding his possessions and believed he had thus secured happiness for his soul. The rich man assumed that his wealth would ensure comfort and pleasure "for many years" (v. 19), but his life was cut short and his worldly treasure was immediately useless to him.

Jesus cautioned that the rich man's path was the path of the fool. The human soul was made for better things than money.

Learn instead a life of generosity, a way of being rich toward God and his creatures, and you will find a richness welling up within you, something more lasting and more satisfying. And when your soul is required of you by the Father, you won't hear a chilling rebuke like the one in this parable but instead words brimming with love and joy: *Well done.*

Pray:

Deliver us, O Lord, from the love of money, which is the root of all evil. May we value our substance, not as the medium of pride and luxury, but as affording us the means of support and usefulness; and may we guide our affairs with discretion, that we may owe no man anything, and be able to give to him that needs. Establish in us the royal law; may we love our neighbors as ourselves, and feel it, not only our duty, but our pleasure, as we have opportunity, to do good unto all men, especially unto them that are the household of faith. Amen.

(William Jay)

Ordinary Time Day 107

KARI WEST

Read: *Luke 12:22–34*

And he said to his disciples, "Therefore I tell you, do not be anxious about your life, what you will eat, nor about your body, what you will put on. For life is more than food, and the body more than clothing. Consider the ravens: they neither sow nor reap, they have neither storehouse nor barn, and yet God feeds them. Of how much more value are you than the birds! And which of you by being anxious can add a single hour to his span of life? If then you are not able to do as small a thing as that, why are you anxious about the rest? Consider the lilies, how they grow: they neither toil nor spin, yet I tell you, even Solomon in all his glory was not arrayed like one of these. But if God so clothes the grass, which is alive in the field today, and tomorrow is thrown into the oven, how much more will he clothe you, O you of little faith! And do not seek what you are to eat and what you are to drink, nor be worried. For all the nations of the world seek after these things, and your Father knows that you need them. Instead, seek his kingdom, and these things will be added to you.

"Fear not, little flock, for it is your Father's good pleasure to give you the kingdom. Sell your possessions, and give to the needy. Provide yourselves with moneybags that do not grow old, with a treasure in the heavens that does not fail, where no thief approaches and no moth destroys. For where your treasure is, there will your heart be also."

Reflect:

Anxiety can feel like a constant weight in your life, dragging on your heart as you move through your days. What if I lose my job? What if I lose my home? Will my children learn well in school this year? What if my parents get sick? Will life ever feel safe and hopeful?

What did Christ tell us to do in the midst of this torrent of anxious thoughts? Consider the ravens. God feeds them, though they don't store up provisions for themselves; and he loves you more than he loves them. Consider the lilies. God clothes them with splendor, though their lives are so brief; he loves you more than he loves them. Christ leans down close, takes us by the hand, and gently reminds us that we have a good Father who will feed us and clothe us.

Life is more than food, Jesus said: Seek the kingdom and find glory that will never fail. The Lord forged our hearts to be filled with richer fare. Instead of chewing on worry after worry after worry, Jesus urged us to remember the loving providence of God and to live a life of generosity. And as we trust in God's provision and act on that trust by openhanded living, we will store up for ourselves a treasure trove in the heavens.

As you pray, bring your anxiety to the Lord because he cares for you. Confess your knee-jerk reaction of self-sufficiency. Ponder the ravens and the lilies and ask God for a fresh awareness of his lavish, loving, perfectly timed provision for you, his cherished child.

Pray:

God, thank you that you array the lilies in splendor and that you feed the ravens from your abundant storehouses. Thank you that it is your good pleasure to give us the kingdom. Give us hearts of trust in you, for Jesus's sake. Amen.

Ordinary Time Day 108

KARI WEST

Read: *Luke 12:35–40*

"Stay dressed for action and keep your lamps burning, and be like men who are waiting for their master to come home from the wedding feast, so that they may open the door to him at once when he comes and knocks. Blessed are those servants whom the master finds awake when he comes. Truly, I say to you, he will dress himself for service and have them recline at table, and he will come and serve them. If he comes in the second watch, or in the third, and finds them awake, blessed are those servants! But know this, that if the master of the house had known at what hour the thief was coming, he would not have left his house to be broken into. You also must be ready, for the Son of Man is coming at an hour you do not expect."

Reflect:

If you love Christ, you'll want him back.

The men in this story were intently awaiting the return of their beloved master. They were straining their ears for the sound of that familiar knock. They couldn't wait to throw open the door and welcome him home. They didn't know how many more long hours of the night they would have to endure before his return, but they were ready for him.

Jesus said the Master would come back in joy, don a servant's garb, and bid those faithful followers to recline at the table, where he would serve them a feast. This parable promises a greater, almost outrageous honor that no one could have expected.

The Son of Man is like the master of the house, but he's also like a thief in the night. No one knows when he's coming. Of course, no one would leave their home if a thief were coming to steal their possessions. So in the same way, keep watch. Christ will return at an hour we do not expect.

As you pray, ask the Lord for keen ears and a longing heart. Ask that you would be like a servant who strains to hear the sound of the beloved master coming home to stay. Ask for readiness, no matter the hour, for Christ's joyful return.

Pray:

May we be united to the Savior by living faith, and bring forth daily the fruits of righteousness to the glory of your name. May we strive more and more to grow in grace, laying aside every weight, and the sin that does most easily beset us, and running with patience the race that is set before us, looking unto Jesus the author and finisher of our faith. And grant, Lord, that we may all live under a becoming conviction of the shortness and uncertainty of life, and be aware that death and eternity are at hand. May we continually bear in mind that we know not how soon we shall be called away. May we live therefore as those who wait for the coming of the Lord Jesus Christ with our loins girded and our lamps burning. Amen.

(William Wilberforce)

Ordinary Time Day 109

KARI WEST

Read: *Luke 12:57–59*

"And why do you not judge for yourselves what is right? As you go
with your accuser before the magistrate, make an effort to settle with
him on the way, lest he drag you to the judge, and the judge hand
you over to the officer, and the officer put you in prison. I tell you,
you will never get out until you have paid the very last penny."

Reflect:

Jesus never shied away from telling his listeners the truth. Here he warned
them: *Judgment is coming. You have the chance now to be reconciled. Take it! If
you don't, you will pay the full penalty.*

Can you feel the tension in this short story? There's not much time left.
The accused and the accuser are on their way to trial. Each step brings them
closer and closer to court. If they reach the judge and the sentencing, there
will be no hope of escape for the accused.

It's a loving act to warn a person when they are running out of time. The
truth is, without Jesus, we stand rightly accused before God. Romans 6:23
tells us clearly that the wages of sin is death. If we do not seek reconciliation
by trusting in the work of Christ, then we will know the judgment of God.

Christ uttered this story as he neared the end of his life. Within the
warning was a promise: We don't have to be dragged before the judge, hopeless as we face a guilty sentence. The free gift of God is eternal life in Jesus
Christ our Lord. Through his blood, Jesus has made a way for our reconciliation. Through Jesus, the penalty for our sins has already been paid.

Romans 8:1–2 proclaims the following good news: "There is therefore
now no condemnation for those who are in Christ Jesus. For the law of the
Spirit of life has set you free in Christ Jesus from the law of sin and death."
We who are in Christ Jesus have been set free!

As you pray, heed his urgent warning and consider this incredible promise. Embrace the life Jesus offers through faith. Believe in Christ and know the warm welcome of the Father, our just and merciful Judge.

Pray:

O God, gracious and merciful, give us, we entreat you, a humble trust in your mercy, and suffer not our heart to fail us. Though our sins be seven, though our sins be seventy times seven, though our sins be more in number than the hairs on our head, yet give us grace in loving penitence to cast ourselves down into the depth of your compassion. Amen.

(Christina Rossetti)

Ordinary Time Day 110
ART GOING

Read: *1 Peter 1:3–7, 13–16, 22–23*

Blessed be the God and Father of our Lord Jesus Christ! According to his great mercy, he has caused us to be born again to a living hope through the resurrection of Jesus Christ from the dead, to an inheritance that is imperishable, undefiled, and unfading, kept in heaven for you, who by God's power are being guarded through faith for a salvation ready to be revealed in the last time. In this you rejoice, though now for a little while, if necessary, you have been grieved by various trials, so that the tested genuineness of your faith—more precious than gold that perishes though it is tested by fire—may be found to result in praise and glory and honor at the revelation of Jesus Christ.

Therefore, preparing your minds for action, and being soberminded, set your hope fully on the grace that will be brought to you at the revelation of Jesus Christ. As obedient children, do not be conformed to the passions of your former ignorance, but as he who called you is holy, you also be holy in all your conduct, since it is written, "You shall be holy, for I am holy."…

Having purified your souls by your obedience to the truth for a sincere brotherly love, love one another earnestly from a pure heart, since you have been born again, not of perishable seed but of imperishable, through the living and abiding word of God.

Reflect:

Peter wrote his first letter to people scattered among the nations. They were uncertain about their future, marginalized in society, alienated in their relationships, and threatened with loss of socioeconomic standing and honor.

Despite these circumstances, Peter proclaimed a "living hope" (v. 3) to these believers, and he insisted our identity is rooted and renewed in Christ. His encouragement and challenges still speak clearly to us today, who are also aliens in an increasingly hostile world. We are:

- *People with a past:* We are "born again to a living hope" (v. 3) through Jesus's resurrection. Do we lean into our new identity?
- *People who have been transformed:* We are no longer captive to our "former ignorance" (v. 14); rather, we are called to embrace holiness. Are there places in our lives where we need to invite God's Spirit to work?
- *People with a love:* We are God's beloved children, so we can learn to love others as we are loved. What does it mean for us to "love one another earnestly from a pure heart" (v. 22)?
- *People with a purpose:* We are a people called to "declare the praises of him who called [us] out of darkness into his wonderful light" (1 Peter 2:9 NIV). Are we eager to share God's mercy and hope with others?

Jesus's resurrection gave us a radically better future than anything we could have dreamt of or imagined. It guaranteed us a new future together and a salvation to rejoice in, no matter what griefs and trials we face today. Living hope arises from being born anew through the resurrection of Jesus. Living hope comes not from surveying the world around us but from believing in the resurrection. And living hope leads to rejoicing, even when trials come.

You can't rejoice in trials unless your love has been transformed, unless your hope is in Jesus and you trust him even though you have not seen him. You possess inexpressible joy in an invisible (but risen) Christ!

As you pray, ask the Lord to kindle in you a living hope, and then beg the Spirit for joy, even in the midst of sorrow.

Pray:

May the Son of God, who is already formed in you, grow in you, so that for you he will become immeasurable, and that in you he will become laughter, exultation, the fullness of joy which no one will take from you. Amen.

(Isaac of Stella)

Ordinary Time Day 111
ART GOING

Read: *1 Peter 2:9–17, 21–25*

But you are a chosen race, a royal priesthood, a holy nation, a
people for his own possession, that you may proclaim the excellen-
cies of him who called you out of darkness into his marvelous light.
Once you were not a people, but now you are God's people; once
you had not received mercy, but now you have received mercy.

Beloved, I urge you as sojourners and exiles to abstain from the
passions of the flesh, which wage war against your soul. Keep your
conduct among the Gentiles honorable, so that when they speak
against you as evildoers, they may see your good deeds and glorify
God on the day of visitation.

Be subject for the Lord's sake to every human institution, whether
it be to the emperor as supreme, or to governors as sent by him to
punish those who do evil and to praise those who do good. For this
is the will of God, that by doing good you should put to silence
the ignorance of foolish people. Live as people who are free, not
using your freedom as a cover-up for evil, but living as servants of
God. Honor everyone. Love the brotherhood. Fear God. Honor the
emperor....

For to this you have been called, because Christ also suffered for
you, leaving you an example, so that you might follow in his steps. He
committed no sin, neither was deceit found in his mouth. When he
was reviled, he did not revile in return; when he suffered, he did not
threaten, but continued entrusting himself to him who judges justly.
He himself bore our sins in his body on the tree, that we might
die to sin and live to righteousness. By his wounds you have been
healed. For you were straying like sheep, but have now returned to
the Shepherd and Overseer of your souls.

Reflect:

Peter didn't address his friends in terms of their ancestry, social status, or
wealth, but as strangers and resident aliens, as "sojourners and exiles" (v. 11).

They existed on the sideline and were beginning to experience persecution. God sent them into a world that didn't receive the good news of the gospel and therefore rejected its messengers. Their persecution would only intensify.

If these new believers were going to be faithful witnesses, they would need to understand who they were and what their world was like. They were chosen, by the mercy of God, to be made holy by the Spirit for a particular purpose.

Christians live a double life as dual citizens: We are inhabitants of a specific place *and* citizens of God's new world. We are pointers to a new reality, a new creation still coming into being.

There is no universal blueprint for exilic living. The particulars of what it means to be a Christian exile must be worked out in each context. As exiles we are still embedded in the authority structures of the society we inhabit. We're called to submission, not separation, and we may feel the tension of our dual citizenship keenly.

But remember Peter's description in verse 9: We are also "a chosen race, a royal priesthood, a holy nation, a people for [God's] own possession" who are instructed to proclaim God's mercy. We are a people with a story to tell.

We are called to be like Jesus—following the pattern he established, walking in his footsteps, patiently bearing suffering. As you pray, pause to name your suffering, then pray for a Spirit-endowed capacity to bear it with equanimity and patient endurance. Pray that God will use you as a signpost to point others toward his heavenly kingdom.

Pray:

Hasten, O Father, the coming of your kingdom; and grant that we your servants, who now live by faith, may with joy behold your Son at his coming in glorious majesty; even Jesus Christ, our only Mediator and Advocate. Amen.

(Anglican Church in North America Book of Common Prayer)

16th Sunday of Ordinary Time

MADISON PERRY

Read: *Psalm 88:1–13*

O LORD, God of my salvation,
 I cry out day and night before you.
Let my prayer come before you;
 incline your ear to my cry!
For my soul is full of troubles,
 and my life draws near to Sheol.
I am counted among those who go down to the pit;
 I am a man who has no strength,
like one set loose among the dead,
 like the slain that lie in the grave,
like those whom you remember no more,
 for they are cut off from your hand.
You have put me in the depths of the pit,
 in the regions dark and deep.
Your wrath lies heavy upon me,
 and you overwhelm me with all your waves. *Selah*
You have caused my companions to shun me;
 you have made me a horror to them.
I am shut in so that I cannot escape;
 my eye grows dim through sorrow.
Every day I call upon you, O LORD;
 I spread out my hands to you.
Do you work wonders for the dead?
 Do the departed rise up to praise you? *Selah*
Is your steadfast love declared in the grave,
 or your faithfulness in Abaddon?
Are your wonders known in the darkness,
 or your righteousness in the land of forgetfulness?
But I, O LORD, cry to you;
 in the morning my prayer comes before you.

Reflect:

Psalm 88 is dark; it seems hopeless. What other god would accept this kind of prayer? Some faiths preach a law of attraction, where we must think positive thoughts if we are to attract positive outcomes. Others say darkness can be avoided if we mutter the right formula, jump through the right hoops, or do enough good. Why would anyone pray such depressing thoughts?

Yet the historical church has prayed Psalm 88 each morning as a reminder of death—our own deaths and the death of our Savior. Note the psalm's beginning, "O Lord, God of my salvation" (v. 1). There is no better encapsulation of who God is than this single line. God has saved us, saves us now, and will save us. We remain rooted in God even when our lives spiral downward. As the psalm leads us, we see that the weight of death is the judgment of God. As we pray, we feel death wrap itself around us, ending our prayer in darkness.

Yet for all this, God's goodness is not spent, for Christ is still with us. As surely as we begin with this psalm turning toward God, Jesus joins us there and sustains us through these profoundly heavy lines. These lines eventually end, yet we do not. For just when death thinks it has pinned us down, it finds that it no longer has hold of us because of Jesus. Jesus, the firstborn from the dead, inverts this movement of sin and death. He thrusts us up into the light, infinitely exceeding the power of death all the way through to complete and total life.

Because of the God of our salvation, we can look unflinchingly on death. Because of our victorious Savior, we can speak honestly about the fullness of sin, knowing that death's ultimate power has been defeated. Praise be to the God of heaven and earth, the God of our salvation.

Pray:

O God, who by the glorious resurrection of your Son Jesus Christ destroyed death and brought life and immortality to light: Grant that your servants, being raised with Christ, may know the strength of his presence and rejoice in his eternal glory; who with you and the Holy Spirit lives and reigns, one God, for ever and ever. Amen.

(Anglican Church in North America Book of Common Prayer)

Ordinary Time Day 113

ART GOING

Read: *1 Peter 3:8–9, 13–18*

Finally, all of you, have unity of mind, sympathy, brotherly love, a tender heart, and a humble mind. Do not repay evil for evil or reviling for reviling, but on the contrary, bless, for to this you were called, that you may obtain a blessing....

Now who is there to harm you if you are zealous for what is good? But even if you should suffer for righteousness' sake, you will be blessed. Have no fear of them, nor be troubled, but in your hearts honor Christ the Lord as holy, always being prepared to make a defense to anyone who asks you for a reason for the hope that is in you; yet do it with gentleness and respect, having a good conscience, so that, when you are slandered, those who revile your good behavior in Christ may be put to shame. For it is better to suffer for doing good, if that should be God's will, than for doing evil.

For Christ also suffered once for sins, the righteous for the unrighteous, that he might bring us to God, being put to death in the flesh but made alive in the spirit.

Reflect:

Peter knew how we yearn to be blessed. But he also knew something we must pray to learn or discover—namely, that blessing is not the presumption of privilege or the acquisition of material things. He offered startling advice in his letter: "Do not repay evil for evil or reviling for reviling, but on the contrary, bless, for to this you were called, that you may obtain a blessing" (v. 9).

Peter instructed his friends to expect blessing from God, but it was the blessing born out of suffering. In Peter's economy of salvation, blessing was related to how we respond to mistreatment.

Remember how frequently, in his first letter, Peter held up the example of Jesus's quiet and patient endurance of suffering on our behalf? He challenged us to be willing to suffer like Christ, but he also offered the comforting promise that "even if you should suffer for righteousness' sake, you will be blessed" (v. 14).

Peter wanted to remind believers that nothing in heaven or earth is more important than honoring Christ as Lord. Jesus's death and resurrection secured an eternal hope that no earthly pain could diminish, and believers can reflect his glory even in their suffering. So Peter encouraged, "Always be prepared to give an answer to everyone who asks you to give the reason for the hope that you have. But do this with gentleness and respect" (v. 15 NIV).

We usually read this instruction as a model of evangelism. But surely Peter also had in mind gentle and hopeful testimony of redemptive suffering.

Pray for the power to suffer this way, hoping in Christ.

Pray:

O God our Father, whose Son forgave his enemies while he was suffering shame and death: Strengthen those who suffer for the sake of conscience; when they are accused, save them from speaking in hate; when they are rejected, save them from bitterness; when they are imprisoned, save them from despair; and to us your servants, give grace to respect their witness and to discern the truth, that our society may be cleansed and strengthened. This we ask for the sake of Jesus Christ, our merciful and righteous Judge. Amen.

(Book of Common Prayer)

Ordinary Time Day 114
ART GOING

Read: *1 Peter 4:7–11*

> The end of all things is at hand; therefore be self-controlled and sober-minded for the sake of your prayers. Above all, keep loving one another earnestly, since love covers a multitude of sins. Show hospitality to one another without grumbling. As each has received a gift, use it to serve one another, as good stewards of God's varied grace: whoever speaks, as one who speaks oracles of God; whoever serves, as one who serves by the strength that God supplies—in order that in everything God may be glorified through Jesus Christ. To him belong glory and dominion forever and ever. Amen.

Reflect:

We are called not to separation from the world but to *submission*. Everywhere we turn, we are embedded in relationships and instructed to follow the pattern of Jesus's own humble and patient submission. We are called to suffer in the same manner as Jesus.

And now we discover another essential word in our life as God's people in the world: *stewards*—stewards of the manifold grace of God. Pause and reflect on that job description! We are called to be stewards and caretakers of this glorious grace in all its hues and shapes. The Lord of resurrection, who has launched the new creation in and among us, has entrusted to us the task of tending his gifts to and for others. In all his manifold goodness, he has distributed his unimaginably diverse gifts to us. Your gifts are not my gifts. But each of us is called to use the gifts we have received "to serve one another" (v. 10).

Gifts are for serving, not merely for having, or even enjoying. We're to give our lives away, and God has given us the means—his own gifts of grace. Some of us do this with words; others, through acts of mercy; and still others through teaching or preaching. Love binds us together, and hospitality is the open door of our lives. God is glorified when we invite others in, welcome them with their gifts, and receive them as a part of our family.

Don't miss Peter's reminder to be disciplined in our praying: "Be self-controlled and sober-minded for the sake of your prayers" (v. 7). There will be many times in our life where we feel helpless or confused about how to serve, how to make relational inroads, or how to witness. We may feel that we have no resource left but our prayers, and even our prayers may be overwhelmed by grief for our hurting world. In the darkest moments we trust that the Spirit will pray for us with sighs too deep for words. But during the other days, offering disciplined prayers for our families, friends, neighbors, and enemies is itself a precious stewardship of grace.

Imagine the extraordinary richness of a life in which your gifts are discovered, nurtured, and offered in service to others. As you pray, ask for eyes to see how you have been gifted, and pray for opportunities to give your life away.

Pray:

Almighty and eternal God, so draw our hearts to you, so guide our minds, so fill our imaginations, and so control our wills that we may be wholly yours, utterly dedicated to you. And then use us, we pray, as you will, and always to your glory and the welfare of your people. Through our Lord and Savior Jesus Christ. Amen.

(Book of Common Prayer)

Ordinary Time Day 115
ART GOING

Read: *1 Peter 5:1–11*

> So I exhort the elders among you, as a fellow elder and a witness
> of the sufferings of Christ, as well as a partaker in the glory that is
> going to be revealed: shepherd the flock of God that is among you,
> exercising oversight, not under compulsion, but willingly, as God
> would have you; not for shameful gain, but eagerly; not domi-
> neering over those in your charge, but being examples to the flock.
> And when the chief Shepherd appears, you will receive the unfading
> crown of glory. Likewise, you who are younger, be subject to the
> elders. Clothe yourselves, all of you, with humility toward one
> another, for "God opposes the proud but gives grace to the humble."
>
> Humble yourselves, therefore, under the mighty hand of God so
> that at the proper time he may exalt you, casting all your anxieties
> on him, because he cares for you. Be sober-minded; be watchful.
> Your adversary the devil prowls around like a roaring lion, seeking
> someone to devour. Resist him, firm in your faith, knowing that the
> same kinds of suffering are being experienced by your brotherhood
> throughout the world. And after you have suffered a little while, the
> God of all grace, who has called you to his eternal glory in Christ,
> will himself restore, confirm, strengthen, and establish you. To him
> be the dominion forever and ever. Amen.

Reflect:

Peter offered a strong exhortation to his elders: Be humble shepherds!

Humble shepherds. "Shepherd" is what the word *pastor* means. We all
need leaders who live as examples of Jesus-centered compassion and tenderness and who watch over us. Do you welcome oversight? Do you seek it out
from your pastor, a spiritual director, or a friend?

In our celebrity culture, it's easy for pastors to become absorbed in devel-
oping careers, acquiring followers, or "building a platform." Social media has
magnified these efforts. In light of this, we all need the kind of pastor who

recognizes that leadership is not acquiring a name but rather tending the flock entrusted to one's care. Pastors, be humble shepherds!

Though we are not all pastors, each one of us has received a calling from God. Our calling is not primarily about gifts, passions, or fulfillment; rather, our calling is to tend to those who have been entrusted to our care. We are to listen to their longings and fears, love them, and serve them as Christ served his church.

Just as he exhorted the elders, Peter also offered instructions for the rest of the believers: Stay awake! Peter warned, "Be sober-minded; be watchful. Your adversary the devil prowls around like a roaring lion, seeking someone to devour" (v. 8). His warning applies to believers today: Stay awake, stand firm in God's power, be resolute in faithfulness, and be mindful of suffering brothers and sisters in the world. Stay alert to the prowling evil one, who wants nothing more than to devour us—to seduce us into self-serving and self-promoting.

As you pray, ask for protection. Pray for your pastor and for your willingness to be pastored. And pray for the people God has entrusted to your care.

Pray:

Visit this place, O Lord, and drive far from it all snares of the enemy; let your holy angels dwell with us to preserve us in peace; and let your blessing be upon us always; through Jesus Christ our Lord. Amen.

(Anglican Church in North America Book of Common Prayer)

Ordinary Time Day 116
ART GOING

Read: *2 Peter 1:1–12*

Simeon Peter, a servant and apostle of Jesus Christ,

To those who have obtained a faith of equal standing with ours by the righteousness of our God and Savior Jesus Christ:

May grace and peace be multiplied to you in the knowledge of God and of Jesus our Lord.

His divine power has granted to us all things that pertain to life and godliness, through the knowledge of him who called us to his own glory and excellence, by which he has granted to us his precious and very great promises, so that through them you may become partakers of the divine nature, having escaped from the corruption that is in the world because of sinful desire. For this very reason, make every effort to supplement your faith with virtue, and virtue with knowledge, and knowledge with self-control, and self-control with steadfastness, and steadfastness with godliness, and godliness with brotherly affection, and brotherly affection with love. For if these qualities are yours and are increasing, they keep you from being ineffective or unfruitful in the knowledge of our Lord Jesus Christ. For whoever lacks these qualities is so nearsighted that he is blind, having forgotten that he was cleansed from his former sins. Therefore, brothers, be all the more diligent to confirm your calling and election, for if you practice these qualities you will never fall. For in this way there will be richly provided for you an entrance into the eternal kingdom of our Lord and Savior Jesus Christ.

Therefore I intend always to remind you of these qualities, though you know them and are established in the truth that you have.

Reflect:

It's always helpful to keep the big picture in view: what God wants *for*—not *from*—his people. Peter wrote that "his divine power has given us everything we need for a godly life" (v. 3 NIV).

God provides all we need for an abundant and flourishing life. To that end, he has granted to us "his precious and very great promises" (v. 4), as follows:

- Provision: We are called to Jesus's glory and excellence (v. 3) and given all that we need to obtain it.
- Power: We can forgive, speak the gospel, and be God's healing presence; we have become "partakers of the divine nature" (v. 4).
- Promises: We are born anew into hope. Jesus will return, and we will live forever with him in a new heaven and new earth. In the meantime, no one can take away our joy.

What is the ultimate goal of this provision, this power, and these promises? That we may become partakers in the divine nature, so we can become ever more like Jesus. That is God's purpose for God's people: Christlikeness.

Look at the virtues Peter called for as confirmation of our calling. Do you hear echoes of the fruit of the Spirit from Galatians 5? Life in Christ forms us and shapes us into his image. When we live like him, we begin to look more like him.

Pray now for a deeper awareness of the promises, the power, and the constant provision you have received from God.

Pray:

Keep, O Lord, your household the Church in continual godliness, that through your protection it may be free from all adversities, and devoutly serve you in good works, to the glory of your Name; through Jesus Christ our Lord, who lives and reigns with you and the Holy Spirit, one God, now and for ever. Amen.

(Anglican Church in North America Book of Common Prayer)

Ordinary Time Day 117
ART GOING

Read: *2 Peter 2:1–3, 10–19*

But false prophets also arose among the people, just as there will be false teachers among you, who will secretly bring in destructive heresies, even denying the Master who bought them, bringing upon themselves swift destruction. And many will follow their sensuality, and because of them the way of truth will be blasphemed. And in their greed they will exploit you with false words. . . .

Bold and willful, they do not tremble as they blaspheme the glorious ones, whereas angels, though greater in might and power, do not pronounce a blasphemous judgment against them before the Lord. But these, like irrational animals, creatures of instinct, born to be caught and destroyed, blaspheming about matters of which they are ignorant, will also be destroyed in their destruction, suffering wrong as the wage for their wrongdoing. They count it pleasure to revel in the daytime. They are blots and blemishes, reveling in their deceptions, while they feast with you. They have eyes full of adultery, insatiable for sin. They entice unsteady souls. They have hearts trained in greed. Accursed children! Forsaking the right way, they have gone astray. They have followed the way of Balaam, the son of Beor, who loved gain from wrongdoing, but was rebuked for his own transgression; a speechless donkey spoke with human voice and restrained the prophet's madness.

These are waterless springs and mists driven by a storm. For them the gloom of utter darkness has been reserved. For, speaking loud boasts of folly, they entice by sensual passions of the flesh those who are barely escaping from those who live in error. They promise them freedom, but they themselves are slaves of corruption. For whatever overcomes a person, to that he is enslaved.

Reflect:

We need no reminder that there are false prophets and deceptive teachers who bring swift destruction down on themselves and their ministries, for their stories sadly abound. Leaders who have wielded global influence fall hard, leaving a wake of disheartened followers and, too often, damaged victims, not to mention the flood of defectors from the faith.

Peter called them "waterless springs" (v. 17), who "promise … freedom, but they themselves are slaves of corruption" (v. 19). We must pray fervently that we will not be deceived by such folly or be sucked in by false promises; we must pray for discerning minds and hearts.

But where does such discernment come from? Peter wrote, "I want you to recall the words spoken in the past by the holy prophets and the command given by our Lord and Savior" (2 Peter 3:2 NIV). Jesus gave this same encouragement to his disciples before his ascension: "I will not leave you as orphans; I will come to you.…But the Helper, the Holy Spirit, whom the Father will send in my name, he will teach you all things" (John 14:18, 26).

There is only one sure way to maintain our faith and spot false teaching: Read the Scriptures! Meditate on God's Word and let it shape your vision. We are perennial amnesiacs who need daily reminders of the promises, the presence and power of Jesus's own Spirit, our calling as believers, and the grace we are given to follow Christ.

How we live as we wait for the coming of the Lord matters. Peter charged us to live not casually or presumptuously but in hopeful anticipation of the new heaven and the new earth. In the meantime, we must not be carried away by the empty promises of false teachers but rather "grow in the grace and knowledge of our Lord and Savior Jesus Christ" (2 Peter 3:18).

Pray:

Grant us, Lord, not to be anxious about earthly things, but to love things heavenly; and even now, as we live among things that are passing away, to hold fast to those that shall endure; through Jesus Christ our Lord, who lives and reigns with you and the Holy Spirit, one God, for ever and ever. Amen.

(Anglican Church in North America Book of Common Prayer)

Ordinary Time Day 118
SALLY BREEDLOVE

Read: *Matthew 13:44–46*

"The kingdom of heaven is like treasure hidden in a field, which a man found and covered up. Then in his joy he goes and sells all that he has and buys that field.

"Again, the kingdom of heaven is like a merchant in search of fine pearls, who, on finding one pearl of great value, went and sold all that he had and bought it."

Reflect:

The kingdom of heaven was Matthew's focus as he wrote his biography of Jesus. He wanted to proclaim that Jesus is King of the cosmos. The kingdom of heaven is present now, in this world, wherever people recognize and follow Christ as King.

This is a radical truth! Life can be impossibly hard; it disappoints and confuses us. Every one of us has wondered, *If God is King, why doesn't he fix things now? What must he be like if he lets such terrible things happen?* We might wonder if there really is a God.

Jesus didn't defend or explain God's kingdom. Instead, he painted pictures to help us recognize that God's kingdom is real, even in still-shattered world. It's like a treasure hidden in an ordinary grain field; we have to buy the whole field in order to obtain the treasure. It's like an exquisite luminous pearl for which we've searched our whole lives; when we find it, it will cost us everything we have.

We think the question is: "Where is God's kingdom in this world of conflict, confusion, and economic pain?" But Jesus offers a different perspective. He wants to know if we are paying attention and if we are willing to pay the price.

Indeed, are we seeing only weeds and missing the good grain? Do we see the world as nothing more than a muddy, uncultivated mess? Are we disappointed because the church seems irreparable, or do we trust that God will sort it out in the end? Does gaining the kingdom feel like too much work; is it too costly?

Are we too bored, too sure of ourselves, too hurt, too angry, or too exhausted to recognize the treasure that can be ours if we trust that God really is at work? Are we willing to let Christ be King, and to search for the signs that God still reigns on earth?

As you pray, ask God to open your eyes to his work in the world. Then commit yourself again to acknowledging Christ as your King. Commit yourself to the work he wants to do in you. Commit yourself to the work he wants to do through you. Count the cost, pay the price, and pray.

Pray:

Almighty Father, enter our hearts, and so fill us with your love, that forsaking all evil desires, we may embrace you, our only good. Show unto us, for your mercies' sake, O Lord our God, what you are unto us. Say onto our souls, "I am your salvation." So speak that we may hear. Our hearts are before you; open our ears; let us hasten after your voice, and take hold of you. Amen.

(Augustine)

17th Sunday of Ordinary Time

KARI WEST

Read: *Psalm 89:20–29*

"I have found David, my servant;
　with my holy oil I have anointed him,
so that my hand shall be established with him;
　my arm also shall strengthen him.
The enemy shall not outwit him;
　the wicked shall not humble him.
I will crush his foes before him
　and strike down those who hate him.
My faithfulness and my steadfast love shall be with him,
　and in my name shall his horn be exalted.
I will set his hand on the sea
　and his right hand on the rivers.
He shall cry to me, 'You are my Father,
　my God, and the Rock of my salvation.'
And I will make him the firstborn,
　the highest of the kings of the earth.
My steadfast love I will keep for him forever,
　and my covenant will stand firm for him.
I will establish his offspring forever
　and his throne as the days of the heavens."

Reflect:

Why should we care about a poem about a long-dead king from a distant time?

Scholars understand King David of the Old Testament as a forerunner of Christ. Psalms like these—though truly a promise to David—find their ultimate fulfillment in Jesus. He would become the most exalted King on the earth, his covenant will never fail, and his line and his throne will be established throughout all the ages.

This is a beautiful and important psalm because Christ's victory is our victory. Christ's supremacy and exaltation are what our hearts desire in their inmost places. Here God promised that what we most long for would come to pass—the everlasting reign of King Jesus. Nothing will stop God's plan from unfolding in the fullness of time.

Even now we share in Christ's righteousness; a miracle of our salvation is that—through the death and resurrection of Jesus—the Lord sees all believers in the same way that he sees his resurrected Son. God promised his faithful love would always be with Christ, so we can be confident that his faithful love is always with us as well. We are his beloved ones, hidden in Jesus.

As you pray, meditate on the surety of Christ's present and coming kingdom and kingship. Ask the Lord for specific ways Christ's supremacy can encourage you to live faithfully and joyfully as you wait. Proclaim with David, "You are my Father, my God, and the Rock of my salvation" (v. 26). And above all, rest in God's forever love for you, his child.

Pray:

Lord God, as we turn to you in purity of heart, we give you our highest and most abundant thanks, as best as we are able in our frailty. Our whole mind prays for your unmatched goodness, that by your power you would drive out the enemy from our thoughts and deeds. Father Almighty, enlarge our faith, direct our minds, and help us focus our thoughts on your kingdom. And, in the end, bring us safe to your place of endless blessings, through your Son Jesus Christ. Amen.

(Augustine)

Ordinary Time Day 120
ELIZABETH GATEWOOD

Read: *Matthew 14:10–20*

[Herod] sent and had John beheaded in the prison, and his head was brought on a platter and given to the girl, and she brought it to her mother. And his disciples came and took the body and buried it, and they went and told Jesus.

Now when Jesus heard this, he withdrew from there in a boat to a desolate place by himself. But when the crowds heard it, they followed him on foot from the towns. When he went ashore he saw a great crowd, and he had compassion on them and healed their sick. Now when it was evening, the disciples came to him and said, "This is a desolate place, and the day is now over; send the crowds away to go into the villages and buy food for themselves." But Jesus said, "They need not go away; you give them something to eat." They said to him, "We have only five loaves here and two fish." And he said, "Bring them here to me." Then he ordered the crowds to sit down on the grass, and taking the five loaves and the two fish, he looked up to heaven and said a blessing. Then he broke the loaves and gave them to the disciples, and the disciples gave them to the crowds. And they all ate and were satisfied. And they took up twelve baskets full of the broken pieces left over.

Reflect:

Herod served up the grotesque at his banquet. He had wanted to avoid killing John the Baptist so as not to arouse the anger of the people who considered John a prophet. But caught in the web of an adulterous relationship with his sister-in-law and a swaggering promise, Herod kept his word in order to impress his guests. He offered John's head on a platter. His narcissism, violence, and insecurity leap from the pages of Scripture.

We have seen his type before. We have been invited to his banquet. Though its pleasures rarely last beyond the morning, its destruction endures.

But Jesus offered a different sort of banquet. In grief over the beheading of his cousin John, Jesus went away. He didn't compete for attention, sponge up influence, or grab power; he sought solitude.

A great crowd gathered around him all the same. The multitudes pursued Jesus because they were hungry—hungry for this person who emptied his power and took the form of a servant. They quite literally followed him because they wanted to be in his presence. Despite his mourning, Jesus had compassion on them and healed their sick (v. 14). He met their physical and spiritual needs.

Jesus's banquet was an unexpected feast in the wilderness. At his banquet, Jesus served real food and real teaching. There was abundance for all. Jesus himself was the feast.

As you pray, consider where you are feasting on the fare of destruction instead of on the nourishing banquet of Christ. Pray that the Lord would increase your appetite for his Word and his presence.

Pray:

Father, Son, and Holy Spirit, so often we are enticed by the banquets served up by our world, banquets of showy power, cheap entertainment, and grotesque spectacle. Yet you invite us to taste the simple fare of your body and blood, broken for us. Let us hunger for this banquet that will transform us and enliven us. Thank you that through this banquet, you unite us to yourself and your body, the church. Amen.

Ordinary Time Day 121

ELIZABETH GATEWOOD

Read: *Matthew 15:1–8, 10–20*

Then Pharisees and scribes came to Jesus from Jerusalem and said, "Why do your disciples break the tradition of the elders? For they do not wash their hands when they eat." He answered them, "And why do you break the commandment of God for the sake of your tradition? For God commanded, 'Honor your father and your mother,' and, 'Whoever reviles father or mother must surely die.' But you say, 'If anyone tells his father or his mother, "What you would have gained from me is given to God," he need not honor his father.' So for the sake of your tradition you have made void the word of God. You hypocrites! Well did Isaiah prophesy of you, when he said:

"'This people honors me with their lips,
but their heart is far from me.'" . . .

And he called the people to him and said to them, "Hear and understand: it is not what goes into the mouth that defiles a person, but what comes out of the mouth; this defiles a person." Then the disciples came and said to him, "Do you know that the Pharisees were offended when they heard this saying?" He answered, "Every plant that my heavenly Father has not planted will be rooted up. Let them alone; they are blind guides. And if the blind lead the blind, both will fall into a pit." But Peter said to him, "Explain the parable to us." And he said, "Are you also still without understanding? Do you not see that whatever goes into the mouth passes into the stomach and is expelled? But what comes out of the mouth proceeds from the heart, and this defiles a person. For out of the heart come evil thoughts, murder, adultery, sexual immorality, theft, false witness, slander. These are what defile a person."

Reflect:

The Pharisees asked a version of this question to Jesus: "Did you wash your hands before dinner?" They ended up in deep waters, in a theological debate with Jesus. But Jesus was not worried about germ transmission; he was worried about heart contamination.

The disease that the Pharisees had wasn't transmitted by touching the wrong surfaces; it was a disease that originated in their hearts. It was the disease of spiritual idolatry. They had begun to worship their tradition and had ceased to be in relationship with the living God. Jesus went so far as to say that their tradition-worship had nullified the Word of God. Jesus insisted that holiness is not about having the right soap or the right washing process.

Do we, like the Pharisees, sometimes try to become holy from the outside in through idolatrous traditions or misguided spiritual practices?

What is the answer? How do we root out the evil thoughts that defile us? Jesus wants people to turn their attention to the heart, to be holy and clean from the inside out. But how can we become holy and clean from the inside out?

Jesus introduced plant imagery in this passage, noting that the weeds of tradition-worshippers would be uprooted, but the plants lovingly established and tended by the Father would remain.

The way to be holy and fruitful is to be a vine planted by the Father, connected to the Son, and nourished and enlivened by the Holy Spirit. This was beyond what the Pharisees could imagine; yet for us, the invitation is clear. We bear fruit by remaining in Christ.

As you pray, consider where you are captured by religious or social conventions and how these things might be cutting you off from worshipping the triune God.

Pray:

Father, Son, and Holy Spirit, often we squabble among ourselves about the right ways to do things. We might worship tradition or eschew it, and in either case, we often miss you. Yet you are in our midst, showing us how to be clean from the inside out and inviting us to a relationship with the living God. Please lovingly graft us to Jesus Christ, the True Vine. Amen.

Ordinary Time Day 122

ELIZABETH GATEWOOD

Read: *Matthew 15:30–36*

And great crowds came to him, bringing with them the lame, the blind, the crippled, the mute, and many others, and they put them at his feet, and he healed them, so that the crowd wondered, when they saw the mute speaking, the crippled healthy, the lame walking, and the blind seeing. And they glorified the God of Israel.

Then Jesus called his disciples to him and said, "I have compassion on the crowd because they have been with me now three days and have nothing to eat. And I am unwilling to send them away hungry, lest they faint on the way." And the disciples said to him, "Where are we to get enough bread in such a desolate place to feed so great a crowd?" And Jesus said to them, "How many loaves do you have?" They said, "Seven, and a few small fish." And directing the crowd to sit down on the ground, he took the seven loaves and the fish, and having given thanks he broke them and gave them to the disciples, and the disciples gave them to the crowds.

Reflect:

Jesus had a big agenda: to usher in salvation for the healing and redemption of the world. But Jesus attended to the crowds right in front of him—the mute, the crippled, the lame, and the blind.

He also attended to the hungry. He had a mass of people in front of him, hungry for bread and for something they couldn't quite put their fingers on.

Jesus didn't give them a comprehensive explanation or a sign from heaven, despite their desire for one. Jesus offered them presence, healing, compassion, and nourishment. Ultimately, he offered them himself.

It is Ordinary Time. And indeed, perhaps your days feel all too ordinary. They are filled with tedious, repetitive, seemingly insignificant tasks: slogging through emails, changing diapers, waiting in carpool lines, serving meals, navigating bureaucracy, or managing small tasks that seem disconnected from a meaningful whole. Perhaps you long to do work of importance, to move the needle toward achieving personal goals, or to heal the systemic and personal ills and injustices of your community.

As you pray, consider what you might learn from Jesus—very God and very human—who took time to attend to the people and things in front of him. Consider where you may be missing the invitation to attend to the smaller things in your life. What do you begrudge because it feels beneath you? With whom do you become impatient because your agenda is interrupted?

Pray:

Heavenly Father, we want to be important. We passionately care about certain issues, businesses, subjects, places, and people. And we have been told that we can make a difference. Yet you show us a way of meekness. Your agenda isn't fulfilled by executing a strategic plan but by loving and attending to the things in front of you. Refine our attention. Give us humility to attend to the needs that you have placed in front of us. Amen.

Ordinary Time Day 123
ELIZABETH GATEWOOD

Read: *Matthew 16:13–24*

Now when Jesus came into the district of Caesarea Philippi, he asked his disciples, "Who do people say that the Son of Man is?" And they said, "Some say John the Baptist, others say Elijah, and others Jeremiah or one of the prophets." He said to them, "But who do you say that I am?" Simon Peter replied, "You are the Christ, the Son of the living God." And Jesus answered him, "Blessed are you, Simon Bar-Jonah! For flesh and blood has not revealed this to you, but my Father who is in heaven. And I tell you, you are Peter, and on this rock I will build my church, and the gates of hell shall not prevail against it. I will give you the keys of the kingdom of heaven, and whatever you bind on earth shall be bound in heaven, and whatever you loose on earth shall be loosed in heaven." Then he strictly charged the disciples to tell no one that he was the Christ.

From that time Jesus began to show his disciples that he must go to Jerusalem and suffer many things from the elders and chief priests and scribes, and be killed, and on the third day be raised. And Peter took him aside and began to rebuke him, saying, "Far be it from you, Lord! This shall never happen to you." But he turned and said to Peter, "Get behind me, Satan! You are a hindrance to me. For you are not setting your mind on the things of God, but on the things of man."

Then Jesus told his disciples, "If anyone would come after me, let him deny himself and take up his cross and follow me."

Reflect:

In the course of Jesus's ministry, people struggled to understand who he was and what he was about. The disciples and the Pharisees constantly attempted to tame Jesus and fashion him to fit their preconceived categories. They wanted a prophet who conformed to their experience and expectations, but Jesus continually resisted their pigeonholing.

Peter understood. He didn't seek to explain Jesus; he simply proclaimed him: "You are the Christ" (v. 16). Our understanding of God comes not from slotting him into our existing categories for deity but from heavenly revelation.

Even after this earth-shattering proclamation, Jesus desired hiddenness. Perhaps he didn't want throngs of people following him for the wrong reasons, projecting their agendas and hopes onto him. And even after his moment of clarity, Peter got things wrong. He rebuked Jesus when Jesus predicted his own death. But Jesus was quick to instruct his disciples that following this Messiah means sacrifice, not glory. It means God's masterful plan, not human agendas.

As you pray, remember that you are in the presence of the living God. Take a moment to be still before God.

Pray:

Father, Son, and Holy Spirit, you are the living God. We confess that so often we approach you with our own agendas and plans. We slot you into our categories of "deity" and decline your invitation for relationship with the living God. Forgive us. Let our idolatry and our agendas for you fade away. Let us joyfully proclaim, "You are the Christ, the Son of God," Give us the courage to follow Jesus Christ, who takes us not on a path of glory but on a path to the cross. Amen.

Ordinary Time Day 124
WILLA KANE

Read: *Matthew 20:25–28*

But Jesus called them to him and said, "You know that the rulers of the Gentiles lord it over them, and their great ones exercise authority over them. It shall not be so among you. But whoever would be great among you must be your servant, and whoever would be first among you must be your slave, even as the Son of Man came not to be served but to serve, and to give his life as a ransom for many."

Reflect:

Does our list of heroes need to change? Instead of admiring sports figures or performers, politicians or CEOs, should we instead learn to value and respect those who serve their neighbors at great cost to themselves?

Jesus is the epitome of true greatness; he came not to be served but to serve, and he gave up his life for others.

Christ turned our human understanding of greatness upside down. If we want our lives to look like Jesus's, then we, too, need this great reversal in our thinking about purpose and position.

What would Jesus do if he were to walk in the flesh in our world today? Would he head up a large church or work at a rescue shelter? Would we see him on prime-time television, or would he be chatting with the children at the elementary school where he was a teacher? Whether he was a hospital's CEO or a sanitation worker, he would serve the least and the lost.

Is there a way you are being called to let go of narrow self-interest and small ambitions to extend grace beyond the circle of those you know and trust? As we lay down our lives for others, we become conduits of Christ's love to a world that is lost and dying.

Pause to think about those you know who serve selflessly. Thank God for them. Ask Jesus to give you a servant's heart, to fill you with compassion for those around you. Pray that we would be willingly upended by the gospel and that we would joyfully give our lives away in service to others, empowered by the Spirit of Christ as we follow his example.

"Whoever wants to be great must become a servant. Whoever wants to be first among you must be your slave. That is what the Son of Man has done: He came to serve, not be served—and then to give away his life in exchange for the many who are held hostage" (Matthew 20:26–28 MSG).

Pray:

Lord, high and holy, meek and lowly, You have brought me to the Valley of Vision, where I live in the depths but see You in the heights; hemmed in by mountains of sin I behold Your glory. Let me learn by paradox that the way down is the way up, that to be low is to be high, that the broken heart is the healed heart, that the contrite spirit is the rejoicing spirit, that the repenting soul is the victorious soul, that to have nothing is to possess all, that to bear the cross is to wear the crown, that to give is to receive, that the valley is the place of vision. Lord, in the daytime stars can be seen from deepest wells, and the deeper the wells the brighter Your stars shine; let me find Your light in my darkness, Your life in my death, Your joy in my sorrow, Your grace in my sin, Your riches in my poverty, Your glory in my valley. Amen.

(The Valley of Vision)

Ordinary Time Day 125
KARI WEST

Read: *Matthew 22:34–40*

But when the Pharisees heard that he had silenced the Sadducees, they gathered together. And one of them, a lawyer, asked him a question to test him. "Teacher, which is the great commandment in the Law?" And he said to him, "You shall love the Lord your God with all your heart and with all your soul and with all your mind. This is the great and first commandment. And a second is like it: You shall love your neighbor as yourself. On these two commandments depend all the Law and the Prophets."

Reflect:

Here again a religious leader was testing Christ. But this time, Jesus gave a direct answer to his question, though it was not asked out of a desire to understand. We can almost picture this man asking his question and then sitting back, arms folded, ready to weigh Christ's response and judge his character accordingly.

But Jesus offered an answer that had sifted souls for centuries. He laid two commandments at the feet of this teacher, so simple—and yet profound enough that we will never fully delve the depths of these few words: "Love God with all you are and love your neighbor likewise."

As you come to pray, what stirs in you as you read these two greatest of commandments? Do they simply slip out of your sight and mind, too well-worn by familiarity for you to grasp their profundity?

Ask the Lord for fresh insight into these commands. Do they stir up guilt or perhaps desperation within you? How could you ever love God with all your heart, soul, mind, and strength? How could you ever suspend your own navel-gazing long enough to love your neighbor?

Take your feelings of inadequacy to the Lord, and with Saint Augustine pray that God will command what he will and grant what he commands.

Most of all, come to Christ and thank him that he has fulfilled these two vast and paramount commandments. He has loved the Lord God with everything, and he has loved all his neighbors perfectly, including you.

Come and partake of his righteousness through the free gift of salvation.

Pray:

May peace and prosperity, friendship and faith always flourish in this neighborhood and city. Fill my neighbors' troubles with compassion, Lord, so they may exchange joy for mourning, and beauty for ashes. So that those who lament may rejoice with you, and that at length you may share with them the security and joy of the city of God, the heavenly Jerusalem, where no flames will be felt except those of love. In the meantime, may our eyes be lifted up to heaven, in the humble hope and fervent prayer for those around us, that true Christian faith would spread throughout the entire world. And may that faith prevail in our own hearts, that we may faithfully practice and grow in you. Amen.

(Philip Doddridge)

18th Sunday of Ordinary Time
KARI WEST

Read: *Psalm 106:36–47*

They served their idols,
    which became a snare to them.
They sacrificed their sons
    and their daughters to the demons;
they poured out innocent blood,
    the blood of their sons and daughters,
whom they sacrificed to the idols of Canaan,
    and the land was polluted with blood.
Thus they became unclean by their acts,
    and played the whore in their deeds.
Then the anger of the LORD was kindled against his people,
    and he abhorred his heritage;
he gave them into the hand of the nations,
    so that those who hated them ruled over them.
Their enemies oppressed them,
    and they were brought into subjection under their power.
Many times he delivered them,
    but they were rebellious in their purposes
    and were brought low through their iniquity.
Nevertheless, he looked upon their distress,
    when he heard their cry.
For their sake he remembered his covenant,
    and relented according to the abundance of his steadfast love.
He caused them to be pitied
    by all those who held them captive.
Save us, O LORD our God,
    and gather us from among the nations,
that we may give thanks to your holy name
    and glory in your praise.

Reflect:

God called the Israelites to be set apart and to show the world a wholly different way to live. His laws for his people were meant to demonstrate his holiness and to portray a better way to be human

Instead, God's people chose to conform to the cultures around them, ultimately turning to the most vicious sort of idol worship—sacrificing their own infant boys and girls to demons on the Canaanite altars. The psalmist used graphic language: "they poured out innocent blood, the blood of their sons and daughters" (v. 38), they "played the whore in their deeds" (v. 39).

Perhaps we are tempted to sit in judgment of the Israelites. How could they have done such a thing? How could they have descended to the point of performing such horrific deeds? How had they failed so devastatingly?

But the truth is, our hearts are terribly powerful things, able to bear much good fruit when cleansed by Christ's blood and empowered by his Spirit but also capable of the darkest depravity when twisted and corrupted by idolatry.

What we give ourselves to in worship matters so very much. But what matters even more is what the psalmist said about God. God didn't forget his covenant; he returned and rescued his people again, pouring out his mercy on his stubborn people. His immense love led him to Golgotha, where he finally freed our idolatrous hearts once and for all.

As you pray, ask for fresh conviction to know where idolatry has taken hold in your soul. Confess and receive his perfect mercy. Rejoice in his name.

Pray:

What gratitude is justly due from me a sinner, who has been brought from darkness into light, and, I trust, from the pursuit of earthly things to the prime love of things above! O God, purify my heart still more by your grace. Quicken my dead soul, and purify me by your Spirit, that I may be changed from glory to glory, and be made even here in some degree to resemble my heavenly Father. Amen.

(William Wilberforce)

Ordinary Time Day 127
MADISON PERRY

Read: *Hebrews 1:1–4*

> Long ago, at many times and in many ways, God spoke to our
> fathers by the prophets, but in these last days he has spoken to us by
> his Son, whom he appointed the heir of all things, through whom
> also he created the world. He is the radiance of the glory of God and
> the exact imprint of his nature, and he upholds the universe by the
> word of his power. After making purification for sins, he sat down
> at the right hand of the Majesty on high, having become as much
> superior to angels as the name he has inherited is more excellent
> than theirs.

Reflect:

Hundreds of years ago, people aspired to master all fields of knowledge. They
diligently studied philosophy alongside biology, astronomy alongside poetry,
business alongside music. A mature mind would hold a working knowledge
of most areas of learning.

Today, we live in an infinitely more complex world. Everywhere we turn,
we are out of our depth; very few people can explain how water treatment
works, how a person falls in love, or why the gold standard in currency
matters.

The writer of the letter to the Hebrews asserted something striking: Jesus
Christ is at the heart of the universe. When it is all said and done, all matters
practical and beautiful are summed up in him. You can contemplate nothing
richer than the words and person of Jesus Christ. Through the Son and in
the Spirit, God the Father created everything. The Son's power upholds the
universe.

This should move us to worship and to love. If the God we love is
upholding everything, then every person and every dimension of this reality
deserves our steady and affectionate attention.

Praise God—Father, Son, and Holy Spirit. Lift up the name of Jesus Christ where you are, calling to mind the breadth and depth of his reign. Ask that God would protect your heart from worshipping false gods. Ask that God would enliven your heart so that you will love every square inch of his creation and every person made in his image.

Pray:

Glory to you, Lord God of our fathers;
you are worthy of praise; glory to you.
Glory to you for the radiance of your holy Name;
we will praise you and highly exalt you for ever.
Glory to you in the splendor of your temple;
on the throne of your majesty, glory to you.
Glory to you, seated between the Cherubim;
we will praise you and highly exalt you for ever.
Glory to you, beholding the depths;
in the high vault of heaven, glory to you.
Glory to you, Father, Son, and Holy Spirit;
we will praise you and highly exalt you for ever.
Amen.

(Benedictus es, Domine)

Ordinary Time Day 128

MADISON PERRY

Read: *Hebrews 2:1–8*

Therefore we must pay much closer attention to what we have heard, lest we drift away from it. For since the message declared by angels proved to be reliable, and every transgression or disobedience received a just retribution, how shall we escape if we neglect such a great salvation? It was declared at first by the Lord, and it was attested to us by those who heard, while God also bore witness by signs and wonders and various miracles and by gifts of the Holy Spirit distributed according to his will.

For it was not to angels that God subjected the world to come, of which we are speaking. It has been testified somewhere,

"What is man, that you are mindful of him,
or the son of man, that you care for him?
You made him for a little while lower than the angels;
you have crowned him with glory and honor,
putting everything in subjection under his feet."

Reflect:

The writer of Hebrews raised a hard possibility: We may neglect the great salvation offered in Christ and drift away from it. King David's great declaration in Psalm 51:12 had a similar sense of urgency and clarity: "Restore to me the joy of your salvation."

The remedy to this danger? This passage in Hebrews is straightforward in what it recommends that we do: "Pay much closer attention to what we have heard" (v. 1).

How do we pay close attention? The book of Hebrews is a long meditation on the person and work of Jesus Christ. It is persistently prayerful, and the author frequently paused to rehearse psalms and hymns. He focused on God's loving care for his people and recited David's praise, "What is man, that you are mindful of him, or the son of man, that you care for him?" (v. 6; Psalm 8:4).

Is prayer a nourishing activity for you? Are you feasting on your salvation in prayer?

Return to the Author of your salvation, the Perfecter of your faith. Even where you are weak, if you acknowledge him, his faithfulness will overcome your faltering. If you have lost sight of the radiance of God's glory in the face of Christ, ask him to reveal himself. If you have forgotten your need of a Savior, if you have lost an appetite for salvation, confess these things as well. Be patient if the growth of your faith is slow. Be humble and grateful as you begin to taste new life.

Pray:

Have mercy on me, O God,
according to your steadfast love;
according to your abundant mercy
blot out my transgressions.
Wash me thoroughly from my iniquity,
and cleanse me from my sin!
Amen.

(Psalm 51:1–2)

Ordinary Time Day 129
MATT HOEHN

Read: *Hebrews 3:12–15*

Take care, brothers, lest there be in any of you an evil, unbelieving heart, leading you to fall away from the living God. But exhort one another every day, as long as it is called "today," that none of you may be hardened by the deceitfulness of sin. For we have come to share in Christ, if indeed we hold our original confidence firm to the end. As it is said,

"Today, if you hear his voice,
do not harden your hearts as in the rebellion."

Reflect:

Have you ever gone through a prolonged season when you are unable to exercise according to your normal pattern? During such times, muscle groups that have taken years to develop can atrophy quickly.

In today's Scripture reading, the author of Hebrews issued a stark warning against allowing our most important muscle—the heart—to atrophy. The neglect of the heart leads to the direst of all outcomes: "fall[ing] away from the living God" (v. 12).

The atrophy of the heart isn't a passive process as it is in other muscle groups. A corrosive agent actively fuels this process: "the deceitfulness of sin" (v. 13). The heart has no neutral gear; it is always either being strengthened in the faith or withering under the effects of unchecked sin.

How can we fight this atrophy of the heart? The answer is counterintuitive. It is not to work on our hearts harder or to apply some new technique to them; rather, it is to "hold our original confidence firm to the end" (v. 14). The confidence referred to is the confidence of faith—faith in what Christ has done on our behalf in his perfect incarnate life, his atoning death, and his resurrection to the right hand of the Father. It is not confidence in our own innate capacity to repair our hearts. Remembering what Christ has done for us and holding on to faith are the exercises that keep our hearts from atrophying.

We're not isolated or alone in this. We must "exhort one another" (v. 13) in this process through being our brother's or sister's keeper, by sharpening others, and by being sharpened by them. Self-exertion is futile when it comes to strengthening our hearts. Remembering Christ, holding fast to him, and joining in Christ-centered community is the regimen for a healthy heart.

As you pray, open your heart to God. Ask him to strengthen you in the virtues of faith and perseverance and invite him to work in any areas where your heart is directed toward something other than him.

Pray:

Heavenly Father, strengthen my faith in your Son Jesus Christ. Help my unbelief and soften my heart in areas where it has hardened. Grant me the ability to persevere to the end, that I may enter the joy of your presence in the company of all the saints. Amen.

Ordinary Time Day 130
MATT HOEHN

Read: *Hebrews 4:8–13*

> For if Joshua had given them rest, God would not have spoken of another day later on. So then, there remains a Sabbath rest for the people of God, for whoever has entered God's rest has also rested from his works as God did from his.
>
> Let us therefore strive to enter that rest, so that no one may fall by the same sort of disobedience. For the word of God is living and active, sharper than any two-edged sword, piercing to the division of soul and of spirit, of joints and of marrow, and discerning the thoughts and intentions of the heart. And no creature is hidden from his sight, but all are naked and exposed to the eyes of him to whom we must give account.

Reflect:

When you imagine being cut or pierced by a sharp object, what's the first image that comes to your mind? Surely it's not a pleasant one. Whether it's the minor paper cut you received last week or that slice on your finger you got while chopping vegetables, the thought of a cut from a sharp object leads to recoil and squeamishness.

But there is a notable exception to this desire to recoil. If you've ever badly broken a bone or had a serious internal condition, you know the experience of undergoing surgery firsthand. In this instance, the cut of the surgeon's blade is desired; it's an act of compassionate care in repairing what is broken or excising what is unhealthy inside us.

According to the author of Hebrews, God's Word is a form of spiritual surgery. When we spend time communing with God by reading his Word, Scripture operates on us like an active surgical blade. It makes an incision into the hard layers of our hearts, it renews and repairs what is broken inside us, it cuts out the unhealthy growth of sin and disordered desires, and it ultimately leads to health and rest.

We do not simply read the Bible; God's Word also reads us by "discerning the thoughts and intentions of the heart" (v. 12), leading to repentance and true communion with the Father.

As you bow your head, let the Word of God give direction to the words you offer back to God in prayer. Receive God's Scripture as a living and active gift to you today. Rest in the tender care of your heavenly Father.

Pray:

Gracious God and most merciful Father, you have granted us the rich and precious jewel of your holy Word: Assist us with your Spirit, that the same Word may be written in our hearts to our everlasting comfort, to reform us, to renew us according to your own image, to build us up and edify us into the perfect dwelling place of your Christ, sanctifying and increasing in us all heavenly virtues; grant this, O heavenly Father, for Jesus Christ's sake. Amen.

(Anglican Church in North America Book of Common Prayer)

Ordinary Time Day 131
MATT HOEHN

Read: *Hebrews 4:14–16*

    Since then we have a great high priest who has passed through the heavens, Jesus, the Son of God, let us hold fast our confession. For we do not have a high priest who is unable to sympathize with our weaknesses, but one who in every respect has been tempted as we are, yet without sin. Let us then with confidence draw near to the throne of grace, that we may receive mercy and find grace to help in time of need.

Reflect:

Loneliness can be one of the most despair-inducing of all experiences. The feeling of isolation, the sense that no one could possibly understand what we're going through, is among the most difficult lived realities of the human condition.

The feeling of being without connection to others is sometimes related to besetting sin patterns. We feel the pain of our loneliness as our shame plagues us. We think, *If anyone knew about my struggles, they would turn away from me. I'd be exposed and devastated.* So we choose isolation; it's the price we pay to keep parts of our lives hidden.

The Lord God sees all. He knows everything about us, even the things we hide. The good news of the gospel is that God doesn't look on our besetting sin patterns and recoil from us or reject us out of disgust. Actually, precisely the opposite is true: He sent his Son out of love to assume our human nature, to become familiar with our condition, and to redeem us by his perfect incarnate life, atoning death, and victorious resurrection.

We don't have a God who is removed from our fears, our temptations, or our feelings of isolation. We have a God who took on human flesh to calm our fears, to experience our temptations, and thereby to bring us out of the darkness of isolation and into the light of truth.

Because of Jesus, we can draw near to God, not with fearful trepidation but with confidence in the goodness of his grace and in the efficacy of his abundant mercy to forgive.

As you pray, invite the Lord to enter into the hidden and isolated parts of your heart. Meditate on the incarnate humanity of Jesus Christ, who knows temptation firsthand and sympathizes with your struggle. Repent of your sinfulness, draw near to his grace, and receive his mercy.

Pray:

Lord, without you I can do nothing; with you I can do all. Help me by your grace, that I fall not; help me by your strength, to resist mightily the very first beginnings of evil, before it takes hold of me; help me to cast myself at once at your sacred feet, and lie still there, until the storm be overpast; and, if I lose sight of you, bring me back quickly to you, and grant me to love you better. Amen.

(E. B. Pusey)

Ordinary Time Day 132

MATT HOEHN

Read: *Hebrews 6:19–20*

> We have this as a sure and steadfast anchor of the soul, a hope that enters into the inner place behind the curtain, where Jesus has gone as a forerunner on our behalf, having become a high priest forever after the order of Melchizedek.

Reflect:

Do you feel that God is distant from you when you pray?

Many Christians have an easy time grasping God's grandeur, power, and transcendence. Creation testifies to his glorious dominion, as we read again and again in Psalms: "Let the sea roar, and all that fills it; the world and those who dwell in it! Let the rivers clap their hands; let the hills sing for joy together before the LORD" (Psalm 98:7–9). The beauty and splendor we see in the natural world reminds us how big our God is.

But for many, it's God's intimate closeness that's so difficult to believe. We struggle to trust that God knit us together in the womb, that he knows the number of hairs on our heads, and that he cares deeply for our individual fears, questions, and life circumstances. We doubt our own significance in a world that sometimes feels out of control.

The author of Hebrews insisted that the God who created galaxies by his own breath is the very God who sent his Son Jesus to assume our full humanity.

Jesus forged a path for us to his Father. The curtain that once reminded God's people of their sinfulness and inability to be in the presence of God's holiness was torn in two by the atoning death of Jesus. Christ went behind this curtain and now leads us in victorious procession after him, through this curtain, into the welcoming presence and loving embrace of the Father. He is truly "a forerunner on our behalf" (v. 20), leading us where only he himself could.

If God feels distant, impersonal, or inaccessible to you, be reminded that God is not far off: You have been brought near to him through the blood of Christ. As you pray, hold to the truth that God knows you, loves you, and cares for you deeply and personally. Even during challenging times, even amid the darkest nights, you can hold on to this "sure and steadfast anchor of the soul" (v. 19). You can claim this miraculous hope as your own.

Pray:

O Lord, you never fail to support and govern those whom you bring up in your steadfast love and fear: Keep us, we pray, under your continual protection and providence, and give us a perpetual fear and love of your holy Name; through Jesus Christ our Lord, who lives and reigns with you and the Holy Spirit, one God, for ever and ever. Amen.

(Anglican Church in North America Book of Common Prayer)

19th Sunday of Ordinary Time
KARI WEST

Read: *Psalm 107:23–32*

Some went down to the sea in ships,
doing business on the great waters;
they saw the deeds of the LORD,
his wondrous works in the deep.
For he commanded and raised the stormy wind,
which lifted up the waves of the sea.
They mounted up to heaven; they went down to the depths;
their courage melted away in their evil plight;
they reeled and staggered like drunken men
and were at their wits' end.
Then they cried to the LORD in their trouble,
and he delivered them from their distress.
He made the storm be still,
and the waves of the sea were hushed.
Then they were glad that the waters were quiet,
and he brought them to their desired haven.
Let them thank the LORD for his steadfast love,
for his wondrous works to the children of man!
Let them extol him in the congregation of the people,
and praise him in the assembly of the elders.

Reflect:

God is at the helm of the world. His voice stirs the wind, and his whisper commands the oceans. No part of creation is outside the reach of his lordship and no corner of the world is beyond the bounds of his realm.

This isn't just an interesting theological fact; it is a permanent and permeating reality. This truth has the power to shift our understanding of the world and change the way we experience our circumstances. God is the one who rules the world; God is the one who draws near each time we lift our voice to him.

The storm-tossed helpless sailors, staggering like drunkards under the weight of the wind and waves, cried to God, and God answered them: "He delivered them from their distress" (v. 28).

God is compassionate and powerful, merciful and mysterious, loving and mighty. He hears the cries of his people. He stills the storms and hushes the waves of the sea (v. 29); his love is steadfast, and his works are wonderful (v. 31).

Let the reality of God's reign and God's nearness draw you to your knees in prayer. Exalt him for his great love and the wonderful things he has done. Ask him for rescue, for succor, for strength. Be at peace. Live under the rule of our great King.

Pray:

O God, the protector of all those who trust in you, without whom nothing is strong, nothing is holy: Increase and multiply upon us your mercy, that, with you as our ruler and guide, we may so pass through things temporal that we lose not the things eternal; grant this, heavenly Father, for the sake of your Son Jesus Christ, who lives and reigns with you, in the unity of the Holy Spirit, one God, now and for ever. Amen.

(Anglican Church in North America Book of Common Prayer)

Ordinary Time Day 134

MATT HOEHN

Read: *Hebrews 7:25–28*

Consequently, he is able to save to the uttermost those who draw near to God through him, since he always lives to make intercession for them.

For it was indeed fitting that we should have such a high priest, holy, innocent, unstained, separated from sinners, and exalted above the heavens. He has no need, like those high priests, to offer sacrifices daily, first for his own sins and then for those of the people, since he did this once for all when he offered up himself. For the law appoints men in their weakness as high priests, but the word of the oath, which came later than the law, appoints a Son who has been made perfect forever.

Reflect:

In this passage, the author of Hebrews provided us with a litany of reasons to praise the name of the risen Lord Jesus. He is the true "high priest" and is "holy, innocent, unstained, separated from sinners, and exalted above the heavens" (v. 26). Jesus now sits enthroned at the right hand of the Father, and he is worthy of all our praise. He "lives to make intercession" for us (v. 25) and has "been made perfect forever" (v. 28).

As we reflect on the person and work of Jesus, we must not let his ascendant glory obscure the means by which he was exalted to this glory.

In proving himself to be the true High Priest, Jesus was condemned to an unjust death by the corrupt high priest of his day.

Though perfectly holy, he took on human form among the unholiness of the human race.

Though "unstained" by the sin of this world and thus "separated from sinners" (v. 26), he was despised in his day for his notorious reputation as "a friend of tax collectors and sinners" (Matthew 11:19). He suffered an excruciating public humiliation when he died on the cross.

Before he was "exalted above the heavens" (v. 26), Jesus was first suspended underneath the heavens on a gruesome tree, then deposited lifeless below the earth in a tomb.

As you pray, focus on the victory of the true High Priest, who intercedes at the right hand of the Father on your behalf, drawing you into his presence. As you do so, be reminded of the cost Jesus paid in order to do this. Lift your heart to the Father in gratitude.

Pray:

O God, whose blessed Son came into the world that he might destroy the works of the devil and make us children of God and heirs of eternal life: Grant that, having this hope, we may purify ourselves as he is pure; that, when he comes again with power and great glory, we may be made like him in his eternal and glorious kingdom; where he lives and reigns with you and the Holy Spirit, one God, for ever and ever. Amen.

(Anglican Church in North America Book of Common Prayer)

Ordinary Time Day 135

MARY MAC HOEHN

Read: *Hebrews 8:10–12*

> "For this is the covenant that I will make with the house of Israel
>   after those days, declares the Lord:
> I will put my laws into their minds,
>   and write them on their hearts,
> and I will be their God,
>   and they shall be my people.
> And they shall not teach, each one his neighbor
>   and each one his brother, saying, 'Know the Lord,'
> for they shall all know me,
>   from the least of them to the greatest.
> For I will be merciful toward their iniquities,
>   and I will remember their sins no more."

Reflect:

Do you love God's law? Do you long for it to be written on your heart?

So often when we think of God's law, we think of rules and regulations. It can be tempting to think of God's law as a guidebook for how to win his favor, or to think of God as a demanding Judge, watching us and assessing how well we obey the rules. Why would anyone want a list of rules engraved on their heart—at the center of their being?

The author of Hebrews offered us an important insight: "For they shall all know me, from the least of them to the greatest" (v. 11). God reveals himself to us through his law. He does not give us rules to follow for the sake of following rules, but he uses his law to teach us about himself.

Psalm 119 provides us additional understanding: "How sweet are your words to my taste, sweeter than honey to my mouth! Through your precepts I get understanding: therefore I hate every false way" (vv. 103–104). The law of God is sweet—it offers us knowledge of the law's Creator, and it helps us to live a life in accordance with his best for us.

So often we think of the law as being like broccoli or spinach. We eat it because it's good for us, but we do not enjoy the experience. Yet Scripture offers a very different picture of the law: it is honey—sweet, delicious, and pleasing, something to be savored. Why? Because the law is God's gift to us. How gracious of our Creator to show us how to navigate the life he has given us in the world that he created! Through his law we can come to know God; through his law God makes himself known to every one of us, from the least to the greatest.

We will all fall short of full obedience. How gracious is our God? Not only does he engrave his law, which is sweeter than honey, on our frail human hearts, but also, at great cost to himself, he offers us mercy when we fail to obey and instead choose sin.

As you pray, may your heart be moved to worship, to gratitude, and to affection for God as you reflect on his law and his grace to you through his law.

Pray:

Heavenly Father, thank you for your law. Thank you for choosing to write it on our broken human hearts. You are gracious to reveal yourself to us, and, Lord, we long to know you. Would you continue to work in our hearts? Help us to love your Word and to follow you faithfully; reveal more of yourself to us. Thank you for showing us mercy through Christ's sacrifice on our behalf. Hear us, heavenly Father, in the name of your Son Jesus Christ, who lives and reigns with you, in the unity of the Holy Spirit, now and for ever. Amen.

Ordinary Time Day 136

MARY MAC HOEHN

Read: *Hebrews 9:11–14, 24–28*

But when Christ appeared as a high priest of the good things that have come, then through the greater and more perfect tent (not made with hands, that is, not of this creation) he entered once for all into the holy places, not by means of the blood of goats and calves but by means of his own blood, thus securing an eternal redemption. For if the blood of goats and bulls, and the sprinkling of defiled persons with the ashes of a heifer, sanctify for the purification of the flesh, how much more will the blood of Christ, who through the eternal Spirit offered himself without blemish to God, purify our conscience from dead works to serve the living God....

For Christ has entered, not into holy places made with hands, which are copies of the true things, but into heaven itself, now to appear in the presence of God on our behalf. Nor was it to offer himself repeatedly, as the high priest enters the holy places every year with blood not his own, for then he would have had to suffer repeatedly since the foundation of the world. But as it is, he has appeared once for all at the end of the ages to put away sin by the sacrifice of himself. And just as it is appointed for man to die once, and after that comes judgment, so Christ, having been offered once to bear the sins of many, will appear a second time, not to deal with sin but to save those who are eagerly waiting for him.

Reflect:

"He entered the Most Holy Place once for all by his own blood, thus obtaining eternal redemption" (Hebrews 9:12 NIV).

Once for all. What a beautiful reminder to the guilty heart that Christ has paid the price for our sin in a onetime sacrifice—a sacrifice that does not have to be continually repeated.

In our lives with God, we may find it hard to take this beautiful truth to heart. Instead, we may find ourselves ruminating on moments of failure, or continually trapped in feelings of shame. Hebrews 9 offers us a reassuring reminder that Christ has fully paid for our sin in a onetime sacrifice. His sacrifice has sanctified us and purified our consciences.

It can be tempting to continue punishing ourselves and to dwell in shame. But God wants so much more for his people. Christ has "put away sin by the sacrifice of himself" (v. 26).

What do we do with this gracious gift? We put aside "dead works" in order to "serve the living God" (v. 14). We are set free from shame and empowered to serve God with unblemished hearts. The work Christ has done for us was finished on the cross. Rather than languishing in guilt, we are called to walk forward, empowered by God to love and serve him!

How do we serve God? One way we can walk in God's goodness is to practice forgiveness. Not only should we refrain from holding on to our own sins but also we must not hold on to the sins of others. When we forgive someone, we lay aside the hurt we have experienced, and we cling to the love of Christ instead. Christ's sacrifice *once for all* was for us and for the person who has hurt us. May we accept his forgiveness, and may we extend forgiveness to those around us.

As you come before the Lord in prayer, remember God's great act of mercy toward you. Ask him for the power to forgive others as you have been forgiven. Praise him for his grace.

Pray:

Jesus, thank you for offering yourself as a sacrifice once for all. Help me to live in light of this truth. Set me free from guilt and shame, and empower me to serve you. Lord, teach me how to forgive those who have wronged me. Amen.

Ordinary Time Day 137
SALLY BREEDLOVE

Read: *Hebrews 12:1–3, 7–13*

Therefore, since we are surrounded by so great a cloud of witnesses, let us also lay aside every weight, and sin which clings so closely, and let us run with endurance the race that is set before us, looking to Jesus, the founder and perfecter of our faith, who for the joy that was set before him endured the cross, despising the shame, and is seated at the right hand of the throne of God.

Consider him who endured from sinners such hostility against himself, so that you may not grow weary or fainthearted….

It is for discipline that you have to endure. God is treating you as sons. For what son is there whom his father does not discipline? If you are left without discipline, in which all have participated, then you are illegitimate children and not sons. Besides this, we have had earthly fathers who disciplined us and we respected them. Shall we not much more be subject to the Father of spirits and live? For they disciplined us for a short time as it seemed best to them, but he disciplines us for our good, that we may share his holiness. For the moment all discipline seems painful rather than pleasant, but later it yields the peaceful fruit of righteousness to those who have been trained by it.

Therefore lift your drooping hands and strengthen your weak knees, and make straight paths for your feet, so that what is lame may not be put out of joint but rather be healed.

Reflect:

None of us signed up for the impossibly hard things that happen to us, but we still find ourselves in painful places. We experience the brokenness of the world; we are wounded by life's jagged edges.

What do we do in these difficult places? We continue to carry out our responsibilities when life is hard. We are still called to live ordered and humble lives, to do our work well, to care for those around us, and to seek justice for all. We may feel like we are running a marathon with no end in sight.

Yet we are not alone in our suffering. "Consider him who endured," the author of Hebrews instructed us, "so that you may not grow weary or faint hearted" (v. 3).

We are called to follow Jesus, who endured all the way to the cross. And we are called to live in hope. The present distress will not have the last word. As we follow Jesus, we will begin to see where we are headed. The kingdom of joy is before us, where Jesus sits at the right hand of God. We can be honest about the sufferings we are called to endure alongside Jesus in the present moment. We can be energized as we walk toward a joyful eternal future.

As you pray, ask God to make you a follower who endures. Ask him to give you faith to see the kingdom that lies ahead and even now breaks into our world.

Pray:

Lighten our darkness, we beseech you, O Lord; and by your great mercy defend us from all perils and dangers of this night; for the love of your only Son, our Savior Jesus Christ. Amen.

Be present, O merciful God, and protect us through the hours of this night, so that we who are wearied by the changes and chances of this life may rest in your eternal changelessness; through Jesus Christ our Lord. Amen.

(Anglican Church in North America Book of Common Prayer)

Ordinary Time Day 138

SALLY BREEDLOVE

Read: *Hebrews 12:18–29*

> For you have not come to what may be touched, a blazing fire and darkness and gloom and a tempest and the sound of a trumpet and a voice whose words made the hearers beg that no further messages be spoken to them. For they could not endure the order that was given, "If even a beast touches the mountain, it shall be stoned." Indeed, so terrifying was the sight that Moses said, "I tremble with fear." But you have come to Mount Zion and to the city of the living God, the heavenly Jerusalem, and to innumerable angels in festal gathering, and to the assembly of the firstborn who are enrolled in heaven, and to God, the judge of all, and to the spirits of the righteous made perfect, and to Jesus, the mediator of a new covenant, and to the sprinkled blood that speaks a better word than the blood of Abel.
>
> See that you do not refuse him who is speaking. For if they did not escape when they refused him who warned them on earth, much less will we escape if we reject him who warns from heaven. At that time his voice shook the earth, but now he has promised, "Yet once more I will shake not only the earth but also the heavens." This phrase, "Yet once more," indicates the removal of things that are shaken—that is, things that have been made—in order that the things that cannot be shaken may remain. Therefore let us be grateful for receiving a kingdom that cannot be shaken, and thus let us offer to God acceptable worship, with reverence and awe, for our God is a consuming fire.

Reflect:

Hebrews was written to Christians whose faith was wavering: They were struggling to believe in and follow after Jesus. Instead of coddling these dispirited people, the author painted an expansive picture of the beauty of Jesus and all that lies ahead for believers, reminding us that the call to live a faithful life is a serious one. Hebrews never "dumbs down" the cost of discipleship and never takes the focus off Jesus.

Could it be that this writer was speaking directly to our time? Yes, his words are meant for all generations, but our world is awash with a choose-what-you-want-to-believe-about-Jesus discipleship. We live in a time when so much is being shaken to the core and when sin is continually exposed. What do we do in turbulent times like ours?

Can we be faithful, holy people? Ordinary Time reminds us again and again that this is indeed what discipleship is about. The author of Hebrews called out the best in us; he called us to life, to Jesus, to grace, to an unshakable kingdom, and to a coming celebration. Throngs of festive angels and believing people are gathering, and we are invited to join them.

Will we believe what he has promised? Beyond all the destruction, disease, and division of our day, the unshakable kingdom awaits us.

Be sober: God is fire, and he is on an uncompromising mission. But beyond the sifting and the shaking lies the radiant city. If you pay close attention, you will hear, see, and smell the first hints of a huge party, the marriage feast of the Lamb. Have you said yes to your invitation?

As you pray, say yes to the triune God. You are walking toward the party where Jesus is the exalted Bridegroom. He awaits the arrival of his bride, the church. Will you let him make you beautiful? Are you eager to join that celebration?

Pray:

O God, the King of glory, you have exalted your only Son Jesus Christ with great triumph to your kingdom in heaven: Do not leave us comfortless, but send us your Holy Spirit to strengthen us, and exalt us to that place where our Savior Christ has gone before; who lives and reigns with you and the Holy Spirit, one God, in glory everlasting. Amen.

(Anglican Church in North America Book of Common Prayer)

Ordinary Time Day 139
SALLY BREEDLOVE

Read: *Hebrews 13:1–5, 7–19*

Let brotherly love continue. Do not neglect to show hospitality to strangers, for thereby some have entertained angels unawares. Remember those who are in prison, as though in prison with them, and those who are mistreated, since you also are in the body. Let marriage be held in honor among all, and let the marriage bed be undefiled, for God will judge the sexually immoral and adulterous. Keep your life free from love of money, and be content with what you have, for he has said, "I will never leave you nor forsake you."

Remember your leaders, those who spoke to you the word of God. Consider the outcome of their way of life, and imitate their faith. Jesus Christ is the same yesterday and today and forever. Do not be led away by diverse and strange teachings, for it is good for the heart to be strengthened by grace, not by foods, which have not benefited those devoted to them. We have an altar from which those who serve the tent have no right to eat. For the bodies of those animals whose blood is brought into the holy places by the high priest as a sacrifice for sin are burned outside the camp. So Jesus also suffered outside the gate in order to sanctify the people through his own blood. Therefore let us go to him outside the camp and bear the reproach he endured. For here we have no lasting city, but we seek the city that is to come. Through him then let us continually offer up a sacrifice of praise to God, that is, the fruit of lips that acknowledge his name. Do not neglect to do good and to share what you have, for such sacrifices are pleasing to God.

Obey your leaders and submit to them, for they are keeping watch over your souls, as those who will have to give an account. Let them do this with joy and not with groaning, for that would be of no advantage to you.

Pray for us, for we are sure that we have a clear conscience, desiring to act honorably in all things. I urge you the more earnestly to do this in order that I may be restored to you the sooner.

Reflect:

Hebrews 13 offers a vast number of instructions. Listen to the breadth of the directives: Offer generous hospitality, even to people you don't know. Identify with prisoners and victims of abuse. Live by and within God's plan for sex: it's a gift for marriage between a wife and a husband. Give up greed that insists on acquiring more and more. Appreciate and imitate your pastor.

The list continues: Don't be led away from solid truth. Give up your obsession with being an insider to any group. Get a job and work hard. Share. Help build the unity and peace of the church; don't destroy it with your constant critiques. Pray for others, not just for yourself.

After this catalogue of commands, the writer said, "I've kept this as brief as possible; I haven't piled on a lot of extras" (Hebrews 13:22 MSG).

We might want to reply, "Are you kidding? If I live like this, I won't fit in anywhere. I'll be seen as too conservative, too liberal, too supportive of the establishment, too supportive of the disenfranchised, too judgmental, and too dismissive of the values of people whose esteem I really want."

Look at the passage again. The writer gave us many instructions for living a with-God life, but he also assured us that Jesus is the one who will always be faithful, and he promised us that his grace is the only good ground for life. A holy life isn't a duty; it's a joy. It's the pathway to deep intimacy with the Father. We practice living like Jesus because it puts us in sync with Jesus, the one who loved us first.

As you pray, will you speak aloud to God some ways your life needs to change? Will you thank God that Jesus is the one who puts you together and provides for you? You are not alone.

Pray:

Look upon us, O Lord, and let all the darkness of our souls vanish before the beams of thy brightness. Fill us with holy love, and open to us the treasures of thy wisdom. Amen.

(Saint Augustine)

20th Sunday of Ordinary Time
KARI WEST

Read: *Psalm 109:1–5, 26–31*

> Be not silent, O God of my praise!
> For wicked and deceitful mouths are opened against me,
>   speaking against me with lying tongues.
> They encircle me with words of hate,
>   and attack me without cause.
> In return for my love they accuse me,
>   but I give myself to prayer.
> So they reward me evil for good,
>   and hatred for my love....
> Help me, O LORD my God!
>   Save me according to your steadfast love!
> Let them know that this is your hand;
>   you, O LORD, have done it!
> Let them curse, but you will bless!
>   They arise and are put to shame, but your servant will be glad!
> May my accusers be clothed with dishonor;
>   may they be wrapped in their own shame as in a cloak!
> With my mouth I will give great thanks to the LORD;
>   I will praise him in the midst of the throng.
> For he stands at the right hand of the needy one,
>   to save him from those who condemn his soul to death.

Reflect:

It's a hard thing to bear the hatred and accusations of other people, and it's even harder when that vitriol is undeserved and comes from those we love and pray for. How do we handle the anguish of unmerited animosity from those we considered to be friends? Do David's opening words bring a specific situation to your mind?

David spent most of this psalm telling God in detail about the vicious lies and the verbal attacks thrown at him by his false accusers. Perhaps this is our first clue. Before we rush to contemplating God's character or asking for his help, as David did by the end of this psalm, we must be honest with the Lord. We must lay before him the details of our struggles. We must offer up the intricacies of our hardship to the one who cares for us. We must spit out the poison of our anger and bitterness before it takes its toll on our hearts.

After this honesty with God, David then asked him to intervene. He asked for rescue and deliverance. He pleaded with God to work according to his steadfast love and his good character. He said that as long as God rescued him by his love, others could curse him if they liked. With the blessing of God, their hostility no longer mattered. David remembered that God stands beside the needy, giving strength and salvation.

David begged for salvation, for the unfailing love of God. We know even more about God's love than David did. We now know Jesus, our Savior, the perfect image of the Father's love. In our hardships, in our struggles, in those barbed circumstances that David's words call to mind, there is rest to be found in Christ. He bled out on a cross under false accusations and in front of a crowd that spewed mockery and hatred. Our Jesus, who patiently bore each lie and all vitriol, died unjustly to bind himself to us and give us peace with God.

Remember that our God still stands beside the needy. He stands with the mistreated and abused. Pray for honesty toward God, endurance, peace, and justice from God. Pray for a deeper full-being knowledge of Jesus, our sinless sin-bearer, whose blessing is all that we need.

Pray:

O Lord, you alone know the present discomposure of my spirit; rebuke, I implore you, the furious tempest; and restore my soul to that calmness and tranquility, which may capacitate me for the duties of your service and my calling. Amen.

(Henry Scougal)

Ordinary Time Day 141

KARI WEST

Read: *Luke 13:10–17*

Now he was teaching in one of the synagogues on the Sabbath. And behold, there was a woman who had had a disabling spirit for eighteen years. She was bent over and could not fully straighten herself. When Jesus saw her, he called her over and said to her, "Woman, you are freed from your disability." And he laid his hands on her, and immediately she was made straight, and she glorified God. But the ruler of the synagogue, indignant because Jesus had healed on the Sabbath, said to the people, "There are six days in which work ought to be done. Come on those days and be healed, and not on the Sabbath day." Then the Lord answered him, "You hypocrites! Does not each of you on the Sabbath untie his ox or his donkey from the manger and lead it away to water it? And ought not this woman, a daughter of Abraham whom Satan bound for eighteen years, be loosed from this bond on the Sabbath day?" As he said these things, all his adversaries were put to shame, and all the people rejoiced at all the glorious things that were done by him.

Reflect:

Can you imagine what life would have been like for this woman before she encountered Jesus? For eighteen years, day in and day out, she had not been able to stand up straight. She had been bent over, her gaze fixed constantly down.

In our natural state, we suffer from a similar condition; we are largely unable to look outward toward others or upward toward God. We live in a constant state of navel-gazing.

After eighteen years of the woman's suffering, Jesus laid gentle hands on her twisted body, and she raised up her head to see the Savior of the world. Notice the language he used: "Woman, you are *freed*" (v. 12, italics added). The spirit that had disabled her for so long had been banished. It's no wonder that the first thing she did was to glorify the Lord, her healer.

But the religious leader, curved in on himself, rebuked Jesus for his miraculous and gracious act of healing. Rather than join the woman in praise of God, he called wrong what was manifestly right. The ruler of the synagogue was more concerned with broken rules than broken bodies; he was more concerned about the sanctity of his temple than the integrity of the people who worshiped there.

Jesus rebuked this leader for his blindness and lack of compassion, for not recognizing God's great work. Through Christ, God had lifted up a bent head to gaze on the goodness of Jesus, so that his people would glorify his name.

As you pray, ask the Lord to do this work in your own heart. Ask that your eyes would be lifted up and trained on Jesus so that you may glorify your Lord.

Pray:

Almighty God, you have promised to hear the petitions of those who ask in the Name of your Son: Mercifully incline your ear to us as we make our prayers and supplications to you; and grant that what we ask faithfully, according to your will, we may obtain effectually, for the relief of our necessities and the setting forth of your glory; through Jesus Christ our Lord. Amen.

(Anglican Church in North America Book of Common Prayer)

Ordinary Time Day 142

NATHAN BAXTER

Read: *Luke 13:18–21*

> He said therefore, "What is the kingdom of God like? And to what shall I compare it? It is like a grain of mustard seed that a man took and sowed in his garden, and it grew and became a tree, and the birds of the air made nests in its branches."
>
> And again he said, "To what shall I compare the kingdom of God? It is like leaven that a woman took and hid in three measures of flour, until it was all leavened."

Reflect:

If anyone could have confidence to define the kingdom of God, surely it was Jesus. Yet the Son of Man stood with us to ask, to wonder, and to reckon. Jesus invited contemplative comparisons.

Insight grows through gently explored comparisons. Slowly, we see and test the way the more familiar might connect with the less familiar, how the small and simple might imply the larger and more complex.

Jesus began with a seed, which would have been familiar to the farmers and spice market shoppers who were listening. Perhaps it's not familiar to us. The mustard seed is tiny, as small as the period at the end of this sentence.

Can you see it? Something so small requires a season-spanning patience and trust. The harvest that might come of this tiny kernel of life will not be like the wheat or barley. This shrub will take time to mature before it can support perching birds or yield abundant spice. Yet patience and trust will see it. The seed that is received and planted will grow.

How many people bake their own bread? And of those who do, how many bake enough to feed fifty or sixty people for several days? Yet even such an industrious baker must work and then wait. Here we have another contemplative comparison inviting patience and trust. Yeast is mixed into and worked through the dough so that it will rise.

Are you daunted or inspired by small and subtle things? Are you discouraged or enlivened by everyday patience and trust? To what shall you liken the kingdom of God so that you, too, may wonder with Jesus?

As you pray, consider what seems to be too small and insignificant to be of value. Take a moment and pray for eyes to see a small sign that God is present in this broken world and in the challenges you are facing. Hold that "mustard seed" up to your Father and give him thanks.

Pray:

Teach me to seek you, and as I seek you, show yourself to me; for I cannot seek you unless you show me how, and I will never find you unless you show yourself to me. Let me seek you by desiring you, and desire you by seeking you; let me find you by loving you, and love you in finding you. Amen.

(Anselm of Canterbury)

Ordinary Time Day 143

NATHAN BAXTER

Read: *Luke 13:31–35*

At that very hour some Pharisees came and said to him, "Get away from here, for Herod wants to kill you." And he said to them, "Go and tell that fox, 'Behold, I cast out demons and perform cures today and tomorrow, and the third day I finish my course. Nevertheless, I must go on my way today and tomorrow and the day following, for it cannot be that a prophet should perish away from Jerusalem.' O Jerusalem, Jerusalem, the city that kills the prophets and stones those who are sent to it! How often would I have gathered your children together as a hen gathers her brood under her wings, and you were not willing! Behold, your house is forsaken. And I tell you, you will not see me until you say, 'Blessed is he who comes in the name of the Lord!'"

Reflect:

In a swirling storm of rising polarization, Jesus declared, "I will reach my goal" (v. 32 NIV). These words should both hearten and humble.

Earlier in Luke 13, Jesus healed a woman on the Sabbath, who, for eighteen years, had been "bent over and could not straighten up at all" (v. 11 NIV). His action exposed the hypocrisy of some; others were impressed by the miracle. Instead of capitalizing on the favor, Jesus told two parables that invited his listeners to ponder what the kingdom is really like.

In these verses, the Pharisees came to Jesus, saying, "Leave this place and go somewhere else. Herod wants to kill you" (v. 31 NIV). Undaunted, Jesus replied in a way that seemed to confuse rather than clarify. He concluded, "I will reach my goal" (v. 32 NIV).

What was Jesus's main agenda? What stirred his anger and his anguish? What guided his pace and ground his purpose? What made him able to assert, "I will reach my goal"?

Could anyone have even fathomed that course if he'd stated it outright? His close friends didn't understand, even when he told them plainly. "None of the rulers of this age understood it, for if they had, they would not have crucified the Lord of glory" (1 Corinthians 2:8 NIV).

In a swirling storm of rising polarization, Jesus said, "I will reach my goal."

It's a saying that can hearten us. Jesus will keep all of God's promises. "For no matter how many promises God has made, they are 'Yes' in Christ. And so through him the 'Amen' is spoken by us to the glory of God" (2 Corinthians 1:20 NIV).

It's also a saying that can humble us. "Whom did the LORD consult to enlighten him, and who taught him the right way?" (Isaiah 40:14 NIV).

As you pray, bring the concern or conflict weighing on your heart into the wisdom and refuge of Jesus. Remind yourself of a particular promise from God's Word that will steady and encourage your heart. Thank your Father God for what his promise means to you.

Pray:

Our God, in whom we trust: Strengthen us not to regard overmuch who is for us or who is against us, but to see to it that we be with you in everything we do. Amen.

(Thomas à Kempis)

Ordinary Time Day 144

NATHAN BAXTER

Read: *Luke 14:1–11*

One Sabbath, when he went to dine at the house of a ruler of the Pharisees, they were watching him carefully. And behold, there was a man before him who had dropsy. And Jesus responded to the lawyers and Pharisees, saying, "Is it lawful to heal on the Sabbath, or not?" But they remained silent. Then he took him and healed him and sent him away. And he said to them, "Which of you, having a son or an ox that has fallen into a well on a Sabbath day, will not immediately pull him out?" And they could not reply to these things.

Now he told a parable to those who were invited, when he noticed how they chose the places of honor, saying to them, "When you are invited by someone to a wedding feast, do not sit down in a place of honor, lest someone more distinguished than you be invited by him, and he who invited you both will come and say to you, 'Give your place to this person,' and then you will begin with shame to take the lowest place. But when you are invited, go and sit in the lowest place, so that when your host comes he may say to you, 'Friend, move up higher.' Then you will be honored in the presence of all who sit at table with you. For everyone who exalts himself will be humbled, and he who humbles himself will be exalted."

Reflect:

Don't you love how Jesus meddled?

Jesus was a guest in the house of a ruler of the Pharisees, where "they were watching him carefully" (v. 1). It was a Sabbath day, and one of the guests was suffering. Jesus confronted the unspoken prejudice against healing on the Sabbath. Other guests "remained silent" (v. 4).

Then Jesus, the one being carefully watched, revealed his own observational talent. Dinner and conversation had revealed status alignments and ambitions, the thick yet subtle power dynamics of up and down, inside and outside, center and margin. Horizons of honor beckoned some and eluded others. Jesus meddled by pushing those horizons far beyond where strategy might naturally lead.

What do we hear in the punch line of Jesus's parable? "For everyone who exalts himself will be humbled, and he who humbles himself will be exalted" (v. 11).

Can you hear a subtler means for calculating self-promotion? Can you hear thick irony that meddled with the whole game of status-seeking?

Can you hear the heart of God from the lips of the Son of Man? Might a whole world of upside-down honor be entered through a doorway of humility?

As you pray, confess where you seek to secure or promote your own position. Look at Jesus, who lived the upside-down life of choosing the lowest place to serve in obedient love. Ask him to give you a heart that serves more deeply.

Pray:

O God, of your goodness, give me yourself, for you are enough for me. I can ask for nothing less that is completely to your honor, and if I do ask anything less, I shall always be in want. Only in you I have all. Amen.

(Julian of Norwich)

Ordinary Time Day 145
NATHAN BAXTER

Read: *Luke 14:15–24*

> When one of those who reclined at table with him heard these
> things, he said to him, "Blessed is everyone who will eat bread in
> the kingdom of God!" But he said to him, "A man once gave a great
> banquet and invited many. And at the time for the banquet he sent
> his servant to say to those who had been invited, 'Come, for every-
> thing is now ready.' But they all alike began to make excuses. The
> first said to him, 'I have bought a field, and I must go out and see it.
> Please have me excused.' And another said, 'I have bought five yoke
> of oxen, and I go to examine them. Please have me excused.' And
> another said, 'I have married a wife, and therefore I cannot come.'
> So the servant came and reported these things to his master. Then
> the master of the house became angry and said to his servant, 'Go
> out quickly to the streets and lanes of the city, and bring in the poor
> and crippled and blind and lame.' And the servant said, 'Sir, what
> you commanded has been done, and still there is room.' And the
> master said to the servant, 'Go out to the highways and hedges and
> compel people to come in, that my house may be filled. For I tell
> you, none of those men who were invited shall taste my banquet.'"

Reflect:

We dream of the fullness, freedom, and satisfaction promised in the kingdom
of God. We entertain this eternal hope for many reasons.

Perhaps, like the guest who spoke these words to Jesus, we're uncomfortable with our social context, so we look forward—not so much to the
kingdom of God but to something less awkward, less painful, and less
fraught with conflict.

Perhaps, like some who followed Jesus, we have a sense of the nearness
of the kingdom. We desire the feast but we hesitate to "sit down and count
the cost" (Luke 14:28).

Perhaps, like the outcasts of Jesus's day—and those of our own day—we dream of a feast to distract us from our desolation. We dream of a distant future yet we remain resigned to the prospect of never tasting a crumb.

But what if the feast were to materialize in front of us? Would we go in, sit down, and eat?

"But they all alike began to make excuses" (v. 18). What holds our affections so tightly that we can't conceive of actually leaving it behind?

After the master sent his servant to invite strangers to his feast, he received a surprising response. The servant returned to report, "What you commanded has been done, and still there is room" (v. 22). Why was there still room? The world was full of poor, crippled, blind, and lame people. Surely they would partake in the banquet?

Are we so unlike the guests in this story? Are we distracted and full of excuses, loath to accept the gracious invitation we've received? Do we lack the imagination to venture forth in faith and hope? Will we have the courage to go in, sit down, and eat?

Everyone has been invited to the feast. Everyone has been urged to attend a feast unlike any other, to receive the bounty offered by the master: "*Blessed is everyone who will eat bread in the kingdom of God!*" (v. 15, italics added).

As you pray, consider your own heart. Are you eager for the banquet? Are you willing to lay aside whatever you need to let go of to join Jesus in his joyful kingdom?

Pray:

Lord Jesus, come to your church, completely and fully. Send out the word to the highways. Gather everyone, good and bad. Bring the weak, the blind, and the lame into your church. Bring everyone to your supper. Command that your house be filled! Amen.

(Ambrose of Milan)

Ordinary Time Day 146

KARI WEST

Read: *Luke 14:25–33*

> Now great crowds accompanied him, and he turned and said to
> them, "If anyone comes to me and does not hate his own father and
> mother and wife and children and brothers and sisters, yes, and even
> his own life, he cannot be my disciple. Whoever does not bear his
> own cross and come after me cannot be my disciple. For which of
> you, desiring to build a tower, does not first sit down and count the
> cost, whether he has enough to complete it? Otherwise, when he
> has laid a foundation and is not able to finish, all who see it begin
> to mock him, saying, 'This man began to build and was not able to
> finish.' Or what king, going out to encounter another king in war,
> will not sit down first and deliberate whether he is able with ten
> thousand to meet him who comes against him with twenty thou-
> sand? And if not, while the other is yet a great way off, he sends a
> delegation and asks for terms of peace. So therefore, any one of you
> who does not renounce all that he has cannot be my disciple."

Reflect:

We are quick to mitigate the words of Jesus. We sidestep difficult and uncomfortable passages like this one where he commanded us to hate our families
and ourselves in order to take up a symbol of cursed, horrific torture.

If this feels harsh to us in our current cultural context, how much harsher
might it have felt to the largely Jewish audience of Jesus's day who honored
and prized family so highly? They knew the words of the Old Testament,
"Anyone hung on a tree is under God's curse" (Deuteronomy 21:23 csb),
and perhaps had personally witnessed the horrendous spectacle of Roman
crucifixion.

It is good to consider the whole teaching of Scripture and to understand
that Christ is not actually commanding hatred of ourselves and our brothers
and sisters. In other passages, Jesus clearly stated that the whole law and the

prophets can be summed up in the first two commandments—namely, to love God and love our neighbor.

At the same time, we cannot let these words lose their shock value. Christ purposefully chose these statements to shake us from comfort and lethargy, from the complacency that whispers that following Christ need not inconvenience us greatly.

Jesus meant what he said: The cost of following him may be so vast, and the love required of us in obedience so great, that by comparison, our earthly loves will look like hatred. And those who desire to know him must follow him "outside the camp" (Hebrews 13:13) and share in his sufferings. The cost of discipleship is real and greater than we like to believe.

And yet, know the mercy of God in Christ's words. He desires to work in us a lifetime habit of relinquishing ourselves to him. In God's economy, nothing freely given over to him will ever be lost. In the laying down of our lives, as seeds dying in the earth, we will find more life and fullness as beloved disciples of Jesus than we could ever conceive. We will be as new shoots of the new humanity, growing up into the likeness of Christ.

As you pray, meditate on the cost of discipleship and ask for fresh faith to follow Jesus wherever he may lead you.

Pray:

Jesus, let us count the cost of discipleship and find your friendship worthy of any sacrifice. Give us pure hearts and right affections. Enable us to live lives of faithfulness, for that is a work that only your Spirit can do in us; in your precious name and by your blood we pray. Amen.

21st Sunday of Ordinary Time

KARI WEST

Read: *Psalm 113*

> Praise the LORD!
> Praise, O servants of the LORD,
>   praise the name of the LORD!
> Blessed be the name of the LORD
>   from this time forth and forevermore!
> From the rising of the sun to its setting,
>   the name of the LORD is to be praised!
> The LORD is high above all nations,
>   and his glory above the heavens!
> Who is like the LORD our God,
>   who is seated on high,
> who looks far down
>   on the heavens and the earth?
> He raises the poor from the dust
>   and lifts the needy from the ash heap,
> to make them sit with princes,
>   with the princes of his people.
> He gives the barren woman a home,
>   making her the joyous mother of children.
> Praise the LORD!

Reflect:

We are the poor, in the dust; we are the needy, living in ash heaps; we are the barren ones, with little to show for our lives.

While these words may or may not describe our outward circumstances, they declare the deepest, truest condition of all humanity—of us, our families, our coworkers, and our friends.

Do you know your own neediness, your own poverty, your own barrenness? Perhaps your recent experiences have made these realities inescapable, or perhaps you still refuse to accept that left on your own, there is little hope for real, rich, overflowing life.

But hear this even deeper truth: We are not left on our own. We have a King who stoops low and lifts the needy. He takes the poor and sets them among princes. He opens his hand and gives the barren one a family.

He is the life-giver. He is majestic and powerful. He is exalted above all. He earnestly desires to meet you in your need, your poverty, and your barrenness—to give you a hope and a future, to supply all your needs, and to root you more deeply in his blood-bought family.

As you pray, confess how much you need God. Praise him that he bends low to lift up his people. He will not leave us on our own.

Pray:

I need Thee every hour,
In joy or pain;
Come quickly and abide,
Or life is vain.
I need Thee every hour,
Teach me Thy will;
And Thy rich promises
In me fulfill.
I need Thee every hour,
Most Holy One;
Oh, make me Thine indeed,
Thou blessed Son.
I need Thee, oh, I need Thee;
Every hour I need Thee;
Oh, bless me now, my Savior!
I come to Thee.
Amen.

("I Need Thee Every Hour," Annie Sherwood Hawks)

Ordinary Time Day 148

KARI WEST

Read: *Luke 15:1–10*

Now the tax collectors and sinners were all drawing near to hear him. And the Pharisees and the scribes grumbled, saying, "This man receives sinners and eats with them."

So he told them this parable: "What man of you, having a hundred sheep, if he has lost one of them, does not leave the ninety-nine in the open country, and go after the one that is lost, until he finds it? And when he has found it, he lays it on his shoulders, rejoicing. And when he comes home, he calls together his friends and his neighbors, saying to them, 'Rejoice with me, for I have found my sheep that was lost.' Just so, I tell you, there will be more joy in heaven over one sinner who repents than over ninety-nine righteous persons who need no repentance.

"Or what woman, having ten silver coins, if she loses one coin, does not light a lamp and sweep the house and seek diligently until she finds it? And when she has found it, she calls together her friends and neighbors, saying, 'Rejoice with me, for I have found the coin that I had lost.' Just so, I tell you, there is joy before the angels of God over one sinner who repents."

Reflect:

Pause and consider a beautiful truth in this passage: If you have repented of your sin, it means that Jesus has lovingly, urgently, and carefully sought after you as a gentle shepherd for a lost sheep, as a woman for a precious coin. Christ has placed you on his shoulders and brought you back to his fold. Though perhaps you couldn't hear them, shouts of joy rang out through the heavenly realms as you turned from death to life.

Rejoice over the fact that Christ came to welcome sinners and eat with those unworthy of him. If he hadn't, none of us could claim his friendship. Don't be like the Pharisees, who drew lines between themselves and the rest of broken, sinful humanity and who criticized Jesus for his indiscriminate call to repentance and faith. Jesus desired all to be saved.

As you pray, consider the miracle of your own conversion.

Ponder these beautiful pictures of Christ's searching for you and his tender care for you. See in your own faith the undeserved, pressing, rescuing love of the Good Shepherd. Confess any pride or selfishness that would regard another human being as less worthy of our Savior's attention. Delight in the care of your Good Shepherd and pray for your friends and loved ones who still need to be drawn into his fold.

Pray:

Jesus, thank you for not leaving us as sheep wandering or coins forgotten. Thank you for the grace of repentance. Let us see your abiding love in our salvation, for your sake. Amen.

Ordinary Time Day 149
KARI WEST

Read: *Luke 15:11–28, 31–32*

And he said, "There was a man who had two sons. And the younger of them said to his father, 'Father, give me the share of property that is coming to me.' And he divided his property between them. Not many days later, the younger son gathered all he had and took a journey into a far country, and there he squandered his property in reckless living. And when he had spent everything, a severe famine arose in that country, and he began to be in need. So he went and hired himself out to one of the citizens of that country, who sent him into his fields to feed pigs. And he was longing to be fed with the pods that the pigs ate, and no one gave him anything.

"But when he came to himself, he said, 'How many of my father's hired servants have more than enough bread, but I perish here with hunger! I will arise and go to my father, and I will say to him, "Father, I have sinned against heaven and before you. I am no longer worthy to be called your son. Treat me as one of your hired servants."' And he arose and came to his father. But while he was still a long way off, his father saw him and felt compassion, and ran and embraced him and kissed him. And the son said to him, 'Father, I have sinned against heaven and before you. I am no longer worthy to be called your son.' But the father said to his servants, 'Bring quickly the best robe, and put it on him, and put a ring on his hand, and shoes on his feet. And bring the fattened calf and kill it, and let us eat and celebrate. For this my son was dead, and is alive again; he was lost, and is found.' And they began to celebrate.

"Now his older son was in the field, and as he came and drew near to the house, he heard music and dancing. And he called one of the servants and asked what these things meant. And he said to him, 'Your brother has come, and your father has killed the fattened calf, because he has received him back safe and sound.' But he was angry and refused to go in. His father came out and entreated him. . . . And he said to him, 'Son, you are always with me, and all that is mine is yours. It was fitting to celebrate and be glad, for this your brother was dead, and is alive; he was lost, and is found.'"

Reflect:

The words we hear most often are words we may begin to hear not at all. Repetition and familiarity can wear down the sharp meaning in a story, like a stone worn smooth in a riverbed. That's the danger we face when we read the parable of the prodigal son.

Will you pause and try to receive these words as if you'd never come upon this tale before? Can you imagine the searing pain of the father as he watches his son steal away? Can you feel the younger son's pangs of hunger and his despair as he contemplates the pig slop? Can you see the tears brimming in his eyes as his father embraces him again? Can you sense the festering anger of the older brother, roiling in his stomach, as he hears the echoes of feasting and laughter?

Among myriad other things, this story shows us that we are born with hungry souls and that the desires we have for fulfillment, pleasure, and freedom can lead us to the most desperate and terrible places. Our hearts are like broken compasses that no longer recall true north, so they fail us again and again. Whether these hearts lead us to open rebellion and sinful living or to quiet self-righteousness and teeming hatred of our brothers and sisters, we all need the reorienting words of our Father.

As you pray, contemplate which words you need to hear. Do you need to know again the Father's loud shout of joy in your salvation, that you were lost and now are found? That he delights in you, his child? Or do you need to hear afresh his call to you to abandon your hatred and rejoice that all God has is yours in Jesus? Wherever you are today, will you join him in his lavish invitation?

Pray:

Father in heaven, please give us ears to hear anew these familiar words. Let us know your grace, both in your call to renewed repentance and in your words of joy over your children returned; for Jesus's sake. Amen.

Ordinary Time Day 150

KARI WEST

Read: *Luke 16:1–9*

He also said to the disciples, "There was a rich man who had a manager, and charges were brought to him that this man was wasting his possessions. And he called him and said to him, 'What is this that I hear about you? Turn in the account of your management, for you can no longer be manager.' And the manager said to himself, 'What shall I do, since my master is taking the management away from me? I am not strong enough to dig, and I am ashamed to beg. I have decided what to do, so that when I am removed from management, people may receive me into their houses.' So, summoning his master's debtors one by one, he said to the first, 'How much do you owe my master?' He said, 'A hundred measures of oil.' He said to him, 'Take your bill, and sit down quickly and write fifty.' Then he said to another, 'And how much do you owe?' He said, 'A hundred measures of wheat.' He said to him, 'Take your bill, and write eighty.' The master commended the dishonest manager for his shrewdness. For the sons of this world are more shrewd in dealing with their own generation than the sons of light. And I tell you, make friends for yourselves by means of unrighteous wealth, so that when it fails they may receive you into the eternal dwellings."

Reflect:

This is one of the parables of Jesus where we don't see the end coming. We read along, expecting the dishonest manager to get what's coming to him for his double dealings. Instead, he is commended for his shrewdness. What are we to make of this?

The startling twist at the end should make us pause and consider. It is meant to surprise us and to drive us back to reread and reexamine the story. Here we see the manager commended because he knew how to take care of himself, and he uses his master's "worldly wealth" to build friendships and forgive the debts of others in the community.

The focus is not on whether or not the manager was honest but on the fact that he used his intelligence to its highest potential. And Jesus calls his disciples to follow this example, using our wits as well as we can, though for a higher purpose than the manager. Christ calls us to have the same kind of desperate, directed focus so that we might "live, really live, and not complacently just get by on good behavior" (Luke 16:9 MSG).

As you pray, ask the Lord to reveal ways that you've been half-hearted in your obedience. Ask for renewed desire to use your all—intelligence, strategy, and will—to follow him.

Pray:

May the love of Christ henceforth constrain us to live no longer to ourselves, but to him who died for us. May we more and more consider ourselves not as our own, but as bought with a price, and may we use the blessings that you have given us in your fear and love, with gratitude to you the giver of them all. Amen.

(William Wilberforce)

Ordinary Time Day 151

KARI WEST

Read: *Luke 16:10–15*

"One who is faithful in a very little is also faithful in much, and one who is dishonest in a very little is also dishonest in much. If then you have not been faithful in the unrighteous wealth, who will entrust to you the true riches? And if you have not been faithful in that which is another's, who will give you that which is your own? No servant can serve two masters, for either he will hate the one and love the other, or he will be devoted to the one and despise the other. You cannot serve God and money."

The Pharisees, who were lovers of money, heard all these things, and they ridiculed him. And he said to them, "You are those who justify yourselves before men, but God knows your hearts. For what is exalted among men is an abomination in the sight of God."

Reflect:

What comes to your mind when you think about true riches?

In this passage, Christ didn't say to be careful with money because money is precious and a great source of power and comfort. We're not commanded to faithfulness with our finances or presented with a chest of diamonds, sapphires, and rubies and told to keep them safe.

No, instead Christ first offered an observation, "One who is faithful in a very little is also faithful in much, and one who is dishonest in a very little is also dishonest in much" (v. 10).

It's as if Jesus held out money and said, "*Be faithful and honest with this small plaything. Let your love of God be displayed and deepened in handling this toy well, without letting it become too important to you. Then one day, you'll be grown up enough to possess the true treasure, the friendship of God.*"

Jesus followed his observation with a probing question, "If then you have not been faithful in the unrighteous wealth, who will entrust to you the true riches?" (v. 11). Jesus knew the hearts of his listeners; he knew that the human heart will always be mastered by something. He was blunt in his instruction, and we should take his words to heart: "*You cannot serve God and money*" (v. 13, italics added).

Do you want to be entrusted with a real trove of riches all your own? Hold to God as your Master and let faithful dealings with money train you to see a much richer source of goodness on the horizon.

Don't get caught up in serving money. Don't spend your time and energy "justify[ing] yourselves in the eyes of others" (v. 15 NIV). There is something so much better, so much deeper, and so much richer to care about. Hold fast to God and trust that a life of seeking him will one day open onto wide vistas of joy and peace, abounding in his love and care.

Pray:

Most merciful Father, we humbly thank you for all your gifts so freely bestowed upon us: for life and health and safety, for strength to work and leisure to rest, for all that is beautiful in creation and in human life; but above all we thank you for our spiritual mercies in Christ Jesus our Lord; who with you and the Holy Spirit lives and reigns, one God, for ever and ever. Amen.

(Anglican Church in North America Book of Common Prayer)

Ordinary Time Day 152

SALLY BREEDLOVE

Read: *Luke 16:19–31*

"There was a rich man who was clothed in purple and fine linen
and who feasted sumptuously every day. And at his gate was laid
a poor man named Lazarus, covered with sores, who desired to be
fed with what fell from the rich man's table. Moreover, even the
dogs came and licked his sores. The poor man died and was carried
by the angels to Abraham's side. The rich man also died and was
buried, and in Hades, being in torment, he lifted up his eyes and
saw Abraham far off and Lazarus at his side. And he called out,
'Father Abraham, have mercy on me, and send Lazarus to dip the
end of his finger in water and cool my tongue, for I am in anguish
in this flame.' But Abraham said, 'Child, remember that you in your
lifetime received your good things, and Lazarus in like manner bad
things; but now he is comforted here, and you are in anguish. And
besides all this, between us and you a great chasm has been fixed, in
order that those who would pass from here to you may not be able,
and none may cross from there to us.' And he said, 'Then I beg you,
father, to send him to my father's house—for I have five brothers—
so that he may warn them, lest they also come into this place of
torment.' But Abraham said, 'They have Moses and the Prophets; let
them hear them.' And he said, 'No, father Abraham, but if someone
goes to them from the dead, they will repent.' He said to him, 'If
they do not hear Moses and the Prophets, neither will they be
convinced if someone should rise from the dead.'"

Reflect:

This story begs the question: Are we convinced by Scripture and by Christ's
resurrection? Do we possess the kind of conviction that seeps into our hearts
and our bones and changes our affections, our habits, and our whole lives? Or
are we simply giving intellectual assent to these things, as even demons do?

This is a terrifying parable, no doubt. A man who lived wholly opposed to the upside-down values of the kingdom of God died and found himself in eternal torment.

But don't miss the fact that Christ gave this story to us as a gift, a warning: This eternal torture need never happen. Repent, embrace the Scriptures, offer your life to God, and ask for a new heart of careful attention to the needy, the broken, and the poor.

As you pray, confess your hope in the one who returned from the dead—more than that, who crushed death underfoot—so that we could truly be changed. Ask the Spirit to convict you of selfishness and the idol of comfort. Ask for God's heart of love and care for the least of these.

Pray:

O Christ, who trampled death, we ask you again to work in us the life of the kingdom. Let us be your hands and feet; let us portray your love to a hurting and needy world. Walk with us and work through us your good and perfect will. Thank you that you are now and always Immanuel, God with us; in your most precious name. Amen.

Ordinary Time Day 153

SALLY BREEDLOVE

Read: *James 1:16–27*

Do not be deceived, my beloved brothers. Every good gift and every perfect gift is from above, coming down from the Father of lights, with whom there is no variation or shadow due to change. Of his own will he brought us forth by the word of truth, that we should be a kind of firstfruits of his creatures.

Know this, my beloved brothers: let every person be quick to hear, slow to speak, slow to anger; for the anger of man does not produce the righteousness of God. Therefore put away all filthiness and rampant wickedness and receive with meekness the implanted word, which is able to save your souls.

But be doers of the word, and not hearers only, deceiving yourselves. For if anyone is a hearer of the word and not a doer, he is like a man who looks intently at his natural face in a mirror. For he looks at himself and goes away and at once forgets what he was like. But the one who looks into the perfect law, the law of liberty, and perseveres, being no hearer who forgets but a doer who acts, he will be blessed in his doing.

If anyone thinks he is religious and does not bridle his tongue but deceives his heart, this person's religion is worthless. Religion that is pure and undefiled before God the Father is this: to visit orphans and widows in their affliction, and to keep oneself unstained from the world.

Reflect:

Life is a challenge. We encounter difficulties that threaten to swamp us; we find ourselves confused in the midst of the haves and have-nots. We hear the whisper of evil thoughts within our own hearts. "Give in," they say. "This is the way to life."

We forget to listen; we speak hastily and then our anger makes things worse. We study God's Word, but then we're off running our own lives, forgetting what we read just hours before. We parade a spiritual persona and forget to show compassion to the hurting people right under our noses.

What was James's point as he addressed such temptations? Is following Christ as complicated as running through an airplane checklist before takeoff? Is the Christian life a convoluted endeavor with too many particulars to get "just right"? If so, then it's an exhausting self-improvement program.

But what if the Christian life is a far more beautiful and joy-filled endeavor? Read James 1:21: "In simple humility, let our gardener, God, landscape you with the Word, making a salvation-garden of your life" (MSG).

Gardens emerge over time. They change season by season. New plants are added, and weeds are pulled over and over again. Differences abound: cool shade, bright sunshine, spots of color, quiet places. The gardener works with the givens of a particular site. But that same gardener, with time and effort, can transform a littered, wasted place into a place of great beauty. We are not asked to be the gardener, but we can be receptive soil.

Do you insist on being the foreman of a construction site, conforming your life to your own plans? Or will you let the Gardener grow and till your life?

As you pray, offer the givens of your life—your gifting or lack of gifting, your opportunities or lack of opportunities, the things out of your control. Give God both space and time to work in the soil of your life. Ask him to transform you into a salvation garden.

Pray:

Almighty God, you alone can bring into order the unruly wills and affections of sinners: Grant your people grace to love what you command and desire what you promise; that, among the swift and varied changes of this world, our hearts may surely there be fixed where true joys are to be found; through Jesus Christ our Lord, who lives and reigns with you and the Holy Spirit, one God, now and forever. Amen.

(Anglican Church in North America Book of Common Prayer)

22nd Sunday of Ordinary Time

MARY RACHEL BOYD

Read: *Psalm 135:1–7, 19–21*

> Praise the LORD!
> Praise the name of the LORD,
>   give praise, O servants of the LORD,
> who stand in the house of the LORD,
>   in the courts of the house of our God!
> Praise the LORD, for the LORD is good;
>   sing to his name, for it is pleasant!
> For the LORD has chosen Jacob for himself,
>   Israel as his own possession.
> For I know that the LORD is great,
>   and that our Lord is above all gods.
> Whatever the LORD pleases, he does,
>   in heaven and on earth,
>   in the seas and all deeps.
> He it is who makes the clouds rise at the end of the earth,
>   who makes lightnings for the rain
>   and brings forth the wind from his storehouses....
> O house of Israel, bless the LORD!
>   O house of Aaron, bless the LORD!
> O house of Levi, bless the LORD!
>   You who fear the LORD, bless the LORD!
> Blessed be the LORD from Zion,
>   he who dwells in Jerusalem!
> Praise the LORD!

Reflect:

Psalm 135 is an exuberant proclamation of the goodness of God. It is a joyful call for God's people to praise him: "Praise the LORD, for the LORD is good; sing to his name, for it is pleasant!" (v. 3).

God is not only good but also powerful. His earth-shaping and earth-shattering power is on full display in creation, and he is sovereign over it: "Whatever the LORD pleases, he does, in heaven and on earth, in the seas and all deeps" (v. 6).

We who call God "great" and "above all gods" (v. 5) choose to submit to his majesty. But submission in the context of Scripture is beautiful and safe because we are not at the whim of an unpredictable king or ruthless ruler. Our King's sovereignty is just and gracious. At times we don't understand or see clearly his design or direction, but we can trust wholeheartedly, as Paul declared in Romans 8:28, that, "for those who love God all things work together for good."

All of Scripture affirms God's greatness and power. In the stories of the Old Testament, God's greatness is made evident on earth, in the seas, and in all the deep. Think back to the stories of creation, of Jonah and the great fish, and of the parting of the Red Sea for Israel as they escaped the Egyptians. These miracles continue in the New Testament: Jesus calmed storms, he made blind eyes see, and he raised the dead. He himself died but rose again.

In each account, our human frailty and insufficiency was on display, and so was the greatness of God. And yet Jesus himself came in human frailty and lived a life of perfect submission to the Father's will. We are called to full submission just as Christ was. We are safe and we can take comfort, for we are submitting to the one who took on a human body and experienced the shame of human weakness. He knows us, he cares for us, and he will not put us to shame.

Pray:

Lord God, Lamb of God, you take away the sins of the world. Have mercy on us. You are seated at the right hand of the Father: receive our prayer. For you alone are the Holy One, you alone are the Lord, You alone are the Most High, Jesus Christ, with the Holy Spirit, in the glory of God the Father. Amen.

Ordinary Time Day 155
SALLY BREEDLOVE

Read: *James 2:1–13*

My brothers, show no partiality as you hold the faith in our Lord Jesus Christ, the Lord of glory. For if a man wearing a gold ring and fine clothing comes into your assembly, and a poor man in shabby clothing also comes in, and if you pay attention to the one who wears the fine clothing and say, "You sit here in a good place," while you say to the poor man, "You stand over there," or, "Sit down at my feet," have you not then made distinctions among yourselves and become judges with evil thoughts? Listen, my beloved brothers, has not God chosen those who are poor in the world to be rich in faith and heirs of the kingdom, which he has promised to those who love him? But you have dishonored the poor man. Are not the rich the ones who oppress you, and the ones who drag you into court? Are they not the ones who blaspheme the honorable name by which you were called?

If you really fulfill the royal law according to the Scripture, "You shall love your neighbor as yourself," you are doing well. But if you show partiality, you are committing sin and are convicted by the law as transgressors. For whoever keeps the whole law but fails in one point has become guilty of all of it. For he who said, "Do not commit adultery," also said, "Do not murder." If you do not commit adultery but do murder, you have become a transgressor of the law. So speak and so act as those who are to be judged under the law of liberty. For judgment is without mercy to one who has shown no mercy. Mercy triumphs over judgment.

Reflect:

Could any rule set us free? Our world insists that the best life is one where nobody tells anyone what to do. Let's consider this for a moment: If *I* am hurt or diminished by what *you* want, then can we really find a path that leads to freedom and joy for *everyone*?

It's also true that we could never devise enough laws to fully protect us from each other. As this passage makes clear, even our playing favorites—deciding who belongs and who should be excluded—makes us hurtful people who cannot be trusted.

The command to love God and to love others as we love ourselves is the only law that covers everything. But what is love? Our world uses the idea of love to justify so many things that aren't actually love.

Love is not doing what we want to do but learning to be like Jesus. He always loved, and his love was always life-giving, genuine, holy, and sacrificial. It always built up those who received it.

His love never damaged other people's souls or bodies. His love also spoke the truth, and it fiercely opposed all sorts of evil and hypocrisy. Ultimately, God's love triumphed in the most devastating event in history: the death of the beloved Son of God on the cross.

As you pray, sit with your own life this past day and past week. Where have you loved like Jesus loves? Where have you fallen short? Confess to Jesus what your lack of love has done to those around you.

Ask him to teach you to love as he loves.

Pray:

Almighty and everlasting God, whose will it is to restore all things in your well-beloved Son, the King of kings and Lord of lords: Mercifully grant that the peoples of the earth, divided and enslaved by sin, may be freed and brought together under his most gracious rule; who lives and reigns with you and the Holy Spirit, one God, now and for ever. Amen.

(Anglican Church in North America Book of Common Prayer)

Ordinary Time Day 156
SALLY BREEDLOVE

Read: *James 2:14–26*

> What good is it, my brothers, if someone says he has faith but does not have works? Can that faith save him? If a brother or sister is poorly clothed and lacking in daily food, and one of you says to them, "Go in peace, be warmed and filled," without giving them the things needed for the body, what good is that? So also faith by itself, if it does not have works, is dead.
>
> But someone will say, "You have faith and I have works." Show me your faith apart from your works, and I will show you my faith by my works. You believe that God is one; you do well. Even the demons believe—and shudder! Do you want to be shown, you foolish person, that faith apart from works is useless? Was not Abraham our father justified by works when he offered up his son Isaac on the altar? You see that faith was active along with his works, and faith was completed by his works; and the Scripture was fulfilled that says, "Abraham believed God, and it was counted to him as righteousness"—and he was called a friend of God. You see that a person is justified by works and not by faith alone. And in the same way was not also Rahab the prostitute justified by works when she received the messengers and sent them out by another way? For as the body apart from the spirit is dead, so also faith apart from works is dead.

Reflect:

James didn't let us get away with anything, did he? He declared earlier in his letter that hard times help us, that the rich are no more important than the poor, and that we can't blame our sin on situations beyond our control. He instructed us to lead with our ears, not our mouths, and to get our tempers under control. He declared we are to be people of compassion and that we set ourselves against God if we favor the rich.

In this passage, he expanded a point from chapter one: Listening to God's Word, knowing it, and saying we believe it is not the same as receiving it into our hearts and obeying it. To make his point, he gave three examples: demons, the patriarch Abraham, and Rahab the harlot.

Demons accept that God is God—but it doesn't change them. Right doctrine without worship and obedience is frightening. It's the path of demons.

Abraham's faith was not something he could simply hold in his head or heart. It had to make itself known. Real faith is never simply a private or intellectual position. Because his faith was real, Abraham had to obey and choose sacrificial worship.

The harlot Rahab who lived in Jericho was not a Jew, but she believed, and that belief propelled her to act. She hid the Jewish spies when her house was searched, and she put her safety and future in God's hands. Faith involves risk and a deep obedience. It takes us past what we can see and predict.

As you pray, ask yourself if your faith summons you to worship and obedience. Does your faith allow you to believe God even when following him may lead to pain and loss? Does your faith ever take you to risky places?

Are there choices you could make that would increase the ways you live by faith? What are they? How will you choose to follow the living God? Pray for courage and discernment.

Pray:

O Lord, who hast mercy upon all, take away from me my sins, and mercifully kindle in me the fire of thy Holy Spirit. Take away from me the heart of stone, and give me a heart of flesh, a heart to love and adore thee, a heart to delight in thee, to follow and to enjoy thee, for Christ's sake. Amen.

(Ambrose of Milan)

Ordinary Time Day 157
SALLY BREEDLOVE

Read: *James 3:2–18*

For we all stumble in many ways. And if anyone does not stumble
in what he says, he is a perfect man, able also to bridle his whole
body. If we put bits into the mouths of horses so that they obey us,
we guide their whole bodies as well. Look at the ships also: though
they are so large and are driven by strong winds, they are guided by
a very small rudder wherever the will of the pilot directs. So also the
tongue is a small member, yet it boasts of great things.

How great a forest is set ablaze by such a small fire! And the
tongue is a fire, a world of unrighteousness. The tongue is set
among our members, staining the whole body, setting on fire the
entire course of life, and set on fire by hell. For every kind of beast
and bird, of reptile and sea creature, can be tamed and has been
tamed by mankind, but no human being can tame the tongue. It is
a restless evil, full of deadly poison. With it we bless our Lord and
Father, and with it we curse people who are made in the likeness of
God. From the same mouth come blessing and cursing. My brothers,
these things ought not to be so. Does a spring pour forth from the
same opening both fresh and salt water? Can a fig tree, my brothers,
bear olives, or a grapevine produce figs? Neither can a salt pond
yield fresh water.

Who is wise and understanding among you? By his good
conduct let him show his works in the meekness of wisdom. But if
you have bitter jealousy and selfish ambition in your hearts, do not
boast and be false to the truth. This is not the wisdom that comes
down from above, but is earthly, unspiritual, demonic. For where
jealousy and selfish ambition exist, there will be disorder and every
vile practice. But the wisdom from above is first pure, then peaceable, gentle, open to reason, full of mercy and good fruits, impartial
and sincere. And a harvest of righteousness is sown in peace by those
who make peace.

Reflect:

James said our tongues have the power to destroy. They set forests on fire; they offer up polluted water; they are like wild beasts tearing people to shreds. It can't go on like this, James insisted. But where is our hope? James had already declared that the tongue is impossible to master.

Instead of suggesting we tape our mouths shut, James invited us to cultivate wise and humble hearts. Without humility, we are lost. Our need to protect, promote, and present ourselves in a certain way never leads to real friendship or community.

We also need real wisdom. Life is confusing. Mercifully, James described what wisdom looks like. It never tries to be impressive, and it never pits people against each other. Instead, it looks like holiness and decency. Wisdom is steady. Wisdom is kind. It is usually a quiet presence, not a pushy opinion.

In a world like ours that is fractious, angry, and accusatory, what would it be like to live in humility? What would it look like to become a woman or man (or boy or girl) of wisdom? How would being humble and wise deepen your ability to love? How would it bring peace to your community?

As you pray, ask God to make you both wise and humble.

Pray:

O God, without whose beauty and goodness our souls are unfed, without whose truth our reason withers: Consecrate our lives to your will, giving us such purity of heart, such depth of faith, and such steadfastness of purpose that in time we may come to think your own thoughts after you; through Jesus Christ our Savior. Amen.

(Anglican Church in North America Book of Common Prayer)

Ordinary Time Day 158

SALLY BREEDLOVE

Read: *Luke 17:1–6*

And he said to his disciples, "Temptations to sin are sure to come, but woe to the one through whom they come! It would be better for him if a millstone were hung around his neck and he were cast into the sea than that he should cause one of these little ones to sin. Pay attention to yourselves! If your brother sins, rebuke him, and if he repents, forgive him, and if he sins against you seven times in the day, and turns to you seven times, saying, 'I repent,' you must forgive him."

The apostles said to the Lord, "Increase our faith!" And the Lord said, "If you had faith like a grain of mustard seed, you could say to this mulberry tree, 'Be uprooted and planted in the sea,' and it would obey you."

Reflect:

Even if you want to follow Jesus, at times you may find yourself objecting to what he said. You would prefer to gloss over the instructions you find too difficult.

Resist that urge. Listen to Christ.

He called us to love as he loves. That means admitting our sin is never just about ourselves; it always hurts others. Be willing to ask yourself: *Where do I fall short? Is it in my contempt of others? My indifference to the suffering around me? My greed? My private indulgence of secret choices? My settled bitterness? My sense of entitlement? My anger?*

We all need to see that our sin damages those around us. We all need God's forgiveness.

Then Jesus asked another difficult thing. He directed us to care deeply about the sinful choices of others. But instead of judging or fighting back, we are to go to our brother or sister and rebuke him or her. Rebuke means to help set things right. Rebuking is not condemning, judging, or shaming someone; it's caring enough to help a person have a freer heart. A wise rebuke says, "*I love you; I long for you to know blessing.*"

This impossibly hard passage asks even more from us. It asks us to keep forgiving others even if they keep sinning against us or if the memories of what they did keep rising up in us.

Rather than ignoring or explaining away what Jesus has said, the apostles cried out, "Increase our faith!" (v. 5).

And Jesus's response? He says it's not more faith we need. Even a little is enough. What we need is the willingness to use the faith we have already, to obey him.

We live in a broken, divided, and angry world. What if we—and all Christians—decided to live into these words from Jesus?

What if we cared more about protecting the little ones in our world than having our own way? What if we took a serious look at our own lives? What if we loved those we know in the family of God so much that we risked speaking into their lives? What if we believed that every grudge we secretly harbor must be done away with? If we were to live into Jesus's words, who knows what could happen?

As you pray, take Jesus's words to heart and ask him for the strength to follow and obey.

Pray:

O God and Father of all, whom the whole heavens adore: Let the whole earth also worship you, all nations obey you, all tongues confess and bless you, and men, women, and children everywhere love you and serve you in peace; through Jesus Christ our Lord. Amen.

(Anglican Church in North America Book of Common Prayer)

Ordinary Time Day 159

SALLY BREEDLOVE

Read: *Luke 17:7–10*

"Will any one of you who has a servant plowing or keeping sheep say to him when he has come in from the field, 'Come at once and recline at table'? Will he not rather say to him, 'Prepare supper for me, and dress properly, and serve me while I eat and drink, and afterward you will eat and drink'? Does he thank the servant because he did what was commanded? So you also, when you have done all that you were commanded, say, 'We are unworthy servants; we have only done what was our duty.'"

Reflect:

What was Jesus after? Wasn't it enough for the disciples to merely do their duty? Did Christ expect them to exceed expectations in everything they did, or was there something else he wanted from them?

If we say we want to follow Christ, we become his servants for life. That's what the apostle Paul meant when he called himself a bondservant of Jesus. When we become disciples, we also make that same lifetime commitment. Christ is always the Master and leader, and we are his followers.

But in this passage, Jesus also suggested something more. Think about other relationships that involve duty. Parents have a duty to provide for and train their children. Children have a duty to respect and obey their parents. Friends have a duty to be loyal and fair. Husbands and wives have a duty to be faithful and kind and to serve each other. But in these relationships, we are never satisfied with someone merely doing his or her duty toward us. What more do we want? Isn't it love? Isn't it friendship?

Parents long for their children to grow up to be abiding companions through life, and we grieve when it isn't so. A well-married couple doesn't just keep up their half of the marriage; they offer each other friendship year after year.

And Jesus, at that last Passover, said, "No longer do I call you servants ... but I have called you friends" (John 15:15). Jesus desires a life of love together with us. Love includes duty—we are obligated to each other at some level in almost every relationship. But doing our duty is never enough in relationships that are important to us. We all long for love and friendship from those dear to us, not just dutiful behavior.

As you prepare to pray, ask yourself: "Have I made my relationship with Jesus too small?" He offers you love and friendship as well as the opportunity to follow and obey. Will you receive his offer and learn to love him and enjoy his companionship?

Pray:
O Lord my God.
Teach my heart this day,
where and how to find you.
You have made me and re-made me,
and you have bestowed on me all the good things I possess,
and still I do not know you.
I have not yet done that for which I was made.
Teach me to seek you,
for I cannot seek you unless you teach me,
or find you unless you show yourself to me.
Let me seek you in my desire;
let me desire you in my seeking.
Let me find you by loving you;
let me love you when I find you.
Amen.

(Prayer of Saint Anselm)

Ordinary Time Day 160

SALLY BREEDLOVE

Read: *Luke 17:11–19*

> On the way to Jerusalem he was passing along between Samaria and Galilee. And as he entered a village, he was met by ten lepers, who stood at a distance and lifted up their voices, saying, "Jesus, Master, have mercy on us." When he saw them he said to them, "Go and show yourselves to the priests." And as they went they were cleansed. Then one of them, when he saw that he was healed, turned back, praising God with a loud voice; and he fell on his face at Jesus' feet, giving him thanks. Now he was a Samaritan. Then Jesus answered, "Were not ten cleansed? Where are the nine? Was no one found to return and give praise to God except this foreigner?" And he said to him, "Rise and go your way; your faith has made you well."

Reflect:

The apostle Paul was clear: Every human being has an inborn problem called ingratitude. The nine lepers were not the only ones who were ungrateful. Paul wrote,

> For [God's] invisible attributes, namely, his eternal power and divine nature, have been clearly perceived, ever since the creation of the world, in the things that have been made. So [human beings] are without excuse. For although they knew God, they did not honor him as God or give thanks to him, but they became futile in their thinking, and their foolish hearts were darkened. (Romans 1:20–21)

Consider the lepers. If you were embittered in your leprosy, then you might believe healing was simply what you deserved. Why say thank you? If you were lost in despair over your helpless situation, then perhaps you would be skeptical of any healing, afraid it wouldn't last. Bitterness, fear, and despair rarely open the door to gratitude, no matter how great the blessing.

The grateful man in the story was a Samaritan. He knew what it was like to be an outcast for his ethnicity as well as for his disease. The other nine were healed by the broad generosity of God, like rain that falls on the just and the unjust.

But when the Samaritan went back to say thank you, Jesus told him, "Your faith has made you well" (v. 19). Gratitude opened the door into a relationship with Jesus and brought the deeper healing we all need.

If you fear you don't have enough faith or the right kind of faith, if you fear you are an outcast or that your problems are too big, will you turn from your questions and ask God for his help? Then thank him for what he gives you.

Our world is full of sorrow, violence, confusion, and division. But still, there is so much to say thank you for. Gratitude puts us on a road that leads to Jesus. As you pray, say thank you to God for at least ten specific things.

Pray:

Lord, I want to say thank you for the good things I have listed. As James reminded me in his letter, "Every desirable and beneficial gift comes out of heaven. The gifts are rivers of light cascading down from the Father of Light" (James 1:17 MSG). Teach me to praise you for your good gifts. Amen.

23rd Sunday of Ordinary Time

KARI WEST

Read: *Psalm 135:13–18*

Your name, O Lord, endures forever,
your renown, O Lord, throughout all ages.
For the Lord will vindicate his people
and have compassion on his servants.
The idols of the nations are silver and gold,
the work of human hands.
They have mouths, but do not speak;
they have eyes, but do not see;
they have ears, but do not hear,
nor is there any breath in their mouths.
Those who make them become like them,
so do all who trust in them.

Reflect:

We become like that which we worship. This psalm poses a simple yet profound question to us: Will we trust in the everlasting name of the Lord and have confidence that his renown will endure throughout all of eternity? Or will we turn to smaller idols, trusting in the gods we craft for ourselves, and slowly lose our humanity as a result of our misplaced worship?

This psalmist presented a horrifying image to us, and it was meant to awaken us from spiritual slumber. You can become a person with unseeing eyes, unhearing ears, and a mouth without breath. God is the one who first breathed life into his image-bearers; if we turn from this source of life and attempt to find another fount of identity or wholeness, we'll die.

But the opposite is also true, which is why passages like this offer promises as well as warnings. When we turn toward God as the source for our life, when we take the words of the psalmist on our own lips and proclaim the praise of our everlasting, compassionate God, we become more human. We draw closer to the image of Jesus, the only perfect human being who has ever walked the face of the earth.

As you pray, ask the Lord to reveal what you're tempted to worship instead of him. Confess your idolatry and ask him to lead you farther on the path of real humanity. Embrace God as the source of all life and goodness.

Pray:

You are the connector and preserver of all created things, the framer of all. You steer the universe with your wise and steady hand. You are the very principle of all good order. The unbreakable bond of harmony and peace. In you we live, and move, and have our being. So I will glorify you, O Lord my God. I will praise your name. You have done wonderful things. Amen.

(Methodius of Olympus)

Ordinary Time Day 162

SALLY BREEDLOVE

Read: *Luke 17:20–37*

> Being asked by the Pharisees when the kingdom of God would
> come, he answered them, "The kingdom of God is not coming in
> ways that can be observed, nor will they say, 'Look, here it is!' or
> 'There!' for behold, the kingdom of God is in the midst of you."
>
> And he said to the disciples, "The days are coming when you
> will desire to see one of the days of the Son of Man, and you will
> not see it. And they will say to you, 'Look, there!' or 'Look, here!'
> Do not go out or follow them. For as the lightning flashes and
> lights up the sky from one side to the other, so will the Son of Man
> be in his day. But first he must suffer many things and be rejected
> by this generation. Just as it was in the days of Noah, so will it
> be in the days of the Son of Man. They were eating and drinking
> and marrying and being given in marriage, until the day when
> Noah entered the ark, and the flood came and destroyed them all.
> Likewise, just as it was in the days of Lot—they were eating and
> drinking, buying and selling, planting and building, but on the day
> when Lot went out from Sodom, fire and sulfur rained from heaven
> and destroyed them all—so will it be on the day when the Son of
> Man is revealed. On that day, let the one who is on the housetop,
> with his goods in the house, not come down to take them away, and
> likewise let the one who is in the field not turn back. Remember
> Lot's wife. Whoever seeks to preserve his life will lose it, but whoever
> loses his life will keep it. I tell you, in that night there will be two
> in one bed. One will be taken and the other left. There will be two
> women grinding together. One will be taken and the other left."
> And they said to him, "Where, Lord?" He said to them, "Where the
> corpse is, there the vultures will gather."

Reflect:

How will things turn out? Will we ever be as happy or secure as we long
to be? What is Jesus's wisdom to us about the future? In this passage from

336

Luke 17, Jesus addressed both Pharisees and disciples. What he said to them seemed the opposite of what we might expect.

He told the Pharisees that they were looking for the wrong thing. The kingdom of God was already among them, and it was not about power. If we look for the wrong thing, we will rarely find the right thing.

Perhaps we are more like the Pharisees than we'd like to believe. We want a God who shows up to fix things and make things right. But Christ said his rule in this world is already taking place in subtle ways. If we pay attention, we'll learn how to recognize his work and to trust the way he works.

He told the disciples that endurance is hard. They longed to see him reign in power, but the world would seem to continue along the way it always had. He warned them to stay alert; otherwise, they were in danger of being distracted by the daily details of work and weddings, eating and drinking.

Like Lot's wife, we may lose our eager hope for the better world that lies beyond this one. Lot's wife perished because she couldn't let go of the life she had enjoyed in Sodom. Even as her sinful city was being destroyed, she looked back with longing.

Like the Pharisees and the disciples, we are too often blind to God's clear invitation to join him in his kingdom work. We have no guarantees about the future. Are we ready, Jesus asked, for his return?

As you pray, ask Jesus to make you ready for your own death or for his coming. Ask him to help you see that you have kingdom work to do today. Pray with joy, for the kingdom of God is in the midst of you!

Pray:
Lord, your kingdom come, your will be done on earth as it is in heaven; in Jesus's name. Amen.

Ordinary Time Day 163

SALLY BREEDLOVE

Read: *Luke 18:1–8*

And he told them a parable to the effect that they ought always to pray and not lose heart. He said, "In a certain city there was a judge who neither feared God nor respected man. And there was a widow in that city who kept coming to him and saying, 'Give me justice against my adversary.' For a while he refused, but afterward he said to himself, 'Though I neither fear God nor respect man, yet because this widow keeps bothering me, I will give her justice, so that she will not beat me down by her continual coming.'" And the Lord said, "Hear what the unrighteous judge says. And will not God give justice to his elect, who cry to him day and night? Will he delay long over them? I tell you, he will give justice to them speedily. Nevertheless, when the Son of Man comes, will he find faith on earth?"

Reflect:

We are taught not to beg. Polite people don't demand. We are told to be patient and to take care of our own problems.

But what can we learn from the persistent widow in this parable who bothered the judge until he gave in?

Perhaps a clue lies in Jesus's question in verse 8: "When the Son of Man comes, will he find faith on earth?" The word *faith* can also be translated as "faithfulness." Perhaps Jesus was asking, *When I return, will I see faithfulness in my people?*

What is faithfulness? At its core, faithfulness is a persistent waiting and trusting, waiting and trusting, waiting and trusting. Faithfulness leads to hope.

Jesus's first question in this parable was rhetorical: "And will not God bring about justice for his chosen ones, who cry out to him day and night?" (v. 7 NIV). The answer is, "Of course! A good God will give justice."

Jesus's second question was not at all rhetorical, and it is pointed directly at us. When the Son of Man returns, will he find faithful people who continually turn to God? Who constantly expect him to be the good and beautiful God he is?

We need to answer both questions. Do we believe God is good? Do we believe that, like a good father, he longs to hear our hearts cry out to him? Or have we regarded him as a harsh judge whom we must badger?

The second question prompts us to examine our own hearts: Will we persist in asking for what we need? Will we wait for God to answer? Will we choose faithfulness to our God and Savior, no matter how long the wait?

As you pray, ask the Lord to strengthen the hearts of his people so we may stay faithful to him. Pray especially for the people you know who are struggling to faithfully follow Jesus.

Pray:

Most loving Father, you will us to give you thanks for all things, to dread nothing but the loss of you, and to cast all our care on the One who cares for us. Preserve us from faithless fears and worldly anxieties, and grant that no clouds of this mortal life may hide from us the light of that love which is immortal, and which you manifested unto us in your Son, Jesus Christ our Lord. Amen.

(Anglican Church in North America Book of Common Prayer)

Ordinary Time Day 164
SALLY BREEDLOVE

Read: *Luke 18:9–14*

> He also told this parable to some who trusted in themselves that they were righteous, and treated others with contempt: "Two men went up into the temple to pray, one a Pharisee and the other a tax collector. The Pharisee, standing by himself, prayed thus: 'God, I thank you that I am not like other men, extortioners, unjust, adulterers, or even like this tax collector. I fast twice a week; I give tithes of all that I get.' But the tax collector, standing far off, would not even lift up his eyes to heaven, but beat his breast, saying, 'God, be merciful to me, a sinner!' I tell you, this man went down to his house justified, rather than the other. For everyone who exalts himself will be humbled, but the one who humbles himself will be exalted."

Reflect:

Jesus told this parable for those who "trusted in themselves that they were righteous, and treated others with contempt" (v. 9). He gave us this story to reshape the way we see ourselves and others.

Perhaps you are a fairly good person. You do your best. You're reasonably honest and kind; you know you aren't perfect, but your intentions are good. If you wonder about God, you assume he knows how hard you're trying and that he's reasonably happy with you.

Christ called this attitude trusting oneself instead of God.

The Bible makes it clear—no one is good enough. We've all fallen short of God's holiness. Our personal goodness, love, commitment to justice, or purity is useless when held up to the light of God. Our righteousness is like having twenty-seven cents in our pocket when what we really need is one million dollars.

True Christ-followers know they aren't good enough. We're thankful we have a Savior who died for our sins and who gave us new life in his name.

But if we do a full stop at this point, we haven't listened to the whole parable.

Jesus also told the parable for those who looked at others with contempt. Does Christ have our full attention now?

What person hasn't muttered in his or her own heart, if not aloud, "Well, I know I'm not perfect, but at least I'm better than _____." We fill in the blank with a certain type of people or the name of a particular person. We judge those around us by what news outlets they choose, whom they voted for, how they raise their children, their ideas about God, their T-shirt logo, tattoos, or five-hundred-dollar shoes.

We will certainly deeply disagree with others about their choices, their beliefs, or their values. But when we treat them with contempt because of those differences, we are wrong. We are no better than anyone else.

As you pray, be honest. Do you trust you are "good enough"? Do you justify yourself by how hard you try or how good your intentions are? Do you spend your life defending yourself or do you trust Christ to save you?

Ask yourself: Whom do you think you're better than? Our hearts all have ranking systems; we rarely see ourselves as bottom-rung people. Repent of your pride. Pray for the mercy of God to teach you mercy toward others.

Pray:
Most merciful God,
we confess that we have sinned against you
in thought, word, and deed,
by what we have done, and by what we have left undone.
We have not loved you with our whole heart;
we have not loved our neighbors as ourselves.
We are truly sorry and we humbly repent.
For the sake of your Son Jesus Christ,
have mercy on us and forgive us;
that we may delight in your will, and walk in your ways,
to the glory of your Name. Amen.

(Anglican Church in North America Book of Common Prayer)

Ordinary Time Day 165
SALLY BREEDLOVE

Read: *Luke 18:15–17*

> Now they were bringing even infants to him that he might touch
> them. And when the disciples saw it, they rebuked them. But Jesus
> called them to him, saying, "Let the children come to me, and do
> not hinder them, for to such belongs the kingdom of God. Truly,
> I say to you, whoever does not receive the kingdom of God like a
> child shall not enter it."

Reflect:

The stories in Luke 18 and 19 were the last encounters between Jesus and ordinary people recorded for us. These encounters revealed the heart of Christ.
They remind us that humility, not accomplishment, is required to enter the
kingdom.

"Now they were bringing even infants to him that he might touch them"
(v. 15). People brought their babies to Jesus; it was something that happened
continually.

Why? The love of Jesus drew them.

In Jesus's day, an important rabbi would never concern himself with little
children. But Jesus welcomed the young even as his disciples rebuked their
parents. He beckoned, "Let the children come to me, and do not hinder
them, for to such belongs the kingdom of God" (v. 16).

Even as Jesus's time on earth grew short, he made time to care for children. He himself was humble of heart, so he stopped to teach. What lesson
did he share as he looked toward the cross? Those who are humble—help-
lessly dependent and without a list of accomplishments or achievements—
are welcome in his kingdom. The kingdom belongs to them.

Jesus told us not only to come as a child, trusting and dependent, but also
to receive as a child. Picture the way a child receives a gift—not in cautious

consideration of what he deserves, but with exuberance, joy, and delight. Children receive what they are given. They trust the giver and the gift.

How does your own heart see Christ? Trust is confidence in the reliability of someone or something. Do you trust the Giver and the gift? Let go of anything else you're trusting in for entrance to the kingdom, for membership in God's family.

Pray. Acknowledge your helpless dependence on Christ. Let his love draw you in. With open hands and an open heart—in faith, with joy—trust him as your Savior. Receive with gratitude and delight the gift of grace. Enter the kingdom as a little child.

Pray:

Gentle Jesus, meek and mild,
Look upon a little child,
Pity my simplicity,
Suffer me to come to thee.
Fain I would to thee be brought,
Gracious Lord, forbid it not;
In the Kingdom of thy grace
Give a little child a place.
Loving Jesus, gentle Lamb,
In thy gracious hands I am;
Make me, Savior, what thou art,
Live thyself within my heart.
Amen.

("Gentle Jesus, Meek and Mild," Charles Wesley)

Ordinary Time Day 166

WILLA KANE

Read: *Luke 18:18–27*

And a ruler asked him, "Good Teacher, what must I do to inherit eternal life?" And Jesus said to him, "Why do you call me good? No one is good except God alone. You know the commandments: 'Do not commit adultery, Do not murder, Do not steal, Do not bear false witness, Honor your father and mother.'" And he said, "All these I have kept from my youth." When Jesus heard this, he said to him, "One thing you still lack. Sell all that you have and distribute to the poor, and you will have treasure in heaven; and come, follow me." But when he heard these things, he became very sad, for he was extremely rich. Jesus, seeing that he had become sad, said, "How difficult it is for those who have wealth to enter the kingdom of God! For it is easier for a camel to go through the eye of a needle than for a rich person to enter the kingdom of God." Those who heard it said, "Then who can be saved?" But he said, "What is impossible with man is possible with God."

Reflect:

It's no coincidence that this passage follows the story about childlike faith as the requirement to enter the kingdom of God.

The man in this story appeared to have everything—wealth, an outwardly righteous life, respect, and prestige. But he realized he lacked something. "What must I do to inherit eternal life?" he asked. He thought there had to be something he could do to enter the kingdom, some way he could measure up.

He viewed Jesus as a "good teacher" but not as Lord.

He was wrong about himself, he was wrong about Jesus, and he was wrong about life.

In love, Jesus put his finger on the young man's errors. Entering the kingdom is not about looking good or being good. The only way to enter is on bended knee, like a little child. It requires absolute allegiance to God, the only one who is good; it demands loving him with one's heart, soul, and mind.

There can be no substitute gods or idols, nothing we hold dearer than Jesus.

Instead of entering the kingdom in joy with a promise of eternal riches, this young man grasped earthly wealth and departed in sorrow.

Jesus knows what is competing for your affections. As you pray, ask the Spirit to show you. Turn and accept anew the grace Christ offers. Choose eternal riches, not the poverty of worldly gain. Put your trust in Jesus as your Savior and Lord.

Pray:

O God, you have prepared for those who love you such good things as surpass our understanding: Pour into our hearts such love towards you, that we, loving you in all things and above all things, may obtain your promises, which exceed all that we can desire; through Jesus Christ our Lord, who lives and reigns with you and the Holy Spirit, one God, for ever and ever. Amen.

(Anglican Church in North America Book of Common Prayer)

Ordinary Time Day 167
ALYSIA YATES

Read: *Luke 18:27–34*

But he said, "What is impossible with man is possible with God." And Peter said, "See, we have left our homes and followed you." And he said to them, "Truly, I say to you, there is no one who has left house or wife or brothers or parents or children, for the sake of the kingdom of God, who will not receive many times more in this time, and in the age to come eternal life."

And taking the twelve, he said to them, "See, we are going up to Jerusalem, and everything that is written about the Son of Man by the prophets will be accomplished. For he will be delivered over to the Gentiles and will be mocked and shamefully treated and spit upon. And after flogging him, they will kill him, and on the third day he will rise." But they understood none of these things. This saying was hidden from them, and they did not grasp what was said.

Reflect:

Jesus's life was reflected in his teaching, and his teaching was an embodiment of his life. Luke 18 allows us to experience this seamlessness.

There was no difference between Jesus's parables and his loving engagement with others in Luke 18. His stories and interactions modeled the faithful life: the persistent widow and the unjust judge, the proud Pharisee and the repentant tax collector, Jesus receiving babies and calming irritated disciples, and Jesus speaking kindly to the rich young ruler who tried to squeeze his camel through the needle's eye.

Jesus knew that the kingdom of God would cost his followers everything. He knew that his disciples didn't yet understand. But he reassured them, "What is impossible with man is possible with God" (v. 27).

His disciples "did not grasp what was said" (v. 34). Peter responded, perhaps in exasperation, with a reminder to Jesus of what he had given up: "We have left all we had to follow you!" (v. 28 NIV). He felt the need to justify himself and rehearse his sacrifices. This was a not-so-subtle reminder, in case Jesus had overlooked Peter's efforts to follow him; it was a plea for recognition and credit.

Jesus answered without patronizing. He acknowledged the cost of the kingdom. And he promised a beautiful reward: "There is no one who has left house or wife or brothers or parents or children, for the sake of the kingdom of God, who will not receive many times more in this time, and in the age to come eternal life" (vv. 29–30).

As you pray, consider the people we met in Luke 18: the widow, the judge, the Pharisee, the tax collector, parents, babies, disciples, and the rich young ruler. What about their interactions with Jesus feels familiar to you? What questions would you ask if you were as bold as Peter? Confess your fears and anxieties, or those things you are holding back from Jesus. Pray for the courage to follow Christ with your whole life.

Pray:

O God, the light of the minds that know you, the life of the souls that love you, and the strength of the wills that serve you: Help us so to know you that we may truly love you, and so to love you that we may fully serve you, whom to serve is perfect freedom; through Jesus Christ our Lord. Amen.

(Anglican Church in North America Book of Common Prayer)

24th Sunday of Ordinary Time

KARI WEST

Read: *Psalm 139:13–18*

> For you formed my inward parts;
>> you knitted me together in my mother's womb.
> I praise you, for I am fearfully and wonderfully made.
> Wonderful are your works;
>> my soul knows it very well.
> My frame was not hidden from you,
> when I was being made in secret,
>> intricately woven in the depths of the earth.
> Your eyes saw my unformed substance;
> in your book were written, every one of them,
>> the days that were formed for me,
>> when as yet there was none of them.
> How precious to me are your thoughts, O God!
>> How vast is the sum of them!
> If I would count them, they are more than the sand.
>> I awake, and I am still with you.

Reflect:

You were formed by the hand of God, "knitted . . . together" in your mother's womb (v. 13).

Take a few moments to meditate on that reality. Do you believe that you are "fearfully and wonderfully made" (v. 14)? Do you ever consider the fact that you are one of God's wonderful works? That you are a part of his magnificent creation?

Know the nearness of God. Remember who carved every intricate way in you, who searched out the depths of you, who crafted the inmost parts of your soul and your being, and who knows you more fully than anyone has ever known you, including yourself. God saw your "unformed substance" (v. 16); he knew each of the days that were written for you before you lived a single one of them.

And now let the truth of God as your near and intimate Creator give you a deeper trust in his thoughts and commands. They are for your good. They fit with what it means to be human. They will satisfy your soul. They will carry you farther into the life you actually long for, even if you don't have the words for it—a life where you are free to become a deeply godly person.

Let the unfailing love of God be your consolation today. Seek a wholehearted life of love and obedience toward your Creator, who is your Father. Hope in the Lord's promises, ask for his comfort, and rest in his gracious compassion.

Pray:

O King, you are the great giver of good gifts to us all, and Lord of the good. You are our Father and maker of all. By your word you made heaven and everything in it. You brought forth sunshine and the day. You appointed the course of the stars, showed the earth and sea their places. You decided when the seasons should come in their circling courses, winter and summer, autumn and spring. You created this sphere out of a confused heap, and adorned the universe from a shapeless mass.

Grant to me life—a life well spent, always enjoying your grace. Help me to act and speak in all things as your Holy Scriptures teach. May I ever praise you, and praise your co-eternal Word, who proceeds from you. Amen.

(Clement of Alexandria)

Ordinary Time Day 169
WILLA KANE

Read: *Luke 19:1–10*

> He entered Jericho and was passing through. And behold, there
> was a man named Zacchaeus. He was a chief tax collector and was
> rich. And he was seeking to see who Jesus was, but on account of
> the crowd he could not, because he was small in stature. So he ran
> on ahead and climbed up into a sycamore tree to see him, for he
> was about to pass that way. And when Jesus came to the place, he
> looked up and said to him, "Zacchaeus, hurry and come down, for
> I must stay at your house today." So he hurried and came down
> and received him joyfully. And when they saw it, they all grum-
> bled, "He has gone in to be the guest of a man who is a sinner." And
> Zacchaeus stood and said to the Lord, "Behold, Lord, the half of
> my goods I give to the poor. And if I have defrauded anyone of
> anything, I restore it fourfold." And Jesus said to him, "Today salva-
> tion has come to this house, since he also is a son of Abraham. For
> the Son of Man came to seek and to save the lost."

Reflect:

Zacchaeus was not a cute little man who climbed a tree to see Jesus, but a
crooked tax collector, chief among those who defrauded his neighbors to
become rich. A known sinner, he was despised by all. He had fallen to the
bottom rung of society by dishonestly climbing the ladder of success. If you
had lived in Jericho, you would have written him off.

Jesus was traveling through Jericho to Passover in Jerusalem, where he
would become the Passover Lamb. But before he reached Jerusalem to suffer
and die, his larger mission was on view as he called to Zacchaeus. Jesus did
not write him off but drew him in.

The Son of Man came to seek and to save the lost.

This is the gospel: Jesus rescues sinners like us. It's why he came.

The story of Zacchaeus is powerful in its message and position. Following
encounters with a blind beggar trapped in poverty and a rich young ruler

trapped by his wealth, this is the last personal encounter we witness before the Passion Week begins to unfold.

The disciples had asked, "Who can be saved?" (Luke 18:26). Encounters with these people gave the answer. Those who are saved first acknowledge they are lost. They turn to Jesus.

Your sin is not a barrier to Christ's seeking you; it's what beckons him. Jesus came to seek Zacchaeus, a sinner, and he came to seek you, a sinner. He came to save Zacchaeus, a sinner, and he came to save you, a sinner. He is the friend of sinners. His love is directed toward sinners.

When Jesus, who did not count equality with God as a thing to be grasped, meets the humble and contrite heart of a sinner, divine love takes root and changes lives.

Pray. Acknowledge your sin before Christ. Thank him that he came to seek and to save. Open your heart to the God who sees you and knows you. In humility, receive his forgiveness and let his love change you.

Pray:

May the Father of the true light—who has adorned day with heavenly light, who has made the fire shine which illuminates us during the night, who reserves for us in the peace of a future age a spiritual and everlasting light— enlighten our hearts in the knowledge of truth, keep us from stumbling, and grant that we may walk honestly as in the day. Thus we will shine as the sun in the midst of the glory of the saints. Amen.

(Basil of Caesarea)

Ordinary Time Day 170

WILLA KANE

Read: *Luke 19:11–27*

As they heard these things, he proceeded to tell a parable, because he was near to Jerusalem, and because they supposed that the kingdom of God was to appear immediately. He said therefore, "A nobleman went into a far country to receive for himself a kingdom and then return. Calling ten of his servants, he gave them ten minas, and said to them, 'Engage in business until I come.' But his citizens hated him and sent a delegation after him, saying, 'We do not want this man to reign over us.' When he returned, having received the kingdom, he ordered these servants to whom he had given the money to be called to him, that he might know what they had gained by doing business. The first came before him, saying, 'Lord, your mina has made ten minas more.' And he said to him, 'Well done, good servant! Because you have been faithful in a very little, you shall have authority over ten cities.' And the second came, saying, 'Lord, your mina has made five minas.' And he said to him, 'And you are to be over five cities.' Then another came, saying, 'Lord, here is your mina, which I kept laid away in a handkerchief; for I was afraid of you, because you are a severe man. You take what you did not deposit, and reap what you did not sow.' He said to him, 'I will condemn you with your own words, you wicked servant! You knew that I was a severe man, taking what I did not deposit and reaping what I did not sow? Why then did you not put my money in the bank, and at my coming I might have collected it with interest?' And he said to those who stood by, 'Take the mina from him, and give it to the one who has the ten minas.' And they said to him, 'Lord, he has ten minas!' 'I tell you that to everyone who has, more will be given, but from the one who has not, even what he has will be taken away. But as for these enemies of mine, who did not want me to reign over them, bring them here and slaughter them before me.'"

Reflect:

The encounters we've considered in Luke 18 and 19 lead us to the lesson of this parable: Humility is required for stewardship.

A humble Savior entrusts his followers with capital to invest. That sacred deposit is primarily the gospel, but it is also our lives, our influence, our time, our resources, and our talents.

Until Jesus returns, we are responsible to use all these things under his lordship and for his glory.

Humble servants steward these gifts, and they will be rewarded for doing so. Enemies of Christ will be punished.

Enemies of Christ aren't always openly hostile. They can be politely indifferent or casually irresponsible with gifts of grace.

Take inventory of the trust account Christ has put in your hands. On days that are difficult, is the deposit he has given you working hard for his benefit? How are you investing the gifts he has given? Are you indifferent or irresponsible with opportunities to share the gospel? Have you ignored the gift of salvation?

As you pray, ask Jesus to guide you into faithful and trustworthy stewardship of all he's given. Confess where you've fallen short, and in humility, embrace with joy the role of a servant in the kingdom of God.

Pray:

O merciful Creator, your loving hand is open wide to satisfy the needs of every living creature: Make us always thankful for your loving providence, and give us grace to honor you with all that you have entrusted to us; that we, remembering the account we must one day give, may be faithful stewards of your good gifts; through Jesus Christ our Lord, who with you and the Holy Spirit lives and reigns, one God, for ever and ever. Amen.

(Anglican Church in North America Book of Common Prayer)

Ordinary Time Day 171
ABIGAIL HULL WHITEHOUSE

Read: *Luke 19:29–44*

> When he drew near to Bethphage and Bethany, at the mount that
> is called Olivet, he sent two of the disciples, saying, "Go into the
> village in front of you, where on entering you will find a colt tied,
> on which no one has ever yet sat. Untie it and bring it here. If
> anyone asks you, 'Why are you untying it?' you shall say this: 'The
> Lord has need of it.'" So those who were sent went away and found
> it just as he had told them. And as they were untying the colt, its
> owners said to them, "Why are you untying the colt?" And they said,
> "The Lord has need of it." And they brought it to Jesus, and throwing
> their cloaks on the colt, they set Jesus on it. And as he rode along,
> they spread their cloaks on the road. As he was drawing near—
> already on the way down the Mount of Olives—the whole multi-
> tude of his disciples began to rejoice and praise God with a loud
> voice for all the mighty works that they had seen, saying, "Blessed is
> the King who comes in the name of the Lord! Peace in heaven and
> glory in the highest!" And some of the Pharisees in the crowd said
> to him, "Teacher, rebuke your disciples." He answered, "I tell you, if
> these were silent, the very stones would cry out."
>
> And when he drew near and saw the city, he wept over it, saying,
> "Would that you, even you, had known on this day the things that
> make for peace! But now they are hidden from your eyes. For the
> days will come upon you, when your enemies will set up a barricade
> around you and surround you and hem you in on every side and
> tear you down to the ground, you and your children within you.
> And they will not leave one stone upon another in you, because you
> did not know the time of your visitation."

Reflect:

Our reading from Luke 19, including Jesus's triumphal entry, seems a little out
of step with Ordinary Time and more fitting for Lent, the season contemplating

Christ's death. But the words of warning we find in these verses speak well into the call to faithful following that is the hallmark of Ordinary Time.

Seated on a lowly donkey like his mother before him, Christ looked over the city of Jerusalem and wept. He said, "Would that you, even you, had known on this day the things that make for peace! But now they are hidden from your eyes" (v. 42). We sense a deep sadness in Jesus because they had missed him and his time of visitation. If only they had seen! If only they had heard! If only their hearts had been open enough to receive the presence of God in their midst! But, tragically, "the things that make for peace"—Christ himself and the meaning of his sacrificial death—were hidden from their eyes.

Like the city of Jerusalem, we, too, can become blind to the very presence of God in our midst. Caught up in the swirl and burden of our daily lives, we forget that God is in the room with us, watching and waiting to be recognized and invited in, waiting to be praised.

Take a moment to center yourself in God's loving presence and let the frustrations and stresses (and all that you did or did not accomplish) fade away. Imagine gathering up all the tasks, concerns, worries, and questions in your mind, and setting them aside.

Now invite the Prince of Peace to come in a powerful and personal way. Repent of the ways that you've become distracted by lesser things and ask God for eyes to see and a heart to praise. Be honest with him about the areas where you've struggled today, and trust that he will draw close to you as you draw close to him in this time of prayer (James 4:8).

Pray:

I hand over to your care, Lord, my soul and my body, my mind and my thoughts, my prayers and my hopes, my health and my work, my life and my death, my parents and my family, my friends and my neighbors, and my country and all humankind. Today and always, I offer this time, and all that I am, to you. Consecrate my life and give me the grace to seek you first. Amen.

(Adapted from Saint Benedict's Prayer Book)

Ordinary Time Day 172
BILL BOYD

Read: *John 2:1–11*

> On the third day there was a wedding at Cana in Galilee, and the
> mother of Jesus was there. Jesus also was invited to the wedding
> with his disciples. When the wine ran out, the mother of Jesus said
> to him, "They have no wine." And Jesus said to her, "Woman, what
> does this have to do with me? My hour has not yet come." His
> mother said to the servants, "Do whatever he tells you."
>
> Now there were six stone water jars there for the Jewish rites
> of purification, each holding twenty or thirty gallons. Jesus said
> to the servants, "Fill the jars with water." And they filled them up
> to the brim. And he said to them, "Now draw some out and take
> it to the master of the feast." So they took it. When the master of
> the feast tasted the water now become wine, and did not know
> where it came from (though the servants who had drawn the water
> knew), the master of the feast called the bridegroom and said to him,
> "Everyone serves the good wine first, and when people have drunk
> freely, then the poor wine. But you have kept the good wine until
> now." This, the first of his signs, Jesus did at Cana in Galilee, and
> manifested his glory. And his disciples believed in him.

Reflect:

Jesus responded to invitations to dinners and festivals of all sorts. He talked,
listened, ate, and drank, just as we all do. And he performed many miracles.

Yet the small Galilean village of Cana is revered and celebrated as the
place of Jesus's first miracle. That miracle—the transformation of water into
wine at a wedding—is undoubtedly the prototype for the Son of God's life
and ministry, and a proclamation of the real truth about kingdom life.

The message of Jesus's first miracle is profoundly simple: The wine of
human hopes always runs out, and usually at the worst possible moment.
The help we need will never come through human effort, but through divine

love. We are invited to ask for help, as Mary did, when we are dismayed by the circumstances of life.

"Do whatever he tells you" (v. 5), Mary instructed the servants at the wedding. Isn't she speaking to us as well?

Christ desires to bless us and help us when things are out of control, when our resources dry up, when the unexpected crashes down on us. As you pray, ask yourself, "What do I do when the wine runs out?"

John began his gospel with a wedding story. Why? Could it be that Christ wanted to emphasize the great gift God has given us in marriage and family? And could it be that the blessing of this Galilean marriage points us toward the union of Christ and the church? We see the lavish love of Jesus: He is the Bridegroom who will provide for his bride on her wedding day.

Turn to Jesus. Listen for his voice. Obey. Seek blessing and restoration for yourself and for others. Rejoice in the extravagant provision of your heavenly Father.

Pray:

Almighty and eternal God, so draw our hearts to you, so guide our minds, so fill our imaginations, so control our wills, that we may be wholly yours, utterly dedicated to you; and then use us, we pray, as you will, and always to your glory and the welfare of your people; through our Lord and Savior Jesus Christ. Amen.

(William Temple)

Ordinary Time Day 173
WILLA KANE

Read: *John 5:2–17*

Now there is in Jerusalem by the Sheep Gate a pool, in Aramaic called Bethesda, which has five roofed colonnades. In these lay a multitude of invalids—blind, lame, and paralyzed. One man was there who had been an invalid for thirty-eight years. When Jesus saw him lying there and knew that he had already been there a long time, he said to him, "Do you want to be healed?" The sick man answered him, "Sir, I have no one to put me into the pool when the water is stirred up, and while I am going another steps down before me." Jesus said to him, "Get up, take up your bed, and walk." And at once the man was healed, and he took up his bed and walked.

Now that day was the Sabbath. So the Jews said to the man who had been healed, "It is the Sabbath, and it is not lawful for you to take up your bed." But he answered them, "The man who healed me, that man said to me, 'Take up your bed, and walk.'" They asked him, "Who is the man who said to you, 'Take up your bed and walk'?" Now the man who had been healed did not know who it was, for Jesus had withdrawn, as there was a crowd in the place. Afterward Jesus found him in the temple and said to him, "See, you are well! Sin no more, that nothing worse may happen to you." The man went away and told the Jews that it was Jesus who had healed him. And this was why the Jews were persecuting Jesus, because he was doing these things on the Sabbath. But Jesus answered them, "My Father is working until now, and I am working."

Reflect:

"Do you want to be healed?" (v. 6).

On the surface, this seems like an unnecessary—even cruel—question for Jesus to ask of the lame man. He had been an invalid for thirty-eight years, lying right by water that reportedly had healing powers, and yet he was never able to get into the pool before someone else beat him to it. How frustrating and humbling this man's life must have been! He was so close to what he believed might bring him healing and yet he was unable to grasp it.

His answer was telling. Instead of a resounding, "Yes! I want to be healed!" the man said that it was impossible. There would be no healing for him because he didn't have help and couldn't help himself. Can you feel the resigned despair in his answer?

Perhaps Jesus's question was meant to rekindle this man's desire for restoration and new life. But the focus of the story shifts, from a healing pool and a hopeless man to Jesus, the compassionate healer who offers eternal hope. The one who knitted this man together in his mother's womb stood before him, full of power and love. He commanded, "Get up" (v. 8), and the man found himself healed after thirty-eight years of misery.

Do you find yourself hemmed in by the impossibility of your circumstances? Are your friends and family far away? Are you facing your own helplessness? Look to Jesus, full of grace, for fresh hope. In his command to the invalid, hear his loving commitment to the good of his people. Though his ways are beyond us and he does not always act according to our timetable, he will right wrongs and restore what the locusts have eaten (Joel 2:25).

As you pray, meditate on this act of Jesus. Jesus took what was broken and made it whole again. Consider our good God, our great healer, and rest in his love for you.

Pray:

O Lord, support us all the day long through this trouble-filled life, until the shadows lengthen, and the evening comes, and the busy world is hushed, and the fever of life is over, and our work is done. Then in your mercy grant us a safe lodging, and a holy rest, and peace at the last. Amen.

(John Henry Newman)

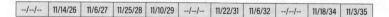
Ordinary Time Day 174

KARI WEST

Read: *John 5:19–29*

So Jesus said to them, "Truly, truly, I say to you, the Son can do nothing of his own accord, but only what he sees the Father doing. For whatever the Father does, that the Son does likewise. For the Father loves the Son and shows him all that he himself is doing. And greater works than these will he show him, so that you may marvel. For as the Father raises the dead and gives them life, so also the Son gives life to whom he will. For the Father judges no one, but has given all judgment to the Son, that all may honor the Son, just as they honor the Father. Whoever does not honor the Son does not honor the Father who sent him. Truly, truly, I say to you, whoever hears my word and believes him who sent me has eternal life. He does not come into judgment, but has passed from death to life.

"Truly, truly, I say to you, an hour is coming, and is now here, when the dead will hear the voice of the Son of God, and those who hear will live. For as the Father has life in himself, so he has granted the Son also to have life in himself. And he has given him authority to execute judgment, because he is the Son of Man. Do not marvel at this, for an hour is coming when all who are in the tombs will hear his voice and come out, those who have done good to the resurrection of life, and those who have done evil to the resurrection of judgment."

Reflect:

Christ, the one through whom the cosmos was wrought, declared in this passage that he can do nothing by himself. Scripture is full of the supernatural stories of Jesus's birth, his miraculous acts of provision and healing, his transfiguration, and his ultimate power over sin, death, and hell. Did he act alone? Not at all. Here in John 5, the Son of God stated that he "can do nothing of his own accord, but only what he sees the Father doing" (v. 19).

This challenges our assumptions: We often equate power with autonomy. But Christ gave us an incredible insight into the perfect, mysterious, and foundational relationship in the Godhead: The Father—out of love—shows the Son his perfect work, and the Son enacts the will of the Father. There is no power grabbing, no usurping, and no one-upmanship.

And what is the great, awe-inspiring work of the Father and the Son? They reach into the grave, knit bones back together, bestow a beating heart, and breathe life into the dead. They raise up a people to join in the vibrant, loving relationship of the Godhead.

As you pray, consider the great work of salvation. Ask yourself if you honor the Son as the bringer of new life to the world, enacting the will of the Father. Ask yourself if you've submitted to his lordship, knowing he will come back as Judge and King. Pray for the great power of the Spirit to walk in humility and love.

Pray:

Grant, Almighty God, that as you have stretched forth your helping hand to us by your only begotten Son, not only binding yourself to us by an oath, but even sealing your eternal covenant by the blood of the same, your Son; grant that we in turn may keep our faith toward you so that we persevere in the undefiled worship of your name, till we attain unto the reward of our faith in your heavenly kingdom, through the same, Christ our Lord. Amen.

(John Calvin)

25th Sunday of Ordinary Time
ALYSIA YATES

Read: *Psalm 143:1–10*

> Hear my prayer, O LORD;
>> give ear to my pleas for mercy!
>> In your faithfulness answer me, in your righteousness!
> Enter not into judgment with your servant,
>> for no one living is righteous before you.
> For the enemy has pursued my soul;
>> he has crushed my life to the ground;
>> he has made me sit in darkness like those long dead.
> Therefore my spirit faints within me;
>> my heart within me is appalled.
> I remember the days of old;
>> I meditate on all that you have done;
>> I ponder the work of your hands.
> I stretch out my hands to you;
>> my soul thirsts for you like a parched land.   *Selah*
> Answer me quickly, O LORD!
>> My spirit fails!
> Hide not your face from me,
>> lest I be like those who go down to the pit.
> Let me hear in the morning of your steadfast love,
>> for in you I trust.
> Make me know the way I should go,
>> for to you I lift up my soul.
> Deliver me from my enemies, O LORD!
>> I have fled to you for refuge.
> Teach me to do your will,
>> for you are my God!
> Let your good Spirit lead me
>> on level ground!

Reflect:

David began Psalm 143 with an urgent plea for mercy: "Hear my prayer, O LORD . . . for no one living is righteous before you" (vv. 1, 2). David's cry for help was also a brutally honest self-assessment, a confession of his own need for redemption and rescue. He admitted his weakness and described his inner state: His heart was appalled, his spirit was faint, and his soul was thirsty (vv. 4, 6).

Despite these afflictions, David trusted the Lord. He focused on God's faithful provision in his past, present, and future. He remembered his own history and meditated on the ways God had already been faithful to him; he pondered the goodness he saw in creation; he declared confidence in the hope he had for rescue.

"*Let me hear in the morning of your steadfast love, for in you I trust*" (v. 8, italics added).

Only those who are lost or distraught need to be rescued; only those who wait through dark nights desperately yearn for the break of day. Do you hear the longing in David's words? Can you sense his unwavering dependence on the Lord?

Perhaps you've experienced the agonized waiting that David described; perhaps you are now walking through a season that seems equally hopeless.

Know that your Father longs to hear from you, wherever you are. Confess your fears, your needs, and your anxieties to him. Turn to him for comfort and remember that you are not alone. Lift up your soul to him and recall his past faithfulness to you. Rejoice in the rescue that will come with the morning.

Pray:

O God, the life of all who live, the light of the faithful, the strength of those who labor, and the repose of the dead: We thank you for the blessings of the day that is past, and humbly ask for your protection through the coming night. Bring us in safety to the morning hours; through him who died and rose again for us, your Son our Savior Jesus Christ. Amen.

(Anglican Church in North America Book of Common Prayer)

Ordinary Time Day 176
SALLY BREEDLOVE

Read: *John 6:26–35*

Jesus answered them, "Truly, truly, I say to you, you are seeking me, not because you saw signs, but because you ate your fill of the loaves. Do not work for the food that perishes, but for the food that endures to eternal life, which the Son of Man will give to you. For on him God the Father has set his seal." Then they said to him, "What must we do, to be doing the works of God?" Jesus answered them, "This is the work of God, that you believe in him whom he has sent." So they said to him, "Then what sign do you do, that we may see and believe you? What work do you perform? Our fathers ate the manna in the wilderness; as it is written, 'He gave them bread from heaven to eat.'" Jesus then said to them, "Truly, truly, I say to you, it was not Moses who gave you the bread from heaven, but my Father gives you the true bread from heaven. For the bread of God is he who comes down from heaven and gives life to the world." They said to him, "Sir, give us this bread always."

Jesus said to them, "I am the bread of life; whoever comes to me shall not hunger, and whoever believes in me shall never thirst."

Reflect:

To trace the story of bread in our world is to delve into the mystery of human history. We lost our first home with all the givenness of the garden's immediate goodness. In exile, how was man to live? He would hunt and forage, but bread represents a more complex gift of God's provision.

What bread is and how to make it was not immediately obvious. No one knows exactly when people began to harvest seeds from field grasses, grind them, and add water and a fermenting agent to catalyze the gluten in those crushed seeds to become elastic and to expand.

Who first "discovered" fermenting agents or understood gluten? Who first realized when yeast was added to flour and water that the mixture would expand so the soft, damp, lumpy mass became a joy to bite into? Who learned that an oven was a better way to cook it than an open flame? Who knew bread would last for several days and could be easily carried around by a nomadic people?

Think more deeply: Who could imagine that a hungry people in the wilderness would be fed manna, the bread of angels? Or who had ever taken a few small loaves, blessed them and broke them, and turned them into food for a multitude on a Judean hillside?

Who could have known that in an upper room during Passover a young rabbi would break a loaf of unfermented bread and call it his body, broken for all of us? That he would leave that meal and walk toward his crucifixion, where his body would indeed be broken?

And who could have imagined that in communion services around the world over two thousand years later, bread would be lifted up and broken with a cry of thanksgiving? That we would still be proclaiming that Jesus is indeed the one broken on the cross to bring life to the world?

Bread is so commonplace in our world, but today as you eat it, remember the mystery of its beginnings and the mystery of the broken body of the Lord Jesus. He indeed is the bread of heaven that gives life to the world.

Pray:

Lord Jesus, stay with us, for evening is at hand and the day is past; be our companion in the way, kindle our hearts, and awaken hope, that we may know you as you are revealed in Scripture and the breaking of bread. Grant this for the sake of your love. Amen.

(Anglican Church in North America Book of Common Prayer)

Ordinary Time Day 177
SALLY BREEDLOVE

Read: *John 8:12–19*

Again Jesus spoke to them, saying, "I am the light of the world. Whoever follows me will not walk in darkness, but will have the light of life." So the Pharisees said to him, "You are bearing witness about yourself; your testimony is not true." Jesus answered, "Even if I do bear witness about myself, my testimony is true, for I know where I came from and where I am going, but you do not know where I come from or where I am going. You judge according to the flesh; I judge no one. Yet even if I do judge, my judgment is true, for it is not I alone who judge, but I and the Father who sent me. In your Law it is written that the testimony of two people is true. I am the one who bears witness about myself, and the Father who sent me bears witness about me." They said to him therefore, "Where is your Father?" Jesus answered, "You know neither me nor my Father. If you knew me, you would know my Father also."

Reflect:

Jesus's startling words "I am the light of the world" (v. 12) were most likely spoken during the Feast of Tabernacles. For five nights during this weeklong celebration, four large golden candlesticks near the bronze altar were lit at twilight to illuminate the temple's outer court. In the surrounding darkness, that light emanated from the Temple Mount, scattering light across the city. The night was filled with dancing, music, and singing, till at dawn a procession moved to the pool of Siloam.

The Feast of Tabernacles was a yearly reminder and enactment of the wilderness wanderings of God's people. For those forty years, the Lord kept them company in a pillar of fire by night and in a pillar of cloud by day. They were not alone. Moses was a remarkably strong leader, but he was only a man. The most distinguishing and comforting reality of their journey was God's presence.

As the candles were lit that night during the Feast of Tabernacles, Jesus declared his own identity. Pay attention: He didn't say he had a light, that he could enlighten, or that he could lead people to the light. He claimed to be light itself. As the apostle John opened his Gospel, he called Jesus the "true light" that has come into the world (John 1:9).

We live in a world flooded with artificial light. But even with all the light we have created, the places that need enlightenment, comfort, and safety are still in so much darkness: our own souls, this broken world we live in, relationships that leave us lonely and confused, the sadness so many of us carry in our hearts.

Walk with Jesus in that singing procession to the pool of Siloam; notice the warmth and joy that emanated from the four large candlesticks. Hear the call of this young rabbi who is urging you to follow him fully. He is the light of the world. He is the light that can never be extinguished.

As you pray, pray the words the church has prayed for centuries.

Pray:

O gladsome light,
    pure brightness of the everliving Father in heaven,
O Jesus Christ, holy and blessed!
Now as we come to the setting of the sun,
    and our eyes behold the vesper light,
    we sing thy praises, O God: Father, Son, and Holy Ghost.
Thou art worthy at all times to be praised by happy voices,
    O Son of God, O Giver of Life,
    and to be glorified through all the worlds.
Amen.

(Phos Hilaron)

Ordinary Time Day 178
WILLA KANE

Read: *John 10:11–18*

"I am the good shepherd. The good shepherd lays down his life for the sheep. He who is a hired hand and not a shepherd, who does not own the sheep, sees the wolf coming and leaves the sheep and flees, and the wolf snatches them and scatters them. He flees because he is a hired hand and cares nothing for the sheep. I am the good shepherd. I know my own and my own know me, just as the Father knows me and I know the Father; and I lay down my life for the sheep. And I have other sheep that are not of this fold. I must bring them also, and they will listen to my voice. So there will be one flock, one shepherd. For this reason the Father loves me, because I lay down my life that I may take it up again. No one takes it from me, but I lay it down of my own accord. I have authority to lay it down, and I have authority to take it up again. This charge I have received from my Father."

Reflect:

On many days and in many places, feelings of fear, helplessness, and loneliness hover in the subconscious or cast dark shadows over waking thoughts.

In this fourth of the "I am" statements, Jesus declared he is the Good Shepherd, appointed by his Father to gather lost sheep, lead them to safety as one flock, and be with them forever.

This Shepherd is innately good. He is wholesome, noble, and selfless. Contrast this image with the religious leaders in first-century Israel, who were hirelings that sold out to satisfy their desire for power and prestige. These false shepherds loved their lives more than they loved their sheep.

But Jesus loves his sheep more than his life. He laid down his life obediently, voluntarily, and sacrificially to erase sin's unpayable debt. With authority he took his life up again to restore what sin destroyed. He went to the cross with the resurrection in mind.

Jesus knows everything about you yet still he came to save you. He knows his own and his own know him, just as the Father knows the Son and the Son knows the Father. He gathers his own in a relationship as all-knowing and intimate as the relationship between Father and Son.

No matter where you are, know this: Jesus welcomes you, "For you were straying like sheep, but have returned to the Shepherd and Overseer of your souls" (1 Peter 2:25).

No matter how dark today feels, know this: Glory awaits, "and when the chief Shepherd appears, you will receive the unfading crown of glory" (1 Peter 5:4).

As you pray, claim Jesus as the Good Shepherd. He is the one who satisfies your deepest wants, makes you lie down in safety beside still waters, restores your soul, leads you in paths of righteousness, and pours out goodness and mercy all your days (Psalm 23). Trust him to be with you this moment, this hour, and into eternity.

Pray:

O God, whose Son Jesus Christ is the Good Shepherd of your people; grant that, when we hear his voice, we may know him who calls us each by name, and follow where he leads; who, with you and the Holy Spirit, lives and reigns, one God, for ever and ever. Amen.

(Anglican Church in North America Book of Common Prayer)

Ordinary Time Day 179
SALLY BREEDLOVE

Read: *John 11:17–27*

Now when Jesus came, he found that Lazarus had already been in the tomb four days. Bethany was near Jerusalem, about two miles off, and many of the Jews had come to Martha and Mary to console them concerning their brother. So when Martha heard that Jesus was coming, she went and met him, but Mary remained seated in the house. Martha said to Jesus, "Lord, if you had been here, my brother would not have died. But even now I know that whatever you ask from God, God will give you." Jesus said to her, "Your brother will rise again." Martha said to him, "I know that he will rise again in the resurrection on the last day." Jesus said to her, "I am the resurrection and the life. Whoever believes in me, though he die, yet shall he live, and everyone who lives and believes in me shall never die. Do you believe this?" She said to him, "Yes, Lord; I believe that you are the Christ, the Son of God, who is coming into the world."

Reflect:

Job asked a question in his anguished lament that stretches over thirty-six chapters of the Bible: If a man dies, can he live again (Job 14:14)?

We live in a world that tries to remove death. We put it out of sight. We accept it as "natural and final." People live; they die; that is all. We also live in a world that increasingly suggests that sometimes death is the best choice a person can make.

As Christians we are to be people of deep compassion who move toward others in their grief and suffering. But we are also called to see death for what it is: the last enemy (1 Corinthians 15:26). And no matter how we try to disguise or avoid it, who has not longed for someone we loved to be with us again? Who has not longed for one more touch, one more conversation, one more everyday connection?

Martha believed in the resurrection as a future promise. But Jesus confronted her on a deeper level—did she believe that her brother was not simply going to live again one day but that even though he was not present, he was still alive? Lazarus was indeed brought back into this life, and that enormous miracle revealed Christ's triumph over the final enemy. But Lazarus would die a second physical death. Jesus's question was one of cosmic proportions. Would Martha believe that Jesus himself could conquer, and even swallow up, death?

Martha would experience Christ's own death and triumphant resurrection. Christ was preparing her, even as he called her brother from the grave. Christ himself is the resurrection and the wellspring of all life; he is not a doctrine to be believed but reality to be embraced.

Will you let Jesus's question to Martha probe your own heart: Do you believe this? And will you trust him and those you love with his promise that he is the resurrection and the life?

Pray:

Lord God, whose Son our Savior Jesus Christ triumphed over the powers of death and prepared for us our place in the new Jerusalem: Grant that we, who have this day given thanks for his resurrection, may praise you in that City of which he is the light, and where he lives and reigns for ever and ever. Amen.

(Anglican Church of North America Book of Common Prayer)

Ordinary Time Day 180
SALLY BREEDLOVE

Read: *John 14:1–7*

"Let not your hearts be troubled. Believe in God; believe also in me. In my Father's house are many rooms. If it were not so, would I have told you that I go to prepare a place for you? And if I go and prepare a place for you, I will come again and will take you to myself, that where I am you may be also. And you know the way to where I am going." Thomas said to him, "Lord, we do not know where you are going. How can we know the way?" Jesus said to him, "I am the way, and the truth, and the life. No one comes to the Father except through me. If you had known me, you would have known my Father also. From now on you do know him and have seen him."

Reflect:

It was Passover night. Jesus was less than twenty-four hours away from his own shameful and unjust execution. But as he spoke these words to his disciples in that upper room, his focus was on their comfort and strengthening.

It would be so natural for a leader headed to his own death to go back over the principles or truths he had taught, to explain what was going on, to defend himself. But Christ did none of these things. Instead, he offered himself to his disciples.

He himself is the way. He doesn't chart the way or guide us on the way. He simply *is* the Way. To be attached to him is to be ushered into the Father's presence.

He himself is the truth. Once again, he doesn't simply teach, defend, or understand truth. He doesn't even embody it in the sense of being a good example. He *is* truth. He is reality. Everything apart from him is tainted with falsehood and confusion.

He himself is life. He doesn't simply show us how to live; attachment to him fills us with life.

Without him, there is no way. Only varying states of exile, loneliness, and lostness. Without him there is no truth. Only lies, manipulation, and confusion. Without him there is no life. Only addiction and cheap, exhausting schemes for happiness.

There are still vestiges of the way, the truth, and the life in this world. But the more they are disconnected from Jesus, the dimmer they become. Will you turn to Jesus? Will you let him be for you what no one or nothing else can be? Only he can take us to the Father. Only he can settle our confused minds and hearts. Only he can offer us the cup of life that brims over with the Father's love.

Pray:

Almighty God, whom truly to know is everlasting life: Grant us so perfectly to know your Son Jesus Christ to be the way, the truth, and the life, that we may steadfastly follow his steps in the way that leads to eternal glory; through Jesus Christ your Son our Lord, who lives and reigns with you, in the unity of the Holy Spirit, one God, for ever and ever. Amen.

(Anglican Church of North America Book of Common Prayer)

Ordinary Time Day 181
WILLA KANE

Read: *John 15:1–11*

"I am the true vine, and my Father is the vinedresser. Every branch
in me that does not bear fruit he takes away, and every branch that
does bear fruit he prunes, that it may bear more fruit. Already you
are clean because of the word that I have spoken to you. Abide in
me, and I in you. As the branch cannot bear fruit by itself, unless
it abides in the vine, neither can you, unless you abide in me. I
am the vine; you are the branches. Whoever abides in me and I in
him, he it is that bears much fruit, for apart from me you can do
nothing. If anyone does not abide in me he is thrown away like a
branch and withers; and the branches are gathered, thrown into the
fire, and burned. If you abide in me, and my words abide in you, ask
whatever you wish, and it will be done for you. By this my Father is
glorified, that you bear much fruit and so prove to be my disciples.
As the Father has loved me, so have I loved you. Abide in my love.
If you keep my commandments, you will abide in my love, just as I
have kept my Father's commandments and abide in his love. These
things I have spoken to you, that my joy may be in you, and that
your joy may be full."

Reflect:

In the upper room with his disciples, Jesus had just instituted the Lord's
Supper; they had drunk the fruit of the vine. And Jesus said, "I am the true
vine" (v. 1).

Final words are important words. These words, the last of the seven "I
am" statements, were among the final ones Jesus spoke to his disciples before
he went to the cross. The road ahead was one of suffering for Jesus and his
followers. He told them to abide in him.

Repeated words are important words. The word *abide* appears ten times
in the first ten verses of John 15 and it means to dwell, to remain, to be
present, and to be held and kept.

If Jesus is the vine, God the Father is the vinedresser, the gardener who removes dead wood and prunes living branches so the vine will produce good and plentiful fruit.

Living branches—true followers of Christ—receive the Spirit's life-giving sap because they have been made clean, as Jesus assured his disciples, "Already you are clean because of the word that I have spoken to you" (v. 3). The gospel cleanses and makes believers in Christ right with God, not because they are fruitful but because they trust Jesus as Savior and abide in him. Fruit-bearing is the result.

In nature, pruning increases abundance. And even though it is painful, the same is true in our lives. Scripture affirms the cost of spiritual fruitfulness: "For the moment all discipline seems painful rather than pleasant, but later it yields the peaceful fruit of righteousness to those who have been trained by it" (Hebrews 12:11).

As you pray, thank God the Father for Jesus the Son—the One whose death and resurrection has cleansed you. Abide in him. Dwell, remain, and be present with him. Allow yourself to be held and kept by your Lord.

Thank God the Father for his careful, purposeful pruning. Name the places you feel his spiritual shears and trust that this is for your good and his glory. He is a sovereign and gracious gardener. He will help you grow and bear fruit—much fruit—that will abide into eternity.

Pray:

O God, from whom to be turned is to fall, to whom to be turned is to rise, and with whom to stand is to abide forever, grant us in all our duties your help, in all our perplexities your guidance, in all our dangers your protection, and in all our sorrows your peace, through Jesus Christ our Lord. Amen.

(Augustine)

26th Sunday of Ordinary Time
WILLA KANE

Read: *Psalm 145:1–10, 18–21*

I will extol you, my God and King,
and bless your name forever and ever.
Every day I will bless you
and praise your name forever and ever.
Great is the LORD, and greatly to be praised,
and his greatness is unsearchable.
One generation shall commend your works to another,
and shall declare your mighty acts.
On the glorious splendor of your majesty,
and on your wondrous works, I will meditate.
They shall speak of the might of your awesome deeds,
and I will declare your greatness.
They shall pour forth the fame of your abundant goodness
and shall sing aloud of your righteousness.
The LORD is gracious and merciful,
slow to anger and abounding in steadfast love.
The LORD is good to all,
and his mercy is over all that he has made.
All your works shall give thanks to you, O LORD,
and all your saints shall bless you! . . .
The LORD is near to all who call on him,
to all who call on him in truth.
He fulfills the desire of those who fear him;
he also hears their cry and saves them.
The LORD preserves all who love him,
but all the wicked he will destroy.
My mouth will speak the praise of the LORD,
and let all flesh bless his holy name forever and ever.

Reflect:

In his last recorded psalm, David extoled the greatness and goodness of God
and called us to join him in praise. In contrast, we live in a world and a time

where real goodness and true greatness seems in short supply. Incivility and violence abound. Fires, floods, natural disasters, and crises in health, peace, and justice spread around the globe. Confidence in the stability of governments ebbs and flows.

Psalm 145 reorients us, calling us to turn our eyes away from a broken world and to look instead at a God of unsearchable greatness who does good because he is good.

We will see evidence of God's greatness when we meditate on his wondrous works in creation. Stop to consider the glorious things God has made. Speak them out loud. Now declare the greatness of the one who made them.

Turn your thoughts to God's goodness. He is righteous, kind, gracious, and merciful. Because of his great love for us, he gives us what we don't deserve and what we could never earn. And blessedly, unbelievably, mercifully, he doesn't give us what we do deserve. The cross of Christ showcases God's grace and mercy. Here we see the steadfast love of God: His Son pays sin's penalty. He laid down his life to be our undeserved ransom.

We were sinners, yet God loved us still. Stop to consider this goodness. Speak it out loud. Declare the goodness of the one whose perfect love, kindness, mercy, and generosity paid for your entrance into his everlasting kingdom. Thank the one who raises you up when you fall, upholds you when days are hard, and satisfies your deepest desires when everyone and everything else falls short. Thank him that he has heard your cry and has saved you.

When Moses asked to see God's glory, God said, "I will make all my goodness pass before you" (Exodus 33:19). God's goodness is his glory.

Our God is great, he is good, and he is glorious. He is worthy of our praise every day and into eternity. Praise him.

Pray:
Holy, gracious, merciful Father, I praise you that you are great, good, and glorious. Thank you for your love poured out to me on the cross. Amen.

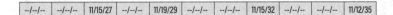

Ordinary Time Day 183

SALLY BREEDLOVE

Read: *1 John 1*

That which was from the beginning, which we have heard, which we have seen with our eyes, which we looked upon and have touched with our hands, concerning the word of life—the life was made manifest, and we have seen it, and testify to it and proclaim to you the eternal life, which was with the Father and was made manifest to us—that which we have seen and heard we proclaim also to you, so that you too may have fellowship with us; and indeed our fellowship is with the Father and with his Son Jesus Christ. And we are writing these things so that our joy may be complete.

This is the message we have heard from him and proclaim to you, that God is light, and in him is no darkness at all. If we say we have fellowship with him while we walk in darkness, we lie and do not practice the truth. But if we walk in the light, as he is in the light, we have fellowship with one another, and the blood of Jesus his Son cleanses us from all sin. If we say we have no sin, we deceive ourselves, and the truth is not in us. If we confess our sins, he is faithful and just to forgive us our sins and to cleanse us from all unrighteousness. If we say we have not sinned, we make him a liar, and his word is not in us.

Reflect:

Jesus called the disciple John and his brother, James, "Sons of Thunder" (Mark 3:17). Perhaps that nickname only meant they were vocal and enthusiastic, but most of us aren't sure we want to be friends with a son of thunder. Such a person would likely be loud, authoritarian, dangerous, and quick-tempered.

How could an aggressive person fitting such a description write the words we read in 1 John 1? Here we find a John who longed for us to know Jesus. He declared that the incarnation of the Son of God is so solidly true that if we had been in Jesus's presence like he was, we would have known

Jesus in his humanity and yet also known so much more. For in Jesus is friendship, life, and light.

We do not have to fear that we are unworthy to be near Jesus. John assured us that if we confess our sins, Jesus is "faithful and just to forgive us our sins and to cleanse us from all unrighteousness" (v. 9). Every one of our sins—past, present, and future—will be taken care of by Jesus's blood and his prayers for us.

John wanted to share his friend Jesus with us—what a transformation! This son of thunder became the kind of friend we long for: humble, quietly confident, and generous. Fellowship with Jesus and with other believers is life-changing indeed.

Perhaps you feel that you've never had a real friend, never been chosen, or never been told you matter. Perhaps you believe you are hopeless; you think your failure and hypocrisy are too much for God. As you pray, listen for the voice of God's Spirit. How is he calling you to a life of greater honesty, obedience, and love? How is he reassuring you that Jesus's death on the cross is more than enough for all your sin and shame?

Thank God for the solid reality of Jesus, for the full forgiveness he offers, and for his ability to transform all of us who are willing to enter into friendship with him.

Pray:
O Father God, transform my life so I am like your Son Jesus Christ. Make me a true friend as he has been to me. In the name of the Father, the Son, and the Holy Spirit. Amen.

Ordinary Time Day 184

KARI WEST

Read: *1 John 2:1–6*

> My little children, I am writing these things to you so that you
> may not sin. But if anyone does sin, we have an advocate with the
> Father, Jesus Christ the righteous. He is the propitiation for our sins,
> and not for ours only but also for the sins of the whole world. And
> by this we know that we have come to know him, if we keep his
> commandments. Whoever says "I know him" but does not keep his
> commandments is a liar, and the truth is not in him, but whoever
> keeps his word, in him truly the love of God is perfected. By this we
> may know that we are in him: whoever says he abides in him ought
> to walk in the same way in which he walked.

Reflect:

What does it mean for the love of God to be "made complete" in us (v. 5 NIV)? It's a strange turn of phrase. Isn't God's love already complete, lacking nothing? And yet here John wrote that by keeping Christ's commands—most notably, his command to love others—the love of God is "perfected" (v. 5) in his people.

John wasn't insinuating that God's love is less than perfect and that we, by our actions, make up for something morally lacking in the love of the Almighty. He meant completion here in terms of finishing a race, of making it to the finish line. The love of God, which God has "poured into our hearts through the Holy Spirit" (Romans 5:5), now must pour from us into the lives of others in order for it to reach its intended end. God's love does not conclude its work with us.

We are to be joyful conduits of God's deep compassion for all people, so that more may know Jesus Christ, our righteous advocate with the Father and the propitiation for the sins of the whole world.

These words are an invitation: Take your place in this great river of gladness. God is continually pouring out grace and mercy over you, treasuring you as his dearly bought child. Now turn and direct that powerful love to those around you, that they may drink the living water and never thirst again.

No person can do this on his or her own, but God longs to meet us in our need. As you pray, ask him for deep, still places in your soul where you may know the riches of his delight in you. Ask him to show you one person in your life who is thirsty for the living water of his presence.

Pray:

Lord of all power and might, the author and giver of all good things: Graft in our hearts the love of your Name, increase in us true religion, nourish us with all goodness, and bring forth in us the fruit of good works; through Jesus Christ our Lord, who lives and reigns with you and the Holy Spirit, one God, for ever and ever. Amen.

(Anglican Church of North America Book of Common Prayer)

Ordinary Time Day 185
SALLY BREEDLOVE

Read: *1 John 2:7–11*

Beloved, I am writing you no new commandment, but an old
commandment that you had from the beginning. The old
commandment is the word that you have heard. At the same time,
it is a new commandment that I am writing to you, which is true in
him and in you, because the darkness is passing away and the true
light is already shining. Whoever says he is in the light and hates
his brother is still in darkness. Whoever loves his brother abides in
the light, and in him there is no cause for stumbling. But whoever
hates his brother is in the darkness and walks in the darkness, and
does not know where he is going, because the darkness has blinded
his eyes.

Reflect:

"What's the goal of life?" All sorts of answers rise up in us when we ask that
question: to be free of our struggles, to find someone who really understands
us, to have children, to have an interesting job, to make a bucket of money,
to be a better person, to have our doubts about God finally resolved, to be rid
of the anxiety we carry, or to get even with the people who have hurt us (or
at least hear them apologize). We want a life that has meaning, a life where
we belong.

But in this passage, John laid out a different goal: to grow in keeping the
greatest commandment. That commandment exhorts us to love God with
all our heart, mind, soul, and strength, and to love our neighbor as ourselves.
John probably heard Jesus speak often about this greatest commandment,
and Jesus confirmed his instructions at the Last Supper before he was crucified. John heard Jesus say the same thing again and again—learn to love.

John modeled this radical love for us in his letter. He addressed his
friends as "beloved" (v. 7) and wrote that "whoever loves his brother abides

in the light" (v. 10). Those who are loved well will learn to love others well; they abide in the light.

Our world runs on the notion that position, power, and privilege are the only things that matter. We are destroying our cities, our cultures, and our relationships with the insistence that we are right and the whole world needs to bow to our beliefs. We are more likely to fear our neighbors than to reach out to them in love.

Are you willing to pray, "Lord, teach me to love like you love"? Will you receive the reality that you are greatly loved by God? Will you let his love touch you so deeply that you are set free to love others?

Pray:

Almighty God our Savior, you desire that none should perish, and you have taught us through your Son that there is great joy in heaven over every sinner who repents: Grant that our hearts may ache for a lost and broken world. May your Holy Spirit work through our words, deeds, and prayers, that the lost may be found and the dead made alive, and that all your redeemed may rejoice around your throne; through Jesus Christ our Lord. Amen.

(Anglican Church in North America Book of Common Prayer)

Ordinary Time Day 186
KARI WEST

Read: *1 John 2:12–14*

> I am writing to you, little children,
>> because your sins are forgiven for his name's sake.
> I am writing to you, fathers,
>> because you know him who is from the beginning.
> I am writing to you, young men,
>> because you have overcome the evil one.
> I write to you, children,
>> because you know the Father.
> I write to you, fathers,
>> because you know him who is from the beginning.
> I write to you, young men,
>> because you are strong,
> and the word of God abides in you,
>> and you have overcome the evil one.

Reflect:

Listen again to the reasons John wrote to these believers. Notice the affectionate way he addressed them as "little children." He offered his dear friends these words—like small benedictions—thousands of years ago, and they are offered again to you today:

- "Your sins are forgiven for his name's sake" (v. 12).
- "You know him who is from the beginning" (v. 13).
- "You have overcome the evil one" (v. 13).
- "You know the Father" (v. 13).
- "You are strong, and the word of God abides in you" (v. 14).

Take each of these declarations and turn them over in your mind. Speak them out loud. Ask the Holy Spirit to bring one in particular to bear.

Which truth do you most need to hear and believe today? That your sins are forgiven? That you know the everlasting Father who is from the beginning? That, through Christ, you have overcome the evil one? That the Word of God lives in you and strengthens you?

We are beloved children of God, and this truth changes everything. We are no longer estranged by our sin; instead, we are rescued and adopted into God's family and invited into relationship with him. His Word abides in us, and he has promised to finish the good work he has begun. He has already given us the strength we need for each day.

Be still and meditate on these verses. Be patient; remain until your mind is quiet and your soul is calm. Then thank the Lord for the gift of his living Word. Thank him for doing its good work in your heart.

Pray:

Truly, Lord, in you and your favor I have life, for you are both my light and my life. My heart trusts in you. Remember me then, Lord, with the favor that you give your people. Visit me with your salvation. Amen.

(Robert Hawker)

Ordinary Time Day 187
KARI WEST

Read: *1 John 2:15–17*

> Do not love the world or the things in the world. If anyone loves
> the world, the love of the Father is not in him. For all that is in the
> world—the desires of the flesh and the desires of the eyes and pride
> of life—is not from the Father but is from the world. And the world
> is passing away along with its desires, but whoever does the will of
> God abides forever.

Reflect:

John's instructions in these verses are startling: "Do not love the world or the things in the world. If anyone loves the world, the love of the Father is not in him" (v. 15).

But when John wrote of "the world" in these verses, he didn't mean our physical environment, bodily existence, or the good creation that God has wrought and sustained. "The world" here means everything that is contrary to the abiding, eternal kingdom of God.

John specified three things that are opposed to God's life-giving and ruling presence: the lust of the flesh, the lust of the eyes (v. 16 NIV), and the pride of life. In other words, evil desires—whether they be rooted in sexual immorality, greed, or covetousness—are rooted in the belief that we don't need our Father.

John didn't attempt to shame or bully us into shallow morality. Instead, he told us very simply that these things don't come from God and that we were made for the abundant life found at God's right hand. The things of this world, on the other hand, will pass away like the mist burned away by the rising sun.

God's kingdom is built through the atoning work of Jesus and the witness of the church; as believers, we participate in this generative work. We who are washed in Christ's blood are called to love as we have been loved.

As you begin your time of prayer, read through these verses again and ask the Holy Spirit to reorient your heart. Confess any love for the things that draw you away from the kingdom of God. Confess all pride and all evil desires. Receive his renewing mercy. Ask for deeper commitment to the way of Christ and a deeper belief that in his steps, true and lasting life will always be found.

Pray:

May we act like children of God, wherever we are, pure and blameless in the midst of a crooked and perverse generation. And may we never be entangled in the snares of the wicked, or bound by the chains of our sins. Amen.

(Gregory Nazianzen)

Ordinary Time Day 188
KARI WEST

Read: *1 John 2:18–29*

Children, it is the last hour, and as you have heard that antichrist
is coming, so now many antichrists have come. Therefore we know
that it is the last hour. They went out from us, but they were not of
us; for if they had been of us, they would have continued with us.
But they went out, that it might become plain that they all are not
of us. But you have been anointed by the Holy One, and you all
have knowledge. I write to you, not because you do not know the
truth, but because you know it, and because no lie is of the truth.
Who is the liar but he who denies that Jesus is the Christ? This is
the antichrist, he who denies the Father and the Son. No one who
denies the Son has the Father. Whoever confesses the Son has the
Father also. Let what you heard from the beginning abide in you. If
what you heard from the beginning abides in you, then you too will
abide in the Son and in the Father. And this is the promise that he
made to us—eternal life.

I write these things to you about those who are trying to deceive
you. But the anointing that you received from him abides in you,
and you have no need that anyone should teach you. But as his
anointing teaches you about everything, and is true, and is no lie—
just as it has taught you, abide in him.

And now, little children, abide in him, so that when he appears
we may have confidence and not shrink from him in shame at his
coming. If you know that he is righteous, you may be sure that
everyone who practices righteousness has been born of him.

Reflect:

John wrote this letter to be circulated among a series of house churches. He
wanted to encourage them because they belonged to the household of God
and to warn them against those who tried to dissuade them from following
Christ. There were some among the believers who denied the deity of Christ
and left the fellowship of the church.

John wanted his friends to understand that Christ is the ultimate reality. Those who belong to God's family will cling to Jesus because God, through Christ, is the one who sustains the church. "You have been anointed by the Holy One," John reminded them, "and you all have knowledge" (v. 20). The very Spirit of Christ indwells believers.

He charged them to keep what they heard in the beginning as central in their lives—namely, the gospel story. As they sought to honor Christ and follow his commands of love and holiness, they would continue to abide in the fellowship of God. When Christ appears, they would have the joy of being confident and unashamed before him. They would know the fullness of God's promise, eternal life with him.

And in the meantime, Christ's righteousness would birth more and more righteousness within them. This was also a distinguishing mark by which they could discern other true followers of Christ.

As you pray, let these words do their work within you. Ask the Holy Spirit for a true understanding of the ultimate centrality of Christ in your life. Thank him for the gift of his anointing. Plead for the power to be steadfast in love and holiness and to trust in his redemption when you fail.

Above all, hope in his coming fullness and in the eternal life that awaits us.

Pray:

O most merciful Redeemer, Friend, and Brother,
May I know thee more clearly,
Love thee more dearly,
And follow thee more nearly:
For ever and ever. Amen.

(Richard of Chichester)

27th Sunday of Ordinary Time
KARI WEST

Read: *Psalm 150*

> Praise the LORD!
> Praise God in his sanctuary;
> > praise him in his mighty heavens!
>
> Praise him for his mighty deeds;
> > praise him according to his excellent greatness!
>
> Praise him with trumpet sound;
> > praise him with lute and harp!
>
> Praise him with tambourine and dance;
> > praise him with strings and pipe!
>
> Praise him with sounding cymbals;
> > praise him with loud clashing cymbals!
>
> Let everything that has breath praise the LORD!
> Praise the LORD!

Reflect:

"Praise the Lord!" We hear that phrase so often in Christian circles that we may forget what it means. Perhaps we only associate it with a certain portion of a church service or a specific kind of music. But praising God encompasses far more. It means seeing something true about God and then communicating gratefulness and gladness in response.

The genesis of praise is God's character and his actions. In this psalm, we are charged to praise God because of his surpassing greatness and his acts of power—in other words, for both his character and how his character is manifested in the world.

But we aren't merely passive observers of God's goodness. The psalmist commanded us to take up our part in the dance of creation and the music of the spheres.

Do we know anything of God's graciousness, his steadfast love, or his mighty acts? Then we can strum a harp, clash some cymbals, tap our feet, and use our breath to praise God for who he is and what he has done. We also praise him for what he is doing and will do.

No matter where you find yourself, you can praise God. Will you read through this psalm again and ask Christ to take your eyes off your circumstances and fix them on him? He is the author and perfecter of your life and faith. Come to Jesus and ask for the ability to praise him, to trust him, and to rest in him. Praise the Lord!

Pray:

We sing to you, the one who is the great King from all eternity, fountain that springs from itself, God of God, Immortal and Glorious One, the only Father's true and only Son!

To you, with him, our praises all belong. We will crown you with the finest flowers of song. Son of the Father, by divine birth, all the Father's bright glories shine in you. Amen.

(Synesius)

Ordinary Time Day 190

KARI WEST

Read: *1 John 3:1–3*

> See what kind of love the Father has given to us, that we should be called children of God; and so we are. The reason why the world does not know us is that it did not know him. Beloved, we are God's children now, and what we will be has not yet appeared; but we know that when he appears we shall be like him, because we shall see him as he is. And everyone who thus hopes in him purifies himself as he is pure.

Reflect:

John could barely contain his effusive awe for the love that God has poured over us: "See what kind of love the Father has given to us, that we should be called children of God" (v. 1). The best thing in the world has happened— God has adopted us! God has brought us into his family. God calls us his own. He delights in us as a father delights in his children. John marveled over this reality. Us—God's kids! That's what we are!

But then John expounded an even greater and more mysterious truth: We will be like Jesus. Christ will appear in glory, we will see him as he truly is, and we will be like him. We don't know the details of that reality. We don't know the fullness of the humanity that we will be drawn into on that glorious day, yet John held out this marvelous truth to us. This is a glorious mystery of salvation, a thing "into which angels long to look" (1 Peter 1:12).

What can we do with these beautiful realities? How do we hold such buoyant hope in our souls? How do we respond to such glad news?

Sit with these truths and invite the Holy Spirit to enlarge your heart to grasp their greatness. Don't let them remain as words on a page or as distant and ethereal ideas. They are meant to make your soul swell with gladness; they are meant to fill your heart with a deep and overflowing joy.

As you hold these truths close, you may find new and holy desires burgeoning within, pulling you toward that coming glory. Full life with our pure and glorious Savior beckons!

Pray:

Expand my heart with love, that I may feel its transforming power, and may even be dissolved in its holy fire! Let me be possessed by your love, and ravished from myself! Let the lover's song be mine, "I will follow my beloved on high!" Let my soul rejoice exceedingly, and lose itself in your praise! Let me love you more than myself; let me love myself only for your sake; and in you love all others, as that perfect law requires, which is a ray of the infinite love that shines in you. Amen.

(Thomas à Kempis)

Ordinary Time Day 191

KARI WEST

Read: *1 John 3:11–18*

> For this is the message that you have heard from the beginning, that we should love one another. We should not be like Cain, who was of the evil one and murdered his brother. And why did he murder him? Because his own deeds were evil and his brother's righteous. Do not be surprised, brothers, that the world hates you. We know that we have passed out of death into life, because we love the brothers. Whoever does not love abides in death. Everyone who hates his brother is a murderer, and you know that no murderer has eternal life abiding in him.
>
> By this we know love, that he laid down his life for us, and we ought to lay down our lives for the brothers. But if anyone has the world's goods and sees his brother in need, yet closes his heart against him, how does God's love abide in him? Little children, let us not love in word or talk but in deed and in truth.

Reflect:

John returned to this theme again and again in this letter: Love is from God; those who love have been born of God. Hatred and murder are from the evil one. Those who remain in hatred remain in death. God has made us alive, and the fruit of that new life is love.

And where do we find the culmination of love? John answered the question directly, "By this we know love, that he laid down his life for us" (v. 16). The apex of love is the person of Jesus Christ, who laid down his life for us.

Unlike the apostle Paul, John didn't construct a thick theological framework. He did not pile one complex truth on another complex truth. Rather, he compelled us with simple language, revealing a simple and yet profound reality. The way we know love is by looking to the cross. We see that our sinless Savior suffered for our wrongs, bore the wrath of God, worked victory over Satan and all forces of evil, and became sin for us so that we might become the righteousness of God. We see Christ crucified; we see the Lamb slain for the life of the world.

Our Jesus did all of this for the joy set before him, the joy of bringing us into the family of God and dwelling with us forever. Christ walked to Golgotha with us in mind.

As Jesus laid down his life for us, so we ought to lay down our lives for our friends (v. 16). John's letter was affectionate but direct: "Little children, let us not love in word or talk but in deed and in truth" (v. 18). We are called to live our love by laying our lives down for our brothers and sisters. We are called not to pretty words but to loving action.

As you pray, consider Jesus. See the wounds in his hands and feet, and know he bled for love, for you. Ask the Holy Spirit to show you one way in these coming days that you may live in this same sacrificial love.

Pray:

O God, who before the passion of your only-begotten Son revealed his glory upon the holy mountain: Grant that we, beholding by faith the light of his countenance, may be strengthened to bear our cross, and be changed into his likeness from glory to glory; through Jesus Christ our Lord, who lives and reigns with you and the Holy Spirit, one God, for ever and ever. Amen.

(Anglican Church in North America Book of Common Prayer)

Ordinary Time Day 192

KARI WEST

Read: *1 John 4:13–21*

By this we know that we abide in him and he in us, because he has given us of his Spirit. And we have seen and testify that the Father has sent his Son to be the Savior of the world. Whoever confesses that Jesus is the Son of God, God abides in him, and he in God. So we have come to know and to believe the love that God has for us. God is love, and whoever abides in love abides in God, and God abides in him. By this is love perfected with us, so that we may have confidence for the day of judgment, because as he is so also are we in this world. There is no fear in love, but perfect love casts out fear. For fear has to do with punishment, and whoever fears has not been perfected in love. We love because he first loved us. If anyone says, "I love God," and hates his brother, he is a liar; for he who does not love his brother whom he has seen cannot love God whom he has not seen. And this commandment we have from him: whoever loves God must also love his brother.

Reflect:

Jesus has given us his Spirit. He still bears the name Immanuel. He is God with us still; "we abide in him and he in us, because he has given us of his Spirit" (v. 13).

Do you know this incredible gift that God has given to you? Take a moment and dwell on this reality—the God who has strewn the stars in the night sky, who turns the hearts of kings, who pulls rain down from the clouds and pushes grass up from underfoot, who trampled death—this God has taken up residence in you, his child.

This God is before, behind, and within you. This God is at hand when you wake up, when you sleep, when you go out and when you come in, when your thoughts race at three in the morning, when your anger spills over in the afternoon, and when the bitterness beckons and envy simmers in the evening. He is there when you feel far too much and when you don't feel anything at all.

This God, by his Spirit, will draw you into deeper and deeper fellowship with him, so that you know and rely on his love. This God will make you like Jesus, and his perfect love will continue to drive away your fear. You have been brought into his family and need fear no punishment, no separation from him: "Whoever confesses that Jesus is the Son of God, God abides in him, and he in God" (v. 15).

This God, by his Spirit, will amplify and complete our fumbling attempts to love one another. And in that love for one another, we will know new depths of the love of God.

Pray these truths back to the Spirit of Christ, the very God who indwells you, and find your hope in him.

Pray:

Almighty God, give us the increase of faith, hope, and love; and, that we may obtain what you have promised, make us love what you command; through Jesus Christ our Lord, who lives and reigns with you and the Holy Spirit, one God, for ever and ever. Amen.

(Anglican Church in North America Book of Common Prayer)

Ordinary Time Day 193
KARI WEST

Read: *1 John 5:13–15*

> I write these things to you who believe in the name of the Son of
> God, that you may know that you have eternal life. And this is
> the confidence that we have toward him, that if we ask anything
> according to his will he hears us. And if we know that he hears us
> in whatever we ask, we know that we have the requests that we have
> asked of him.

Reflect:

The whole book of 1 John was written so that believers may know they have
eternal life in Christ. These words are like a rip in the fabric of the world as
we know it, allowing us to peer through and see the deeper realities that are
often hidden from our earthbound sight.

The believers who originally received John's words were meeting in house
churches strewn around ancient Ephesus. They were facing hostility from the
surrounding culture and experiencing upheaval within their communities
because some members had recently denied Christ's divinity and left the faith.

It is amid these circumstances that John sought to lift their gaze to something more lasting: God had poured out lavish love on them, and the Spirit
of Christ dwelt in them. And their ultimate destiny? Eternal life. Not simply
life that lasts forever, but an unimaginably rich, abundant, deeply joyous life
in the fullness of God's presence, filling their lives to the brim with the fierce
gladness of himself.

We have hints and glimmers of this eternal life now, but we can place
our hope fully in God's fulfillment of this promise on the other side of death,
when he will pull us up from the grave and into his arms.

Each time we pray, we approach this God. We can rest in the truth that
he hears us. If what we ask for will make us more ready for that coming abundance of life, we are given the sure knowledge that we will receive it. Our

God will always answer prayers according to his will, and that is a beautiful truth because his will for us is life beyond what we can now hope or imagine.

Ask the Lord what you should pray for "according to his will" (v. 14). Then ask for a hope rooted in the eternal life promised to each of his children, a treasure trove of his presence to be fully known one day soon.

Pray:

Return, O Lord! How long? Let your kingdom come! Your desolate bride says *come*—for your Spirit within her says *come*—the one who teaches her to pray with groanings which cannot be expressed. The whole creation says *come*, waiting to be delivered from the bondage of corruption into the glorious liberty of the children of God. And you yourself have said, *surely I come*. Amen, even so, come Lord Jesus.

(Richard Baxter)

Ordinary Time Day 194
SALLY BREEDLOVE

Read: *Exodus 35:30–36:2*

Then Moses said to the people of Israel, "See, the Lord has called by name Bezalel the son of Uri, son of Hur, of the tribe of Judah; and he has filled him with the Spirit of God, with skill, with intelligence, with knowledge, and with all craftsmanship, to devise artistic designs, to work in gold and silver and bronze, in cutting stones for setting, and in carving wood, for work in every skilled craft. And he has inspired him to teach, both him and Oholiab the son of Ahisamach of the tribe of Dan. He has filled them with skill to do every sort of work done by an engraver or by a designer or by an embroiderer in blue and purple and scarlet yarns and fine twined linen, or by a weaver—by any sort of workman or skilled designer.

"Bezalel and Oholiab and every craftsman in whom the Lord has put skill and intelligence to know how to do any work in the construction of the sanctuary shall work in accordance with all that the Lord has commanded."

And Moses called Bezalel and Oholiab and every craftsman in whose mind the Lord had put skill, everyone whose heart stirred him up to come to do the work.

Reflect:

We were made for work. Sabbath rest is a necessary and gracious rhythm that turns work from the shrill sounding of a fire alarm into music, but still we need real work.

The creation story is an invitation to engage in satisfying work. The words "tend and watch over" in Genesis 2:15 (NLT) are the same Hebrew words used to describe the work of the priests as they led temple worship. Work matters; it can even be called a holy thing. Work is a way to care for all God has made and to unfold the possibilities contained in the gift of creation.

Moses picked two men to oversee the construction of the tabernacle and the creation of the elaborate artisan work that would adorn it. These two "project managers" were to be men filled with the Spirit of God, with skill, intelligence, and the ability to teach others. Their work depended on God's help; their work looked upward to God for meaning.

In Acts 6, the new deacons who were to care for widows had to be disciples of good reputation, filled with the Spirit and wisdom. Their work mattered, so their character and ability mattered.

We flourish when we engage in good work. So, what do we do when we can't work? What do we do with our restless boredom, with our sense of defeat? Rather than chafe or sink into fear and doom, might we serve those around us by doing the unpaid jobs that need doing?

Pause and consider how to accept the work we have with deep gratitude. Pray in thanksgiving for the gift of work. If you have lost your job or are unsure if you will have a job, pray for courage and strength to face your life as it is.

Pray by name for those who need a job. If you are responsible for other people's employment, pray for God's wisdom and grace as you lead. If you are working, pray for the grace to see your work as a way to love as God loves.

Pray:

Heavenly Father, we remember before you those who suffer from want or anxiety or from lack of work. Guide the people of this land so to use our public and private wealth that all may find suitable and fulfilling employment and receive a just reward for their labor, through Jesus Christ our Lord. Amen.

(Anglican Church in North America Book of Common Prayer)

Ordinary Time Day 195
KARI WEST

Read: *Psalm 145:8–16*

> The LORD is gracious and merciful,
>> slow to anger and abounding in steadfast love.
> The LORD is good to all,
>> and his mercy is over all that he has made.
> All your works shall give thanks to you, O LORD,
>> and all your saints shall bless you!
> They shall speak of the glory of your kingdom
>> and tell of your power,
> to make known to the children of man your mighty deeds,
>> and the glorious splendor of your kingdom.
> Your kingdom is an everlasting kingdom,
>> and your dominion endures throughout all generations.
> [The LORD is faithful in all his words
>> and kind in all his works.]
> The LORD upholds all who are falling
>> and raises up all who are bowed down.
> The eyes of all look to you,
>> and you give them their food in due season.
> You open your hand;
>> you satisfy the desire of every living thing.

Reflect:

Reading, believing, and praying the Psalms is often an act of faith. When life is arduous, we need hearts that trust God. Trust can then lead us to take verses such as these on our lips, even when the truths may feel distant from us. He is with us when we stumble; he "upholds all who are falling and raises up all who are bowed down" (v. 14).

Wherever we are, we can speak the Psalms and hope in God's promise to remove our hearts of stone and give us hearts of flesh. We can declare them, trusting in his Spirit to renew our faith.

The truth is that in all circumstances we have a gracious and compassionate God who is slow to anger and rich in love. The truth is that the Lord is good to his whole creation and his compassion extends to all. The truth is that God's kingdom is marvelous and enduring—stretching throughout all time. The truth is that our God is trustworthy, faithful, and generous; he will uphold us, from this time forth and forevermore.

Our God remains all of these things, even in all our hardest moments. He remains through our doubts, through our struggles, and through our fears. He will remain to the end, until we no longer need eyes of faith, for we will behold his kingdom in its fullness. He will "satisfy the desire of every living thing" (v. 16).

As you pray, take one of these traits of our Father God and meditate on it. Ask him for faith to believe even when it is hard. Rest in the fact that he will always say yes to that prayer.

Pray:

Accept these hymns of praise from me, in your great mercy. Grant me peace, and hold back the tide from this world of trouble—diseases of body and soul, of wealth and poverty—that I may find rest and fill my mind with wisdom from the brook of heaven. Amen.

(Synesius)

Christ the King Sunday:
Final Sunday of Ordinary Time
ABIGAIL HULL WHITEHOUSE

Read: *Psalm 131*

> O Lord, my heart is not lifted up;
> my eyes are not raised too high;
> I do not occupy myself with things
> too great and too marvelous for me.
> But I have calmed and quieted my soul,
> like a weaned child with its mother;
> like a weaned child is my soul within me.
> O Israel, hope in the Lord
> from this time forth and forevermore.

Reflect:

Do you know what it's like to be held by God?

Here the psalmist likened his soul to a weaned child at rest in their mother's arms. His soul was held—cradled in the arms of God—and in that place of perfect security, the psalmist found rest. His soul was weaned from the need to strive, control, fix, or finish.

There was no anxious energy, no pushing past limits, and no drive to achieve or be recognized. Rather, the psalmist acknowledged that there was much "too great and too marvelous" (v. 1) for him—much that he could not conceive of or contain—and he was content with his humble capacity and place. He released the need to be anything other than who he was, and he surrendered completely to the arms of his Father.

The psalmist gave us a picture of the daily invitation at the heart of Christian discipleship: We are invited to come to God exactly as we are, acknowledge where we have fallen short or taken on too much, and rest in the hands of the one who holds us and the world.

As you settle into prayer, become aware of all that you are carrying and how the weight of it registers in your body, heart, and mind. Is there anything you need to release to the Lord in order to rest more fully in his loving presence? Invite the Holy Spirit to guide you through this process of repentance and surrender. Be gentle with yourself as you acknowledge places where you have resisted God's grace, tried to control things, or willfully chosen your own way.

Then take a moment to read through Psalm 131 again. Imagine surrendering all that you are carrying and then crawling into the arms of your loving Father. Rest like an infant in his embrace and let yourself be held. Take as much time as you need in this place of childlike surrender before finishing your time of prayer.

Pray:

Gracious Father, make my heart like a weaned child—content and at rest. Help me to loosen my grasp on the things of this world and to find my security in you alone. Show me what I was meant to carry and what you are asking me now to release. Help me to trust you in all areas of my life and to walk humbly with you as your beloved child; in Jesus's precious and powerful name. Amen.

Ordinary Time Day 197

WILLA KANE

Read: *Isaiah 12*

> You will say in that day:
> "I will give thanks to you, O LORD,
>   for though you were angry with me,
> your anger turned away,
>   that you might comfort me.
> "Behold, God is my salvation;
>   I will trust, and will not be afraid;
> for the LORD GOD is my strength and my song,
>   and he has become my salvation."
> With joy you will draw water from the wells of salvation. And you
>   will say in that day:
> "Give thanks to the LORD,
>   call upon his name,
> make known his deeds among the peoples,
>   proclaim that his name is exalted.
> "Sing praises to the LORD, for he has done gloriously;
>   let this be made known in all the earth.
> Shout, and sing for joy, O inhabitant of Zion,
>   for great in your midst is the Holy One of Israel."

Reflect:

"Sing praise-songs to GOD. He's done it all!" (Isaiah 12:5 MSG). The melody of this message runs from the Old Testament to the New.

God is our strength and our song because he is our salvation. He was angry, and rightly so, when we turned away from him to worship ourselves and to love lesser things. But his anger wasn't forever. He withdrew his anger—and more than that, he moved toward us and brought comfort. What a God! What a Savior!

He brought not just comfort, not merely good feelings, but also salvation. He has made us right. In love, he closed the chasm caused by sin. Salvation is perfect love, and perfect love casts out fear (1 John 4:18).

As you pray, examine your heart and confess any fear that resides within, be it fear that you won't measure up or fear of what the future—or even the next hour—might hold. Let the reality of God's saving love saturate your heart and your soul.

The well of salvation holds springs of living water that we can share as we shout to the nations, telling them what he has done.

Raise the roof; sing your heart out. The greatest—Christ Jesus—lives among you. God—yes, God—is your strength and your song. Best of all, he is your salvation!

Pray:

God our Father, whose Son Jesus Christ gives the water of eternal life, may we also thirst for you, the spring of life and source of goodness, through him who is alive and reigns with you and the Holy Spirit, one God, now and forever. Amen.

Ordinary Time Day 198

SALLY BREEDLOVE

Read: *Isaiah 30:9–11, 15–18*

> For they are a rebellious people,
>> lying children,
> children unwilling to hear
>> the instruction of the LORD;
> who say to the seers, "Do not see,"
>> and to the prophets, "Do not prophesy to us what is right;
> speak to us smooth things,
>> prophesy illusions,
> leave the way, turn aside from the path,
>> let us hear no more about the Holy One of Israel."…
> For thus said the Lord GOD, the Holy One of Israel,
> "In returning and rest you shall be saved;
>> in quietness and in trust shall be your strength."
> But you were unwilling, and you said,
> "No! We will flee upon horses";
>> therefore you shall flee away;
> and, "We will ride upon swift steeds";
>> therefore your pursuers shall be swift.
> A thousand shall flee at the threat of one;
>> at the threat of five you shall flee,
> till you are left
>> like a flagstaff on the top of a mountain,
>> like a signal on a hill.
> Therefore the LORD waits to be gracious to you,
>> and therefore he exalts himself to show mercy to you.
> For the LORD is a God of justice;
>> blessed are all those who wait for him.

Reflect:

We have always believed we could solve our own problems, haven't we? When we face challenges, where do we turn?

In Isaiah's day, Israel faced military annihilation by the ruthless Assyrians. Many were convinced that their salvation would come from Egypt—Egypt, the place of their prolonged captivity and the very power God had told them not to trust.

Israel was deaf to God's voice; they were "a rebellious people," who were like "children unwilling to hear the instruction of the LORD" (v. 9). But in the midst of their stubborn fear and their belief that they could find their own solutions, God continued to offer himself. Their faith would be their salvation, Isaiah declared. "In returning and rest" they would be saved; "in quietness and in trust" they would find their strength (v. 15).

Can we solve the issues of our hurting world and our lives on our own? Can we build a fortress strong enough to protect our health, our economy, or the life we have constructed?

Or will we hear the invitation from God? He longs to show us mercy, he is a "God of justice" who blesses all who wait for him (v. 18).

Draw near to him now. His mercy is exceedingly abundant, not just for you but for his whole created world.

Pray:

O God, the source of all holy desires, all good counsels, and all just works: Give to your servants that peace which the world cannot give, that our hearts may be set to obey your commandments, and that we, being defended from the fear of our enemies, may pass our time in rest and quietness; through the merits of Jesus Christ our Savior. Amen.

(Anglican Church in North America Book of Common Prayer)

Ordinary Time Day 199
WILLA KANE

Read: *Isaiah 45:9; 64:8; & 2 Corinthians 4:7–10*
> "Woe to him who strives with him who formed him,
>> a pot among earthen pots!
> Does the clay say to him who forms it, 'What are you making?'
>> or 'Your work has no handles'?"

> But now, O LORD, you are our Father;
>> we are the clay, and you are our potter;
>> we are all the work of your hand.

> But we have this treasure in jars of clay, to show that the surpassing power belongs to God and not to us. We are afflicted in every way, but not crushed; perplexed, but not driven to despair; persecuted, but not forsaken; struck down, but not destroyed; always carrying in the body the death of Jesus, so that the life of Jesus may also be manifested in our bodies.

Reflect:

Isaiah and Paul taught that we are unformed clay in the hands of the Father. He is our Potter.

Have you ever watched a potter at his wheel? He starts with a lump of clay moistened with water to make it pliable, pounds it onto the wheel with enough force to center it perfectly, and then spins the wheel slowly and carefully as he applies just the right amount of pressure. His fingers push deep inside the ball of clay while his palms hold firmly on the outside. He adds water as he spins and forms a vessel into the shape he desires.

What can we learn as we watch the potter? Water makes clay pliable so it can be molded. Similarly, we need the water of God's Word so his hands can mold us. Clay must be centered on the wheel, and we must be centered in Christ, surrendered to Jesus as our Lord and Savior. Only then can God himself begin to mold, shape, and transform us, as he uses the wheel of time and the pressures of life inside and outside of us.

God knows exactly how and why he's using pressure in our life. Affliction, persecution, and being forsaken and struck down are all things our Lord Jesus experienced. These very things, in the hand of the Master Potter, can be used by God to form us into a perfect vessel for his Spirit.

Will we strive against the Lord and his design for us, or will we submit to the pressures he is using to fit us for the life he has planned? Pause to honestly evaluate your attitude toward the challenges you face. Confess your doubts, resentments, and opposition to his will. Then turn to him in submission. He can't mold you when you resist him. Drink in the living water of his Word. Pray for the desire to cooperate with him, even as the wheel of these hard days turns and the pressure increases.

Trust the hand of the Master Potter to form you, to fill you, and to use you for his purpose.

Pray:
Have thine own way, Lord! Have thine own way!
Thou art the Potter, I am the clay.
Mold me and make me after thy will,
while I am waiting, yielded, and still. Amen.
(From "Have Thine Own Way, Lord," Adelaide Pollard)

Ordinary Time Day 200
SALLY BREEDLOVE

Read: *Daniel 11:33–35; 12:1–3*

And the wise among the people shall make many understand, though for some days they shall stumble by sword and flame, by captivity and plunder. When they stumble, they shall receive a little help. And many shall join themselves to them with flattery, and some of the wise shall stumble, so that they may be refined, purified, and made white, until the time of the end, for it still awaits the appointed time....

"At that time shall arise Michael, the great prince who has charge of your people. And there shall be a time of trouble, such as never has been since there was a nation till that time. But at that time your people shall be delivered, everyone whose name shall be found written in the book. And many of those who sleep in the dust of the earth shall awake, some to everlasting life, and some to shame and everlasting contempt. And those who are wise shall shine like the brightness of the sky above; and those who turn many to righteousness, like the stars forever and ever."

Reflect:

We are unaccustomed to such biting prophetic words. It's good to wonder why.

Are we afraid of talking about a righteous God who works a grand-scale plan of redemption in the midst of terrible evil? Do we resist being a part of a story that is cosmic and eternal, a story that is about much more than ourselves? Or perhaps we resist a Jesus who has more in mind than giving us abundant lives of prosperity and protection from all pain?

We can learn from Daniel. He was born into advantage in the kingdom of Israel, but as a young man he watched his nation fall. Jerusalem was razed. The elite, the educated, and the wealthy were killed or taken captive. Daniel lived in exile from his late teens, at the service of a foreign king. At times he was in favor; at times, he was discarded; at times, he served an insane ruler; and at times, he was in mortal danger from those in power. God also gave him the burden of terrifying and beautiful visions of what lay ahead for humanity.

Perhaps because of all he carried, the "watchers from heaven" came to him at least three times to tell him he was greatly loved. Did the knowledge that he was seen and loved give him the power he needed to endure?

Can we endure like Daniel? We, too, are seen by the triune God. We are greatly loved just as he was. Daniel had his opportunity to live faithfully in the midst of trouble. We have that same opportunity in our lives.

Will you pray for the grit and the courage to endure? Will you ask for the wisdom to live well when life is hard? Will you pray for someone you know who is deeply struggling? Will you pray for all of us who are God's people, that we will stay courageously loyal to him?

Pray:

O God of unchangeable power and eternal light: Look favorably on your whole Church, that wonderful and sacred mystery; by the effectual working of your providence, carry out in tranquility the plan of salvation; let the whole world see and know that things which were cast down are being raised up, and things which had grown old are being made new, and that all things are being brought to their perfection by him through whom all things were made, your Son Jesus Christ our Lord. Amen.

(Anglican Church in North America Book of Common Prayer)

Ordinary Time Day 201

KARI WEST

Read: *Zechariah 10:6–12*

"I will strengthen the house of Judah,
    and I will save the house of Joseph.
I will bring them back because I have compassion on them,
    and they shall be as though I had not rejected them,
    for I am the LORD their God and I will answer them.
Then Ephraim shall become like a mighty warrior,
    and their hearts shall be glad as with wine.
Their children shall see it and be glad;
    their hearts shall rejoice in the LORD.
"I will whistle for them and gather them in,
    for I have redeemed them,
    and they shall be as many as they were before.
Though I scattered them among the nations,
    yet in far countries they shall remember me,
    and with their children they shall live and return.
I will bring them home from the land of Egypt,
    and gather them from Assyria,
    and I will bring them to the land of Gilead and to Lebanon,
    till there is no room for them.
He shall pass through the sea of troubles
    and strike down the waves of the sea,
    and all the depths of the Nile shall be dried up.
The pride of Assyria shall be laid low,
    and the scepter of Egypt shall depart.
I will make them strong in the LORD,
    and they shall walk in his name,"
declares the LORD.

Reflect:

Exile is not the end.

God's promises to gather his people back from the ends of the earth pervade the Scriptures. He will do it because of his great compassion, his great faithfulness, and his great love. He will do it because he desires to make the hearts of his children glad, as glad as with wine (v. 7).

God will whistle for us and gather us in, all those he has redeemed and called by name (v. 8). In the far countries, we will remember the Lord.

This passage was a specific promise to the people of Israel, who were scattered because of their sin and rebellion. And yet it's also a promise for those of us from all the nations whom God has redeemed and brought into his family.

The gathering-in has begun, and Christ has flung wide the door through his death and resurrection, but the job is not yet complete. The sense of not-at-homeness has haunted us all, ever since our first parents were flung out of the garden.

As you pray, ponder these prophetic promises. God will gather you. God will make your heart glad. God will cause you to remember him in all the far places of your soul. He will draw you to himself, and you will live. You will be strong, and you will walk in his name. Allow these promises to fill you with courage, wherever you are today.

Pray:

Remember your church, Lord, to deliver it from all evil and to make it perfect in your love, and gather it together in its holiness from the four winds to your kingdom which you have prepared for it. For yours is the power and the glory forever. Amen.

(The Didache)

Ordinary Time Day 202
SALLY BREEDLOVE

Read: *Revelation 22:1–13*

Then the angel showed me the river of the water of life, bright as crystal, flowing from the throne of God and of the Lamb through the middle of the street of the city; also, on either side of the river, the tree of life with its twelve kinds of fruit, yielding its fruit each month. The leaves of the tree were for the healing of the nations. No longer will there be anything accursed, but the throne of God and of the Lamb will be in it, and his servants will worship him. They will see his face, and his name will be on their foreheads. And night will be no more. They will need no light of lamp or sun, for the Lord God will be their light, and they will reign forever and ever.

And he said to me, "These words are trustworthy and true. And the Lord, the God of the spirits of the prophets, has sent his angel to show his servants what must soon take place."

"And behold, I am coming soon. Blessed is the one who keeps the words of the prophecy of this book."

I, John, am the one who heard and saw these things. And when I heard and saw them, I fell down to worship at the feet of the angel who showed them to me, but he said to me, "You must not do that! I am a fellow servant with you and your brothers the prophets, and with those who keep the words of this book. Worship God."

And he said to me, "Do not seal up the words of the prophecy of this book, for the time is near. Let the evildoer still do evil, and the filthy still be filthy, and the righteous still do right, and the holy still be holy."

"Behold, I am coming soon, bringing my recompense with me, to repay each one for what he has done. I am the Alpha and the Omega, the first and the last, the beginning and the end."

Reflect:

Everything is going to be all right: No longer with there be anything accursed (v. 3), the nations will be healed (v. 2), and night will be no more (v. 5).

What strange words to write or to read in a world like ours. Could it possibly be true that we are headed home, headed to a city brimming with life, where our unquenchable thirst is finally satisfied and where there is nothing we have to earn?

The gates have not yet been flung open to that heavenly city. We are mired in a world of conflict. But John encouraged us. Despite the brokenness and the rebellion all around us, even as "evildoer[s] still do evil, and the filthy [will] still be filthy" (v. 11), God's people are to be like Jesus. We are to be people of whom it is said, "The righteous still do right, and the holy [will] still be holy" (v. 11).

How do we keep our focus as we wait? Can we have any assurance that the future will eliminate the sickness, evil, injustice, and brokenness that plagues our world? Is there a way to live in hope?

Jesus spans the arc of history, making sense of God's work in this world. He is the "Alpha and the Omega . . . the Root and the Offspring of David, and the bright Morning Star" (Revelation 22:13, 16 NIV). He will one day judge evil and cast it into the abyss. The new city he is fashioning—that uncorrupt, incorruptible place—will be ready. We'll be welcomed home.

Turn to Jesus; he will take you home to God. As you pray, pray with the whole church, and with the Spirit, "Come, Lord Jesus."

Pray:

Hasten, O Father, the coming of your kingdom; and grant that we your servants, who now live by faith, may with joy behold your Son at his coming in glorious majesty; even Jesus Christ, our only Mediator and Advocate. Amen.

(Anglican Church in North America Book of Common Prayer)

Acknowledgments

*E*IGHTH *DAY PRAYERS* has been the work of friends coming from a cross section of people, organizations, and churches who hope in the power of Scripture-focused prayer and hunger for the growth of God's church. This prayer guide would not be in print without Willa Kane's faith, generosity, and her ability to call people to action; Madison Perry's leadership, vision, and energy; Sally Breedlove's depth of spiritual insight and writing ability; and Kari West's love for Scripture and the written word. Kari's contributions to this volume in particular were extraordinary.

But these four were not adequate for the work they felt called to. Cassie Lawrence offered her gift of meticulous copy editing, Isabel Yates brought an imagination for beauty and graphic design, and Alysia Yates took this project in hand with her immense skills as an editor and her ability to see the whole.

Eighth Day Prayers began with a simple idea that would have been impossible to execute without the enlivening help of the Holy Spirit. A friend of Willa's asked her if there was a way to call people to pray for eight minutes every night at 8:00 p.m. In 2020 our world was in a crisis of fear, isolation, and confusion, so how could a dream that big come into being? Willa, Madison, and Sally did the simple things. They named and set up a website and posted daily invitations to pray. From the beginning they realized prayer that flowed from reflection on Scripture had the power to draw people to the heart of God. They wrote the first 150 or so calls to prayer, and a growing number of people joined in online.

Out of that online worldwide community of over fourteen thousand people, the idea of a book began to emerge. And more people began to help with this project. Francis Capitanio gave significant creative direction, recommending the seasonal ordering and writing several entries along the way. Other writers for this volume include Nathan Baxter, Bill Boyd, Mary Rachel Boyd, Steven E. Breedlove, Elizabeth Gatewood, Matt Hoehn, Mary Mac Hoehn, Brandon Walsh, and Abigail Hull Whitehouse. Steven E. Breedlove also provided the rich introductions to the Christian year and season. Stephen Macchia graciously provided our introduction to what it means to reflect on Scripture in a prayer-filled way. The North Carolina Study Center, a Christian study center based in Chapel Hill, North Carolina, devoted organizational assistance to bless the global church.

Psalm 110:3 tells us that God's people offer themselves freely on the day of God's power. In the creation of *Eighth Day Prayers*, the triune God has indeed been our King, and his people have freely offered themselves in service. We are grateful.

About the Authors

Willa Kane is a former trustee of the Anglican Relief and Development Fund and is presently a trustee of the American Anglican Council. She is one of the founders of New City Fellows, Raleigh, and a trustee for the ministries of Anne Graham Lotz. She was personally discipled by the late Michael Green in relational evangelism and in a commitment to care for the renewal and protection of the gospel on the global stage. For years, she has taught the Bible to women and mentored them. Together with her husband, John, she has poured her life into community leadership and development. Willa is a mother to four and a grandmother to twelve. She lives in Raleigh, North Carolina.

Sally Breedlove is the author of *Choosing Rest* and one of the authors of *The Shame Exchange*. She is the cofounder of JourneyMates, a Christian soul care and spiritual formation ministry. She serves as a spiritual director and retreat leader and as associate director of Selah-Anglican, a spiritual direction training program. With her husband, Steve, a bishop in the Anglican Church in North America, she has ministered broadly across the United States, in Canada, and overseas. Sally is a mother to five and a grandmother to sixteen. She lives in Chapel Hill, North Carolina.

Madison Perry is the founder and executive director of the North Carolina Study Center, a Christian study center at UNC. He studied theology at Duke and law at UNC. An ordained priest in the Anglican Church in North America, his heart is to see university communities glorify the Lord and become places where young people are brought into God's kingdom, healed, and formed by the power of Jesus. He and his wife, Pamela, have six children and live in Durham, North Carolina. He enjoys talking while walking and reading all kinds of literature.

Alysia Yates is a writer, editor, and mother of four. She earned her graduate degree in church history and works as the project manager for Caritas Foundation International. Alysia has served as an ESL teacher within the refugee community, a facilitator for JourneyMates, and a mentor for the New

City Fellows Program. She lives with her husband, John, and two sons in Raleigh, North Carolina. She enjoys visiting her daughters at their universities, long walks with friends, and the delights of a good book.